The Independent Design Guide

Thames & Hudson

The Independent Design Guide

Innovative Products from the New Generation

Laura Houseley

With 555 colour illustrations

Thank you, firstly, to my parents
for their unswerving support
and enthusiasm. And thank you
to Mark, for his patience and
affection. I couldn't have managed
without my superb editorial
assistant, Tamsin Gear; for her
hard work and commitment I am
especially grateful. Thank you to
all the friends who have diligently
followed the progress of this
book and, lastly, thank you to the
designers who gave me that most
precious of things – their time.

First published in the United Kingdom
in 2009 by Thames & Hudson Ltd,
181A High Holborn, London WC1V 7QX

www.thamesandhudson.com

British Library Cataloguing-in-
Publication Data
A catalogue record for this book is
available from the British Library

ISBN 978-0-500-51457-3

Printed and bound in China by Everbest
Printing Co Ltd
Book design: Unlimited

Contents

6   Introduction
8   A new design landscape
14   Chronology

18   **Furniture**
162   **Lighting**
222   **Accessories**
288   **Utility**
320   **Environment**

338   **References**
340   Glossary
342   Contact information
346   Materials
348   Designer locations
349   Index
352   Credits

Introduction

In putting together this book, I wanted to provide a comprehensive overview of emerging design trends, as articulated by the newest generation of designers.

My own fascination with the fashions and flux of contemporary design was the starting point for this carefully chosen selection. As a design critic, I'm well aware of the increased significance of work produced by our most recent generation of fledgling designers. Neither am I alone in my appetite for the new when it comes to contemporary design objects or theories: the escalation of public interest in new design is one reason why a publication like this is possible. This work is intended as an introduction to the people, the products and the topics that are the vanguard of contemporary design practice – a tantalizing and exclusive first view of what is to come.

There are two ambitions for 'The Independent Design Guide'. The first is to capture the spirit of exhilaration and exploration that currently prevails within the industry. I thought a conscientious study of the immensely skilled, energetic and diverse generation of creatives responsible for this was timely, if not overdue. I want this book to be, at least in part, a dedicated celebration of the ingenuity and resourcefulness of young designers. Secondly, I hoped to make sense of this especially exciting period in design history through a careful review of the products and furniture designs that best express the preoccupations of young designers. I recognized that gathering together the pick of the new brought the opportunity not only to exalt contemporary design but also to explore its motivation, the causes and effects that are currently propelling the discipline forward.

Selecting the new design that was most appropriate for inclusion involved working to a set of criteria that I had best explain. Not surprisingly, choosing 'the best' brought a certain amount of subjectivity into play. So I should say in the frankest way possible that I've chosen the work that I believe to be superior in its expression of new motivations and trends, and the young designers who I believe promise the most.

Originality, the successful articulation of an idea or evolution of a way of working, experimentation, innovation, uniqueness and superior execution are some of the characteristics that made me favour a design and a designer. And if I was confident that a work successfully reflected a relevant design theme or topic, I was more inclined to use it. I didn't ever consider applying age as criteria for the selection of designers, because of obvious reasons of limitation. Whilst all those featured are designers at the beginning of their career and working in new ways, their exact age, I think, has little bearing on the relevance of their work: such overtly strict criteria, as sometimes applied by other collective works, seemed foolishly restrictive. I did, however, set one definite parameter – all the designs featured have been produced since 2005.

In order to achieve as comprehensive an overview as possible, scale was needed: 'The Independent Design Guide' contains over 450 designs by more than 360 designers or design groups. In covering such a large selection of work, of course there will be some variation in the content: inevitably, some designers featured will be more established than others, and some works more familiar than others. Similarly, a designer's 'success' had to be considered. If one young designer has had more success or gained more media attention than another of the same age and experience, is he or she then considered an established designer? This, I admit, was a difficult area to navigate. I certainly didn't want to discriminate against any designers because of their success, but neither did I want to detract from the mission of showcasing new works and designers. And so, mindful of keeping the book fresh, I have selected new work over familiar pieces when faced with a choice, and excluded some designers whom I felt were too established to be relevant here. I fully appreciate that this is a particularly grey area and subjective opinions abound! I should also note the speed with which young designers can quickly become elevated to established ones. While I hope this work is a first introduction to many new products and names, this edit is, by its very nature, time sensitive. Depending on when you come across this title, I'm confident several of the designers I label 'fledgling' will already be on their way to becoming industry heroes. If this sounds like a disclaimer, well, I think it probably is.

Lastly, a quick word on geography. Throughout the editing process, I've remained convinced that in order to reflect the true state of things I should not force any content where I found none. With that in mind, you'll find that while my selection gives a decidedly international perspective and features work produced across the globe, there is a notable mass of content from the conventional design hubs of Europe. I found during my research that although new global design centres are emerging all the time (most notably in Asia), the areas that boast established design education

systems and manufacturing infrastructure continue to produce the most significant quantity and quality of young design talent. This collection is an accurate reflection of the distribution of contemporary design at the moment: to have included more designs than were representative from lesser design hubs, just to appear intrepid or flesh out the global listing, would have been misleading and dishonest.

I sincerely hope my own admiration for the skilled and endlessly innovative work produced by this generation of designers is reflected in 'The Independent Design Guide'. The designs featured are, I believe, demonstration enough of the creative spirit out there. I'd like to thank the hundreds of designers who took the time to explain their work to me and assist in the production of the book. Being afforded a daily insight to their perspectives and original ways of thinking and working was a true pleasure.

Laura Houseley

A new design landscape

The subject of this book is the work produced by young designers as a result of their consideration of the world around them. A study of emerging design talents, the 'The Independent Design Guide' presents a rare opportunity both to examine the current preoccupations of the design world and to take a first look at the future form and function of design.

The emerging talents of contemporary furniture and product design inhabit an exceptional world. Designers have always shaped the environment around us, but in recent years the practice of contemporary design has begun to expand beyond preconceived boundaries of importance and relevance. Offering solutions to the dilemmas of modern life, providing status-indicating products, being at the very forefront of developing technologies, and all the while engaging in an increasingly direct dialogue with a progressively more attentive audience, today's designers provide a more compelling picture of modern life than ever before. Although design remains an intimate part of daily life, a shift in the cultural order means that contemporary design is both a powerful creative force and simultaneously a provider of functional solutions.

The newest generation of designers, therefore, are producing work within an altogether original set of parameters, with new motivations, expectations and resources. The rules that dictated what design could or should be during the last century are now defunct and have not yet been replaced, and the work collected here is indicative of this. Our edit contains the most original and interesting furniture and product designs from an international selection of designers at the beginning of their careers. Individually, each design demonstrates a specific innovation; collectively, they expose the thinking of a generation.

Although these preoccupations manifest themselves in a fantastic array of forms, materials and processes, the accumulated works presented in these pages still reveal clear, distinct patterns. These trends are early indicators of what is to come in contemporary design, and to understand them is to recognize our own cultural and social preoccupations.

The state of contemporary design

The definition of 'design' is in a state of flux; it may even be said to have completely changed. Designers are celebrated as creatives, whose ideas are as valuable as their products, and as engineers in equal measure.

In some instance, their role is seemingly interchangeable between artist and designer. The rise of conceptual design and a resurgence of craft, either in opposition to or in conjunction with mass-production, means that design can be judged on pure creative merit, just like works of art. That is not to say that the importance of functional design has lessened at all – quite the opposite. The expectations of contemporary design have grown to accommodate these previously opposing factors.

The environment fostered by the uncertainty, or ambivalence, about the role of a designer in modern culture is a fertile place for the generation that are the subject here. The fudged boundaries of creativity are represented simply through the wide assortment of work we see, while some seek to make sense of them through their individual work. With the goal posts not so much moved as taken off the pitch, all approaches, all styles and all motivations are valid. There is a prevailing air of experimentation that is refreshing and full of promise for those designers at the beginning of their career.

The design that we, the consumers, choose to surround ourselves with is as valid an indicator of our values and beliefs, and as poignant a tool of individual expression, as fashion, music and art, although less frequently alluded to. Design products are intended to function, but the functions considered necessary by modern society are, perhaps, not as straightforward as those of past generations; function can mean stimulating, titillating, or conferring status or credibility. Design brands seek to establish an emotional connection with their audience, based upon the character of a designer or a brand mission. One result of this is that aesthetic styles are less prescriptive than they previously were. The consumer's desire for individuality and appetite for concept-driven design has resulted in a validation of the designer, too, as individual.

Designers feel an increasing weight of responsibility, as solutions to the problems of contemporary urban society are sought. The motivation for making new products is rarely limited to personal ambition, and this is especially true of young designers. At the beginning of their careers, with the doctrines of their design education still fresh, they are actively seeking to rationalize their future role. Reacting to, or highlighting, wider social, cultural or political issues has become a widespread and popular pursuit and is a telling reflection of the design world's confidence in the capabilities of its oeuvre.

This climate has begun to produce a new crop of designers – a generation who are freer than those who went before them, and are afforded more serious consideration. They are increasingly susceptible to the influences of their environment, and spoilt with more technical innovations and manufacturing opportunities. But what are the preoccupations of this emerging generation of young designers: from where do their influences come, and how do these manifest themselves into recognizable trends? Influences are many and varied, though some key issues can be recognized as shaping this generation of designers and generating common themes.

Common influences

Media influence

The proliferation of new media has played a part in shaping the way designers work, and the ability to share information and ideas has played a huge role in enabling young designers. Although design has always been one of the most global creative disciplines, geographical location means even less thanks to new and accessible tools of communication.

It is in part thanks to such media innovations that fledgling design communities have been established in less probable locations and are no longer tied to manufacturing hubs. Much more than just generating an atmosphere of inclusiveness, the whole geography of the design world has changed as a result. Any feelings of isolation and distance should now be obsolete, and it is no longer necessary for designers to leave their local cultures in order to work. Instead, young designers are increasingly establishing internet-based collaborations: for example Isabelle Olsson and Martin Meier, based in Sweden and Switzerland respectively, claim their design studio exists exclusively thanks to Skype. Of course, the globalization of this creative discipline, like that of so many others, has an ironic reverse effect; for some designers, local influences and inspirations have become all the more relevant because of it.

The appearance of online design magazines and blogs has done much to accelerate the traditionally slow cycles of the design world. These latest media vehicles accommodate our appetite for the new, as products go from concept to online presence within days, shattering the familiar cycle of processes previously needed to bring a product to the public's attention. The effects on new design are many: the process of gaining media attention is democratized, the power of computer-generated images has become substantial, and ideas can be instantly communicated. Another effect is criticism of an internet-based 'speculative and theoretical' design culture.

The proliferation of design media and their perceived importance to the careers of young designers has encouraged this generation to consider their own promotion. The 'stories' behind individual designs or bodies of work are especially important in providing points of differentiation, and as such are carefully premeditated and often elaborately presented.

The role of the media in the definition of contemporary design has been crucial too. On the one hand the discipline is intellectualized, while on the other it is dumbed down; the fashionableness of design is the debate, simultaneously, at international political forums and on frothy morning television shows.

Educational influence

The subjects that occupy young product and furniture designers are quite commonly the evolution of those they have recently studied, and so the subjects taught at certain schools have considerable influence in shaping the course of new design. It would be fair to say that institutions such as Design Academy Eindhoven, Ecole cantonale d'art de Lausanne (ECAL) and the Royal College of Art in London, and the established designers that make up their faculties, play a more pivotal role in influencing emerging design trends than might at first be apparent. By introducing their students to issues and ways of working, they set in motion a chain of events and thinking that will eventually end up in homes around the world.

The theoretical stance of such schools is felt well beyond their classrooms. In the 'Man and Well Being' department of Design Academy Eindhoven, students are taught that the 'discipline of design is rooted in the fine arts [and this] has often been the root of confusion; designers have tended to neglect or skimp on the speculative process that precedes the making of things.' The Academy's move to remedy this must surely be felt in the conceptual work of young Dutch designers and beyond.

The current influence of design schools is conspicuously felt for several more reasons. Designers are finding success early in their careers, which often means that they are more closely affiliated to design schools than to design groups or manufacturing companies, who increasingly often pluck young talents directly from their graduation shows. The schools have also made radical moves to position themselves as brands, their students being emissaries of the values and theories that they promote.

Design education can offer influences beyond practical skills and theoretical approaches. Manufacturing or materials companies often sponsor students to experiment with their product. Take, for example, ECAL's collaboration with Eternit or recent work by the Staatliche Hochschule für Gestaltung (HFG) in Karlsruhe with Rosenthal. Such collaborations, undertaken within the academic atmosphere, can have significant repercussions on the formation of new design trends.

Cultural influences

The shape of the international cultural landscape has much bearing on the state of contemporary design. Most influential of late has been the issue of 'Design Art'. Increasingly shared motivations, platforms and (perhaps most significantly) consumption of high-end design and contemporary art have led to a perceived blurring of boundaries. For young designers this means that a new market for their work has emerged. While few could expect to reap the financial benefits enjoyed by established designers, the way in which design products are bought and presented has meant an increased interest in limited edition designs and a freedom to work in a more creative manner. Concepts and personalities are more saleable commodities than before, and designers enjoy a freedom to produce works for these markets rather than simply working towards a commission for mass-production. Many consider that the supposed grey area has always existed; however, while not necessarily 'new', Design Art is certainly newly commercial.

Further blurring of boundaries between the disciplines of craft, engineering, architecture and design are also perceptible. These mean that the skills and techniques used in many different disciplines, as well as inspirations, are available for use by young designers. See Cris Bartel's fashion inspired stools and Pinar Yar's application of aeronautical engineering. In particular, the influence of the fashion industry is key. Many new design businesses emulate the brand strategy of successful fashion houses, aiming to create the same emotional connections with their customer base.

An increasing number of them, inspired by successful companies like Vitra or Established & Sons, even produce 'lines' and collections, emulating ready-to-wear and haute couture. As more established design businesses in fashion and product design buck a trend for presenting designers as the identifiable figureheads of brands, in the style of Tom Dixon or Marcel Wanders, so young designers are encouraged to promote their own personality and indulge in ever-increasing displays of showmanship.

Because the consumption of design has escalated, young designers are communicating with a more design-literate and, generally, culturally aware end user than ever before. Similarly, the cultural foreshortening of modern society means that designers themselves are able to reference and articulate a diverse range of cultural influences.

Environmental and social influences

Contemporary design is a solution-driven discipline, and as a consequence designers feel an inherent sense of responsibility. Current environmental concerns have been acutely felt by the design industry, which acknowledges its pivotal role in ensuring that the everyday products we use are environmentally sound. Numerous design trends are currently becoming established as a result of this environmental consciousness and young designers are particularly dedicated to developing sustainable methods of manufacturing furniture and products. They are aware that this is likely to be one of the defining issues of their careers.

Designers follow any number of routes in this pursuit. Some point to the longevity of their designs as a clear indication of their sustainability – surely creating a piece that will last a lifetime (no matter where or how it is produced) is an efficient manner of cutting back on consumerism? Others are dedicated to investigating sustainable materials and local manufacturing methods. And some put their efforts into creating products that highlight issues of consumption, such as &made's 'Standby'. The fashion for using recycled products and materials, a kind of 'Frankenstein design', is also linked to issues of sustainability, and the work of Ryan McElhinney or Laura da Monchy are good examples. This efficiently green and visually explicit method of manufacture seems particularly popular. Considering packaging and transportation also drives innovation, like the 'Not A Box' light by David Graas.

Currently the issue of sustainable design is the biggest influence on the industry. The necessity and urgency of finding solutions has had a conspicuous and infectious result, injecting a brand new sense of purpose into the design world, with which a new spirit has come. Awareness of and reaction to commonly debated current affairs, such as issues surrounding security, religion and identity, can be recognized among the designs of this generation. Works that represent traditional or identifiably national aesthetics are often comments on a wider social concern of identity. Designers frequently seek to establish an emotional connection between their work and their audience; see the work of Nacho Carbonell for perfect examples of this growing trend, which has become a shorthand for an observation on a desensitized society. The responsibility felt by new designers is not limited to simply providing solutions to lifestyle problems: their discipline is an unchallenged platform for resolutions and comment on all manner of social issues. Reaction to economic situations, be they those of the designer, of their consumer or of the industrial entities around them, is a further inspiration to new design. New methods of construction are increasingly sought, not only for the benefit of the consumer's pocket but also in order to enable the survival of independent designer-makers and/or manufacturing businesses.

Common themes

The designs presented reveal recurring trends.

Nostalgia

Seen that somewhere before? Many designers inject an instantaneous sentimentality into new work by referencing the familiar, often a traditional design style, or incorporating existing objects into their new designs. The weight of association carries a potent emotional currency, and the ambition is to exploit the potential of a new design to tell a story, create an emotional attachment or share an experience. The nostalgic use of past design aesthetics or forms is also seen as a reverential nod towards design history, and therefore a technique that younger designers are especially fond of.

Recycling

Using found objects and materials in the production of new pieces is, firstly, an economical means of manufacture for young designers with limited resources. It reveals a resourcefulness that is also connected to sustainability, and is frequently a comment on consumerism. It also allows young designers to present their own individual viewpoint on the world around them, to look beyond the perceived value of objects. Where others see an empty oil can, a designer might see a table lamp. This method of making is closely linked to the trends for both nostalgia and experimentation.

Solutions

Solution-driven design is the staple of the discipline, but a new accumulation of problems disrupting modern life brings a need for advanced solutions. Inventive new products that tackle issues of energy consumption are popular. The changing shape of the domestic environment is met with designs that resolve issues of space, storage and (a very popular area) the clutter caused by household technology. Solution-driven design is increasingly conceptual, however. Designs that offer even hypothetical solutions to issues such as globalization, stress and angst are rife; such solution designs are often little acts of rebellion.

Materials

Research and experimentation with materials, both new and old, is the crux of contemporary design. Increasingly, the expression of a material is the underpinning of a design. Young designers feel pressure to differentiate their work from that which has gone before, and so the opportunities offered by new techniques and materials are tantalizing. The extreme of this is the type of designer-maker who chooses to invent their own materials, enabling personal manufacture and ensuring that their role of independent creator is underlined. New composite materials offer uncharted qualities, such as extreme lightness, strength or tactility, and are employed increasingly often in solution-driven designs. The opportunity to revisit traditional materials, with their appealing eco-credentials, is another trend.

Technological Innovations

An ever-increasing spectrum of processes is available as a means of expression. If inspiration is not found in conceptual quarters, then it is most likely to come from the possibilities offered by a specific process of making. Rapid prototyping techniques, which enable quick and easy manufacture, are intended to revolutionize the industrialization of products, while in other cases, the inspirational technology is found outside the manufacturing and design industries but is adapted and applied for a specific purpose. Materials and processes developed especially for the mass manufacturing of

furniture and products are significant because of their projected prevalence, and young designers are keen to test these innovations when given the opportunity. The visualizing of technological processes though complex forms that purposefully reference their digital origins is common.

Process and craft

Elsewhere, mechanical processes are being spurned in favour of 'lo-tech' methods of production, in something of a revival of an Arts and Crafts mentality. This is an especially popular trend among the designers featured in these pages, who are consciously offering alternatives to the proliferation of mass-produced goods, while aiding their own desire for self-expression and self-sufficiency. This is a reactionary trend, supported by a current preoccupation with process and provenance, and also linked to the fashionableness of nostalgia. Championing craft-based methods of making often involves employing material and production innovations in a workshop environment. A return to wholly traditional methods of manufacturing, adapting familiar methods and materials to express new aesthetics and ideas, is equally popular.

Play

Finally, humour and a prevailing light-hearted approach characterize many new products you will see here. As designers feel an increasing freedom, in fact a necessity, to express themselves, much of their work projects a sense of play. This trend is also linked to the desire to create an emotional attachment between consumer and product. Key to the success of such prankish behaviour is the availability of an increasingly responsive and articulate design audience who are in on the joke.

Chronology

The new work you see in this title has been produced between 2005 and 2008. It has not, of course, been created in isolation. The influences of key events, collections, innovations and characters from this short period in design history are significant considerations when trying to understand what motivates and inspires the newest generation of designers. A chronology of important design highlights from the period in question offers an insight into the wider design world from which this work is taken.

2005

February
IKEA expands their product base to include flat-pack houses in an effort to cut the prices of a first home.

Launched at the Stockholm furniture fair, the 'Imprint' chair by Peter Hiort-Lorenzen and Johannes Foersom for Lammhults is made out of Cellupress, a wood-fibre material.

March
The Industrial Designers Society of America (IDSA) announce the winners of the 'Eye for Why' student design competition, which aims to reinvent everyday objects.

April
Ron Gilad's chandelier design 'Dear Ingo' is selected to be part of the new collection from Moooi.

Swarovski's 'Crystal Palace' show in Tokyo includes interactive designs 'Stardust' by Tokujin Yoshioka and 'Miss Haze' by Ron Arad.

Enzo Mari produces a new collection for Japanese brand Hida that makes use of native sugi cypress timber.

At the Milan Salone, Habitat launch their VIP collection of designs created by celebrities. It includes 'Wall Light' designed by the model Helena Christensen.

The launch of the new British design and manufacturing brand Established & Sons is held during the Milan Salone.

Finnish brand Artek unveil their 'Studio' collection, developed under the direction of Tom Dixon.

Cappellini present their New Antiques, modern interpretations of classic furniture designs by Marcel Wanders.

The 'Design Made in Africa' show, produced by Association Française d'Action Artistique (AFAA), Saint-Etienne Métropole and Saint-Etienne International Design Biennale, promotes African crafts.

June
Janneke Hooymans & Frank Tjepkema apply the proportions of modern people to objects around us, resulting in the 'XXL Chair'.

September
The first annual Helsinki Design Week is staged.

Stuart Haygarth's 'Tide Chandelier', made entirely from objects found on the coastline of Kent, is exhibited during London's Design Week.

Inaugurating the London Design Festival, designer Tom Dixon takes over Trafalgar Square with an exhibition of a 75 m (246 ft) seating installation made from 12,000 super-sized rubber bands.

November
The 'Kebab Lights' from Committee are presented at Tokyo Design Week. They are made from a miscellaneous collection of found objects and antique crockery.

December
The first annual Design Miami event, 'the global forum for collecting, exhibiting, discussing and creating design' is staged.

2006

January
B&B Italia invests in the Dutch brand Moooi, creating a new design business model.

Design firm FOC, standing for Freedom Of Creation, win the Interior Innovation award for their digitally generated products.

An agreement with the Triennale di Milano sees the studio of Achille Castiglioni open to the public, and an archiving programme begins.

March
Deyan Sudjic is announced as the new director of The Design Museum in London.

The Design Library, the first Italian library dedicated to design, opens in Milan, with interiors by James Irvine and Maddalena Casadei.

The Haus Der Kunst in Munich presents 'On-Off', a retrospective of Konstantin Grcic's work.

April
FieraMilano, the new Milan Salone building designed by Massimiliano Fuksas, is opened.

Ron Arad shows a comprehensive collection of his Voido designs, including 'Blo Void' and 'Oh Void', in a palette of experimental new materials during the Milan Salone.

Jasper Morrison introduces the 'Crate' sidetable, a homage in Douglas fir to the form of a simple found wine crate.

Vitra launches 'Rocks' a system of 'architecture on demand' by Ronan and Erwan Bouroullec and the 'Polder' sofa and 'Worker Chair' by Hella Jongerius.

The 'Pane Chair' by Tokujin Yoshioka for Moroso is launched during the Milan Salone. The shape is formed by baking it like bread.

The Perished series by Studio Job, featuring inlaid motifs depicting the 'extravagance and violence of our times', are presented at Dilmos.

May
The fourth annual DesignMai festival is held in Berlin, which is also officially declared the UNESCO City of Design. The theme of the exhibition is design and urbanity.

September
Jasper Morrison and Naoto Fukasawa's exhibition 'Super Normal' in London celebrates the best of anonymous design.

London's Aram Gallery hosts Jaime Hayon's major solo show 'Stage'.

Tom Dixon works with expanded polystyrene to demonstrate its possibilities for moulded furniture.

October
The 6th Shanghai Art Biennale uses the theme 'Hyper Design' to invite international designers to work with Chinese craftsmen.

November
The annual international exhibition Design Tide in Tokyo takes as its theme 'Design and Peace'.

London's Design Museum drops its frequently controversial Designer of the Year award.

December
Two important auctions are held in New York. In the Phillips de Pury 'Design & Design' auction Ron Arad's 'This mortal coil' bookshelf sells for $117,600. At Sotheby's 'Important 20th Century Design' auction, Marc Newson's 'Pod of Drawers' sells for a record $632,000.

Joris Laarman's 'Bone Chair' and 'Bone Chaise', produced using car-manufacturing software, are launched at Design Miami as part of 'Smart Deco', co-presented by New York gallery Barry Friedman Ltd and the Dutch design collective Droog.

Marc Newson is named designer of the year at the Design Miami event.

Zaha Hadid presents her 'Seamless' collection for Phillips de Pury during Design Miami.

2007

January
Zaha Hadid's 'Ideal House' concept investigates new typologies of living space and is the centrepiece of the Cologne Design Fair.

February
The 10th Design Indaba in Cape Town features work by Jurgen Bey, Hella Jongerius, Jasper Morrison, Konstantin Grcic and Jaime Hayon.

The Campana Brothers' exhibition at Albion Gallery in London features the 'Cartoon' chairs and new works.

B&B Italia relaunches Mario Bellini's iconic 1970s 'Le Bambole' armchair.

March
Ross Lovegrove produces a new collection of works for a Phillips de Pury selling exhibition in New York.

Designer Moritz Waldemeyer and fashion designer Hussein Chalayan collaborate on a catwalk collection of dresses that combine fashion and complex engineering solutions.

The 'Drawing Water Challenge', an international competition sponsored by Arup for designs to give access to clean water, is won by a device that harvests water from the air.

April
The Campana Brothers are the latest designers to produce objects for 'Design With Conscience', a project by Artecnica that pairs leading designers with artisans in the developing world.

Italian mosaic brand Bisazza presents fantastical installations by Jaime Hayon and Studio Job during the Milan Salone.

Tokujin Yoshioka uses thousands of straws to create an installation in Moroso's Milan showroom.

Marcel Wanders presents 'Personal Editions', a large collection of limited-edition pieces produced under his own name.

The Homework collection of monumental household objects is exhibited by Studio Job.

Carpenters Workshop Gallery in London hosts 'Design Povera', the work of Vincent Dubourg.

Rapid prototyping company Materialise.MGX launch works by various designers, including Dutch architect Luc Merx's 'Damned' lamp.

The Artek Pavilion for the Trienalle Park in Milan is designed by Japanese architect Shigeru Ban, and makes use of a revolutionary method of paper construction.

Ronan and Erwan Bouroullec launch the 'Steelwood' chair for Magis.

May
The International Design Forum in Dubai is dedicated to architecture and design in the Arab world.

The 'So Watt!' design exhibition in Paris aims to raise public awareness of energy consumption issues.

Marc Newson shows a collection of his new work at the Gagosian Gallery in New York.

'Dezeen', a comprehensive, international online architecture and design magazine, launches.

Marcel Wanders turns a five-storey former school in Amsterdam into a base for design creatives and creative industries.

June
Design Miami/Basel uses the theme 'Performance'. Maarten Baas, Max Lamb and Front are among designers who produce live installations of work.

DuPont celebrates the 40th birthday of Corian® by commissioning new works in Corian® from 40 designers.

Vitra shows their Editions collection of limited work by a number of top names including Zaha Hadid and Konstantin Grcic.

August
The first Moss store outside New York's Soho opens in Los Angeles.

September
New work by designer Ettore Sottsass inaugurates the Friedman Benda Gallery in New York.

The 'Trash Luxe' exhibition during London Design Week features work produced by recycling waste materials.

Assa Ashuach presents 'A1', a light that has 'artificial intelligence' and reacts to its users' movements.

Peter Halley and designer Matali Crasset collaborate on 'Rebours', a collection of installations shown at the Ropac Gallery in Paris.

October
The Designhuis gallery and institution for contemporary design opens in Eindhoven.

Martino Gamper exhibits 'One Hundred Chairs in One Hundred Days', each made in a single day from found materials or products.

November
During Tokyo Design Week, Hella Jongerius launches a limited edition collection of ceramics using traditional Japanese enamel techniques.

December
Contemporary glass and ceramic work is presented in the 'Fragiles' exhibition by Die Gestalten Verlag during Design Miami.

Wok Media shows 'Made In China' with Contrasts Gallery during Design Miami.

2008
January
Ettore Sottsass dies aged 90.

Dutch manufacturer Arco launches new works by Bertjan Pot during the Cologne Design Fair.

Spanish ceramic firm Lladró release Re-Cyclos, new collections with designers including Committee.

February
'Contemporary Swedish Handicraft' is presented as a showcase at the Stockholm Furniture Fair.

Ronan and Erwan Bouroullec exhibit new pieces and typologies at Galerie Kreo in Paris.

April
Emeco launch Nine-0, the last range of chairs and stools by late Italian designer Ettore Sottsass.

The Swarovski 'Crystal Palace' at the Milan Salone includes Studio Job's giant 'Globe' and Tokujin Yoshioka's minimal 'Eternal'.

Maarten Baas shows five years worth of work at the Milan Salone.

The online design platform DeTank is launched.

Tom Dixon presents his new collection 'Bit Of Rough' during the Milan Salone.

Meta, a British firm uniting designers with traditional artisans, launches with works by Tord Boontje and BarberOsgerby.

Konstantin Grcic's 'Myto' cantilever chair for Plank is presented at the Milan Salone, together with an insight into its production.

At the Milan Salone, Jaime Hayon presents Lladró 'Re-Deco' pieces, a Bisazza-tiled conceptual aeroplane, and his book 'Jaime Hayon Works'.

May
Industrial Facilities exhibition 'Some Recent Projects' opens at London's Design Museum.

June
Li Edelkoort resigns from Design Academy Eindhoven.

August
The show 'Flexibility: Design in a Fast-changing Society' in Turin, which is World Design Capital 2008, includes work by Ross Lovegrove and Matali Crasset.

September
Droog and communications agency KesselsKramer create the 'S1NGLETOWN' exhibition for the Venice Architecture Biennale.

The first Moscow Design Week attracts 28,000 visitors.

In London, Fumi Gallery's first major exhibition includes works by Max Lamb and Pieke Bergmans.

October
Maarten Baas's 'Chankley Bore' designs for Established & Sons are shown during Frieze Art Fair in London.

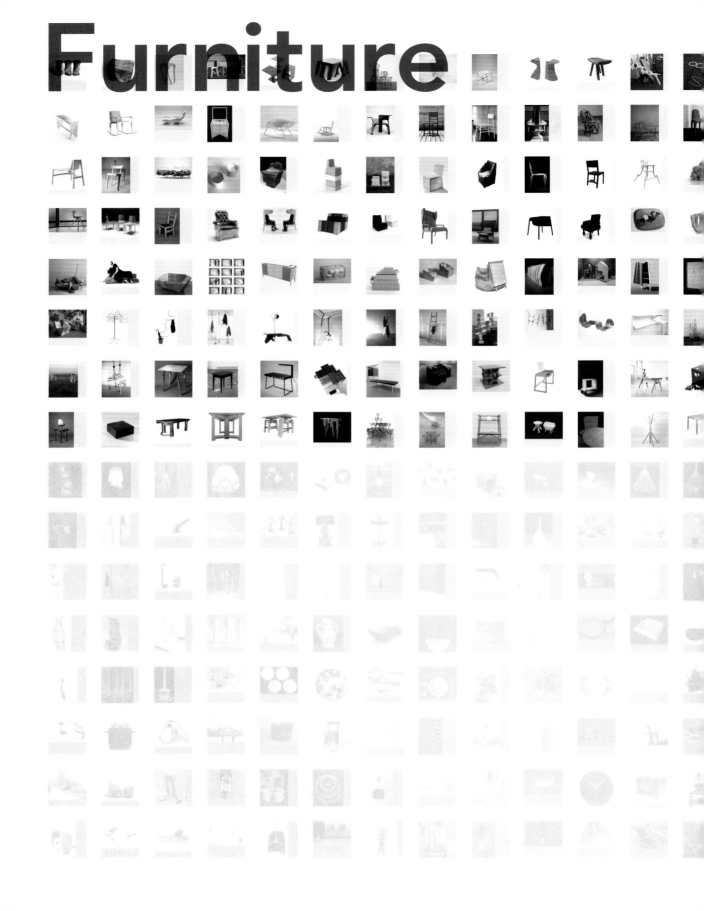

Furniture

(nothing to) HIDE
Willem Derrider
Dutch

The hidden characteristics of a material we think we know well are the focus of this design by Willem Derrider. He asserts that we rarely remember that leather is a product of nature, and that it is most often employed as a material for mass-production in a manner regrettably devoid of its intrinsic identity. The stools exploit the structural strength and malleability of leather, which Derrider sees as forgotten characteristics. The leather is first moulded and then boiled for two minutes. This process alone lends a strength and solidity that allows the stools to function as a seat, without any further frames or supports.

Stool
Leather
www.deridderdesignstudio.com
Location > the Netherlands
In production
By > designer

The Weave Stool
Bikram Mittra
British

The limitations of material, production and technology help create design opportunities, says Bikram Mittra. Here, he has taken a single laminated teak section and repeated it to create the woven pattern of the stool. The process is economical and offers a strong, inherently decorative structure.

Stool
Laminated teak, stainless steel
www.bikrammittra.com
Location > UK
Available to order

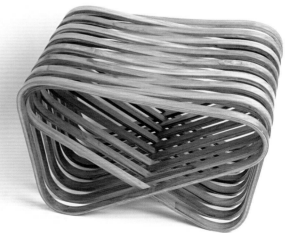

Skinterior
Cris Bartels
Dutch

A slender plastic body is subsidiary to the textile exterior in this Cris Bartels design. Bartels wanted to convey the world of fashion and evoke the image of a fragile body swathed in dominating clothing. The shape of the stool is therefore dictated by its textile mould; it seems clumsy and fragile, and Bartels describes it as 'vulnerable'. The structure is in fact strong, with an appealing, awkward elegance.

Stool
Textile, plastic
www.crisbartels.nl
Location > the Netherlands
Available to order

Bartels's stool was inspired by human anatomy, as is 'Boxed Body' by Björn Rooijackers on p. 127.

Launch Stool
Ben McCarthy
Australian

'The stool came about via a want to push the rotational moulding process' says Australian designer Ben McCarthy. This hollow stool has integral strength but is also lightweight, with an ample volume that is easily achieved using this process. The tapered legs and large, flat seat area give the stool a certain dynamic quality, which McCarthy says is associated with jumping, flying or moving.

Stool
Polyethelene
www.benmccarthy.com
Location > Hong Kong
In production
By > www.go-home.com.au

Pimp
Adrien Rovero
Swiss

The 'Pimp' stool and low table are based upon a simple construction principle; a standard H-profile (often used in the car 'tuning' industry for lightness and strength) and a folded sheet. Brightly coloured anodization is the only decorative element applied to these simply constructed units.

Table, stool
Aluminium, anodized finish
www.adrienrovero.com
Location > Switzerland
Limited edition

Five
Anna Bullus
British

'I wanted to make people stop and think and to challenge perceptions by introducing an element of surprise through the use of optical illusions.' This is a playful piece by Anna Bullus: the four stools can be used individually or come together as a single table.

Stools/table
Medium density fibreboard (MDF), oak veneer, Polyrey laminate
www.annabullusdesign.com
Location > UK
Available to order

This design engages by creating a strong visual illusion; the 'PointOfView Cabinet' on p. 109 is similarly disarming.

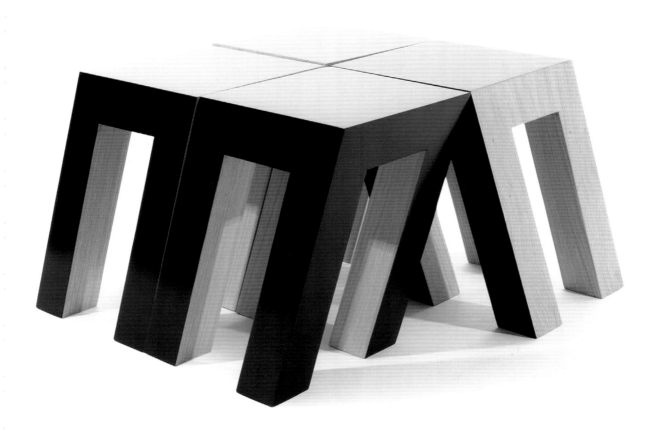

Nido
Eva Marguerre
German

This series of stools and tables
is made by wrapping glass fibre
between fixed points. The stools
are then dipped in coloured epoxy
resin. The effect is reminiscent
of craft-produced wicker furniture,
although the application of
contemporary materials adds
a new dimension. The resulting
structures are extremely light.

Table/stool
Glass fibre, epoxy resin
www.eva-marguerre.de
Location > Germany
Available to order

Letters
Hideyuki Ona, Yu Toida
Japanese

'We want to explore the possibility of lengthening a material's period of usability,' say Japanese design duo Hideyuki Ona and Yu Toida. Methods of recycling and the potential to change the properties of a material were their initial inspirations. The 'Letters' stool is constructed entirely from vulcanized paper, and its shape and scale represent a full wastepaper bin. The designers found the paper to be flexible and adaptable: the stool can be reformed by simply moistening the paper and if it is damaged, new paper can be added to mend it.

Stool
Vulcanized paper
www016.upp.so-net.ne.jp/i-u/
Location > Japan
Limited edition

118
Fabien Caperan
Swiss

The desire to create a stool that functions inside and outside led Fabien Caperan to investigate different upholstery materials. A firefighters' water hose is an unlikely choice, yet the sturdy fabric suits this application perfectly. Foam is injected into sections of hose, which are then attached to a skinny metal structure.

Stool
Foam, fire hose, stainless steel
Location > Switzerland
Available to order

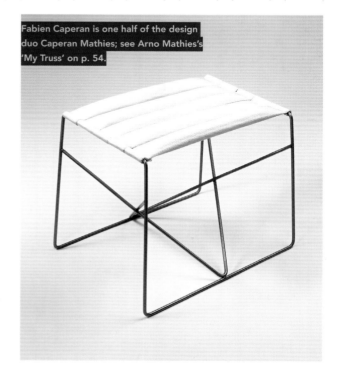

Fabien Caperan is one half of the design duo Caperan Mathies; see Arno Mathies's 'My Truss' on p. 54.

TIK & TAK Stools
Shahira Fahmy
Egyptian

Shahira Fahmy started with a strict rectangular box and subtracted from it to create an uninterrupted, fluid shape that would accurately support the human form. Medium density fibreboard (MDF) was used for the prototype, and it is intended that production versions should be manufactured from rotation-moulded Fordacal®, yet the 'TIK & TAK Stools' share the qualities of hand-crafted furniture. Fahmy describes the design as a reaction to the upright architectural forms surrounding us, 'for example a wall and human body leaning against it and the reshaping of that wall to meet the forces put on it'.

Stool
MDF, high-gloss finish
www.sfahmy.com
Location > Egypt
In development

Qing Zuo!
Judith van den Boom
Dutch

Ceramic designer Judith van den Boom has spent long periods investigating the working practices of both artisans and manufacturers of ceramics in China. Her cultural connection has led to various investigative projects and innovative products. Here she wanted to combine her product-design background with the influences of her explorations and create a functional object that works against the preconceptions of ceramic being a cold material, unattractive for one-to-one use.

Stool
Ceramic, wood
www.judithvandenboom.nl
Location > UK
Available to order

Judith van den Boom is concerned with the industrial use of ceramics; see also 'Floor Motion' on p. 323.

Branch Stools
Jonathan Legge
Irish

This is a 'series of tentative playful characters, with ambiguous functions' says designer Jonathan Legge. He began by considering what could be made with minimal effort or modification from the fallen boughs of trees. He says that the tree 'might not want to become an over-engineered piece of furniture' and so formed these simply bound pieces of wood as ambiguous objects.

Stool
Pine, cotton webbing
www.jonathanlegge.com
Location > UK
Available to order

Gori Stool
Wanju Kim
South Korean

Practicality and versatility were the qualities Wanju Kim wanted to embody in this simple little stool. Ease of manufacture was also a key attribute, so Kim chose to use a single principal material – steel tube – and to minimize the structure. French cane, a traditional upholstery choice, is wrapped around the seat.

Stool
Steel tube, cane
www.wanjukim.com
Location > UK
Available to order

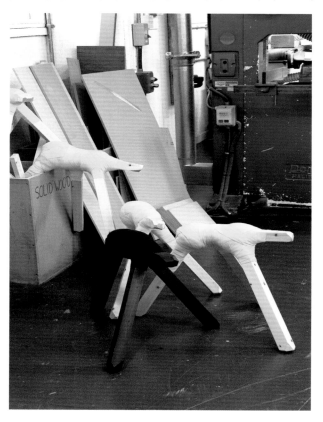

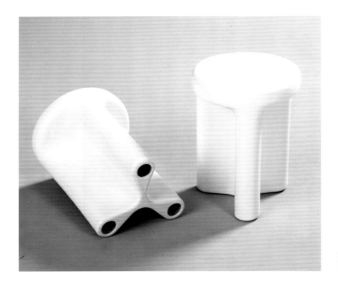

Ceramiko
Moko Sellars
British

In a reaction against disposable furniture, Moko Sellars chose to manufacture her simple and functional stool from ceramic because she feels porcelain has a history of being cherished and passed down through generations. The design itself was influenced by ornamental objects and the process of slip casting, most often used in their manufacture.

Stool
Ceramic
Location > UK
Available to order

Triangular Stool
Nicolas Le Moigne
French

This stool was made using limited materials and under the strict conditions of an academic competition. Nicolas Le Moigne and five fellow graduates were asked to design a piece of furniture using only a single A0 size (841 × 1189 mm or 33.1 × 46.8 in.) sheet of aluminium, of which they had to use at least 70 per cent. The result is a seemingly effortless object that belies great engineering skill.

Stool
Aluminium
www.nicolaslemoigne.com
Location > Switzerland
In production
By > www.inoutdesigners.ch

Using a single sheet of aluminium removes the need for fixtures and fastenings. The same minimal method of construction is used in 'Lia' on p. 149.

Teo Stool
Luciana Gonzalez Franco,
Cristian Mohaded
Argentinian

A flexible material surface dictated the folded form of this stool. The 'Teo Stool' is made from surface-treated cardboard, but the designers intend to create the same form in the future in other, equally pliable materials, such as eco-bonded leather. The limited lifespan of a cardboard stool is part of its appeal, as is the ease with which it can be made, moved and stored.

Stool
Cardboard with surface treatment
Location > Argentina
Limited edition

The process of folding paper also lent inspiration to Sofia Grew for 'A4' on p. 90.

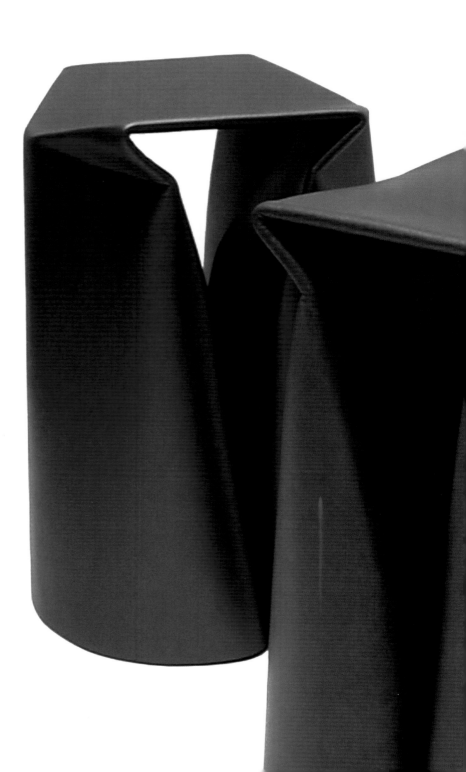

Stack Stool
Ruby and Sather Duke
American

Simple silhouettes turned in a mix of materials and colours, including salvaged wood taken from defunct factories across New York, are stacked together to create these stools. Ruby and Sather Duke of hivemindesign say their interest in the industrial hydroelectric turbines found in dams informed both the shape of the stool and the primary colours used upon them.

Stool
Laminated scrap material, woods including walnut, oak, poplar and pine, water-based lacquer, oil finish
www.hivemindesign.com
Location > USA
In production
By > designer

Cushion
Office Origin Air
Dutch

The traditional milk stool is an anonymous and functional object that has successfully served its purpose for centuries. Ivan Kasner and Uli Budde of the Office Origin Air design studio have illustrated how even the most resolved furniture designs can sometimes benefit from a fresh perspective. Here, the simple addition of a cushion, in a textile by Kvadrat, improves the comfort of the stool.

Stool
Beech, textile
www.officeoriginair.com
Location > the Netherlands
In production
By > designer

Winter Arrives
Outofstock
Tan+Chua – Singaporean
Maggio – Argentinian
Alberdi – Spanish

These pieces represent a romantic
memory of outdoor objects
covered in a thick layer of freshly
fallen snow. The effect was
recreated with steel furniture
and upholstered foam. Outofstock
is a disparate collective whose
members are based in Singapore,
Buenos Aires and Barcelona. This
explains the Outofstock company
ethos: 'we believe in celebrating
both our diversity and similarities,
and our work is largely inspired
by either unique cultural nuances
or shared global experiences.'

Chair, stool
Steel, lacquer, foam, suede
www.outofstockdesign.com
Location > Singapore/Spain/
Argentina/UK
Available to order

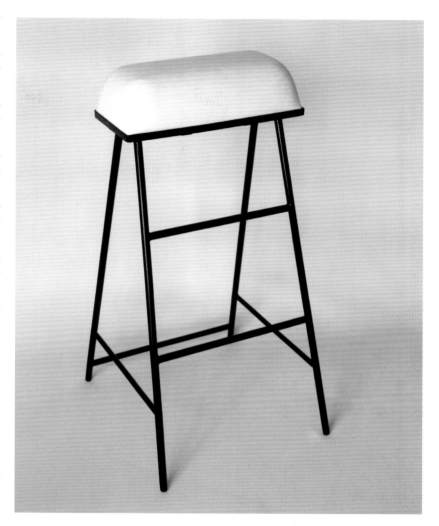

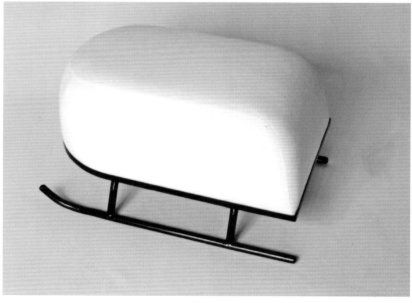

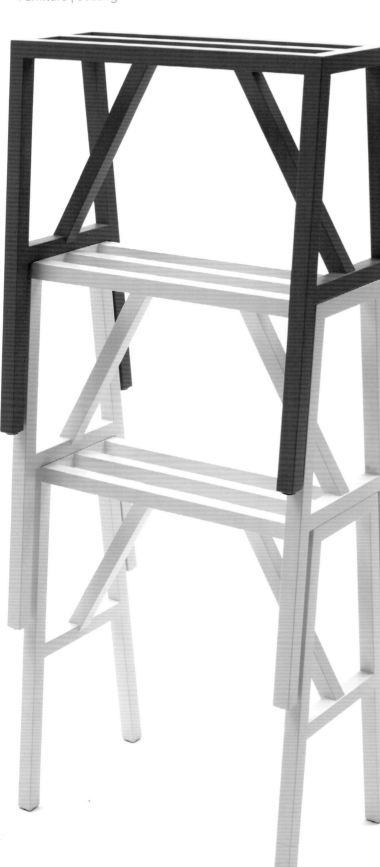

Stool
Kensaku Oshiro
Japanese

This stool by Kensaku Oshiro looks and feels extraordinarily light. The structure is made up of 13 separate sticks that are positioned precisely according to necessity. Together, they create a graphic outline that is minimal and integral.

Stool
Beech, paint
www.kensakuoshiro.com
Location > Italy
Available to order

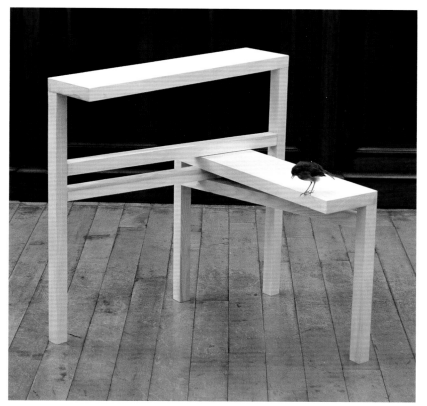

Stile Stool
David Emblin
British

'I believe in simple, accessible and intuitive objects that speak for themselves' says David Emblin. The 'Stile Stool' has a simple remit; to act as both a seat and a table when required, and to fold away when not required. Emblin has set out to embody the inherent functionality of the stile in this design, which is 'a little piece of the countryside for the home'.

Stool/table
Wood
www.davidemblin.co.uk
Location > UK
Available to order

Molto Beene
Julian Appelius
German

When unengaged, four feet of this small stool are in contact with the floor, while the other six are suspended, and the structure is alarmingly unstable. But when the stool is sat upon, the middle legs make contact with the ground and the seat is secure. The flexible seat is made from spring steel.

Stool
Steel, wood
www.julianappelius.de
Location > Germany
Available to order

Wings Bench
Pinar Yar, Tugrul Gövsa
Turkish

This bench pays homage to the lightness and strength of aeroplane wings; the composite material employed in the seat is used in the production of winglets. The addition of a wooden base reflects the use of wood in early aeronautical design, and the combination of this elementary material and the technologically advanced composite creates aesthetic tensions in the design.

Bench
Composite, wood
Location > Turkey
In production
By > www.gaeaforms.com

Bench for two
Céline Dayes,
Romuald Marie
French

Céline Dayes and Romuald Marie work under the studio name '16&12'. Some time ago they decided to take the basic elements of ornamental baroque plasterwork, a seemingly functionless interior element, and give them a purpose. The resulting benches use the familiar forms of the plasterwork, reworked in ceramic, as seats.

Bench
Ceramics, glaze, ebony
www.16et12.com
Location > France
Available to order

Benches
Sylvia Lai
Chinese

The traditional Chinese bench has a simple and enduring structure. It is a nostalgic memory of this form that led Sylvia Lai of Studioroom906 to redesign the bench and increase its value. She has recreated the bench in various heights and sizes – the new topology of the bench offers the possibilities for many new uses including seating, tables and storage.

Bench
Plywood
www.studioroom906.com
Location > China/the Netherlands
Available to order

Many young Chinese designers rework emblematic Chinese iconography in their work. See also Min Chen's 'Stereo Callligraphy' on p. 156.

Eternit
Nicolas Le Moigne
French

A collaboration with Swiss manufacturers Eternit led to the design of these stools and low tables. The Eternit material is a fibre-reinforced cement, here taken in a new direction. Le Moigne investigated original moulding techniques and found that adding a central fold to the form provided additional strength.

Bench, table
Fibre-reinforced cement
www.nicolaslemoigne.com
Location > Switzerland
In production
By > www.garden-styling.ch

A material that mixes cement and fibre offers exciting construction possibilities. See Jaccard Vladimir's 'Birdy' on p. 313.

Fuga
Yeşim Bakirküre
Turkish

Although 'Fuga' appears to be folded from a single sheet of metal, this table is, in fact, constructed from several carefully welded pieces. Perforations along the connection points exaggerate the effect and allow light to permeate the otherwise solid form.

Bench/table
Metal sheet
www.ypsilontasarim.com
Location > Turkey
Available to order

Metal sheets lend themselves to a strong origami aesthetic. See also 'Seam Lights' on p. 165.

Quilt Chair and Stool
Kiki van Eijk
Dutch

These pieces come from a collection by van Eijk named Quality Time. The name refers to both the amount of time lavished on their construction and the intention that the design stand the test of time, and is also reference to past furniture styles, principally the turned wood that characterized Victorian furniture. Van Eijk both updates and personalizes these traditional forms and patterns in powder-coated steel and quilted leather. She summarizes the design as 'hard versus soft, the traditional forms and techniques of the Victorian time transformed into our/my world.'

Rocking chair, stool
Steel, powder-coated finish, leather
www.kikiworld.nl
Location > the Netherlands
Available to order

Kiki van Eijk has extracted characteristics from period furniture and reinterpreted them, one of the most conspicuous recent visual trends. See Adam Rowe's 'Victorian Grandfather Chair' on p. 78 and Mareanne Bosch's 'Tafel-Tafel' on p. 138.

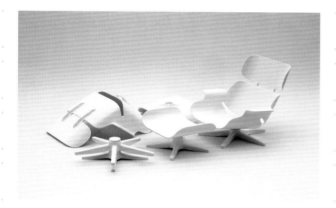

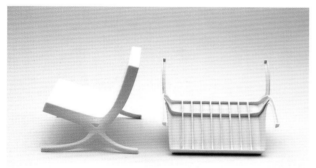

A Stacking Homage
Dirk Winkel
German

Dirk Winkel has taken some of the 20th century's most iconic furniture designs and very cleverly reproduced them in a democratic way that strips them of all of their associated pretension. 'The concept was to transform the original idol's messages; the plastic chairs lose the message of financial power and wealth, they keep their design message.' The chairs are manufactured cheaply from injection-moulded polypropylene, they are stackable and, in an ironic twist, they fulfil an important intention of the original designers that has been lost: they are affordable and accessible for all.

Chair
Polypropylene
www.dirkwinkel.com
Location > Germany
In development

Teotitlan 1
Tanya Aguiñiga
Mexican/American

Designer Tanya Aguiñiga is motivated by a desire to sustain and promote traditional crafts, especially from her native country, Mexico. The 'Teotitlan 1' chair was conceived after a field trip staying with an ancient weaving community in Oaxaca. The chair makes references to the looms and the method of wrapping strings used in that traditional technique.

Chair
Steel, lacquer, nylon rope
www.aguinigadesign.com
Location > USA
Available to order

Traditional craft techniques are a popular preoccupation among young designers. See Simon Hasan's 'Leather Vases' on p. 226 or DFC's Science Series on p. 265.

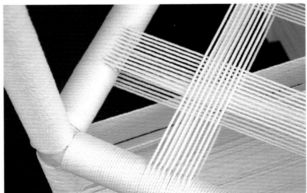

Streamer
Bernhard Schwarzbauer
Austrian

Ribbons of spring-steel streamers
are attached to a tubular steel
frame, creating a dramatic profile
for this chair. The effect of the many
linear streamers is to draw a light
and fluid outline, removed from the
true industrial nature of the piece.
A comfortable, soft-touch synthetic
coating is applied to the surface.

Chair
Steel, soft-touch polyurethane
www.bernhardschwarzbauer.com
Location > Germany
Available to order

Blockhead
Jussi Takkinen
Finnish

What would a rocking chair look like if it were put together with instant glue? Well, a little like this, thinks Jussi Takkinen. His idea was to refresh the image of a traditional wooden rocking chair by reducing the emphasis on the joints. This is achieved by rounding off the ends of the birch sticks that make up its basic skeleton.

Chair
Birch
www.jussitakkinen.com
Location > Finland
In development

The Shuffle Chair
Tanja Schlierkamp
German

This chair is 'an invitation to sit badly' says Schlierkamp. After looking into the restrictions on comfort caused by a normal chair and studying less conventional ways of sitting, Schlierkamp designed a chair to cater for flexible movement. Further experiments in ergonomics included giving the chair three legs and a pair of disconnected footrests (not shown) in contrast to the conventional crossbar that often doubles as a foothold.

Chair
Plywood, stainless steel, lacquer
Location > UK
Available to order

A Restless Chairacter
Pepe Heykoop
Dutch

Pepe Heykoop's chair looks a lot like an old, unstable dining chair, and this product is an effective homage to just that. The principal feature of the chair is its movement; Heykoop has engineered the frame to be exceptionally flexible, allowing and encouraging the sitter to lean, rock and twist in the seat, behaviour usually frowned upon. The flexible casing enclosing the metal skeleton is intrinsic to the flexible nature of the chair, but also contributes to the 'over-painted, aged' effect and general deception.

Chair
Aluminium, steel, polyurethane
www.pepeheykoop.nl
Location > the Netherlands
In development

Ash and Corian Chair
Jon Harrison
British

Harrison sought a perfect marriage of material and aesthetics in a chair 'that wouldn't jump out or jar with its environment'. Ash and Corian® were chosen for their tactile, aesthetic and functional qualities. Usability and manufacture are highly important in Harrison's work: 'I believe if an item is to function correctly it should be able to tell the consumer what it is for and how to use it intuitively – with no need for instructions or explanations.' This simple chair speaks directly in the 'common visual language' Harrison believes we all share.

Chair
Ash, Corian®
www.jon-harrison.com
Location > UK
In development

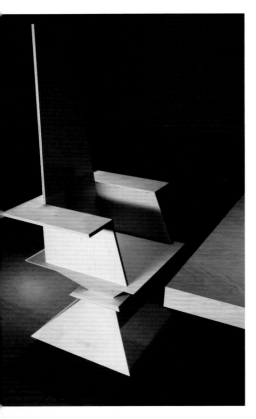

The king in I died
Kostas Tsagkas
Greek

Originally designed for an exhibition in Eindhoven titled 'The Last Supper?', these chairs were intended to sit at either end of a long dining table. Tsagkas came to the conclusion that sitting at the head of such a grand table suggested vanity and distance, and therefore the abstract expression of a throne was a reference during the design process.

Chair
Birch plywood
www.reform.nl
Location > the Netherlands
Available to order

Thonet No.18 (homage)
Matthias Pliessnig
American

The manner in which the steam-bent oak wraps repeatedly around an original Thonet No.18 chair is, says Pliessnig, a response to 'the seductive beauty' of the chair. As he reacts to the curves and structure of the chair in his weaving, he claims he is paying homage to the celebrated form and providing comment on what he sees as the prevalent desire by contemporary designers to over-complicate timeless design.

Chair
Steam-bent oak
www.matthias-studio.com
Location > USA
Available to order

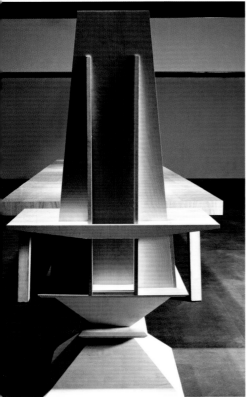

The grandeur of ancient dining chairs was inspiration here. The same traditions inspired Frank Flavell's 'Wingback Chair' on p. 78.

R.A.W. Chair
Haris Rusydin
Indonesian

Haris Rusydin sees the potential of Indonesia's indigenous materials (such as rattan) and industries, and seeks to evolve ways of working with and updating them. The lack of an established contemporary design culture in Indonesia has only strengthened his resolve. This new approach can be seen in the 'R.A.W. Chair' (standing for random arrangement webbing), which uses zip-ties instead of woven rattan. This method of joining allows inexpensive and space saving shipping of the furniture.

Chair
Rattan, zip-ties, wooden dowel
www.roosydinharis.com
Location > Indonesia
Available to order

Bronze Poly Chair
Max Lamb
British

Max Lamb's series of Poly Chairs are hand-carved and beaten out of low-density expanded polystyrene. They are then cast in solid bronze using lost-foam casting, a process that is most typically used to mass-produce aluminium engine parts. Only one bronze can be cast from each mould, making every chair unique. The texture of the fragile polystyrene is captured in a permanent, precious form.

Chair
Bronze
www.maxlamb.org
Location > UK
Limited edition

United We Stand
Rob Southcott
Canadian

Alone, each of these chairs is top-heavy and slightly unstable, but together, their intertwined 'branches' offer each other support; the chairs become a united structure, with each individual unit reliant on its neighbour. 'United We Stand' is a rather poignant visual reminder 'that we can all use a little support' says Rob Southcott.

Chair
Laminated birch, brass
www.robsouthcott.com
Location > Canada
Available to order

Channa Ernstsen's 'InterVases' on p. 231 are similarly co-dependent.

W Lounge
Joel Edmondson
American

This curvaceous chair was initially developed to show off a laminate product. Bent plywood with a laminate finish offers a surprisingly sturdy construction, despite the cantilevered form of the chair.

Chair
Plywood, glass fibre, laminate
Location > USA
In development

Sled
Merit Milla Vaahtera
Finnish

The spring Nordic sun can be warm even when there is still snow on the ground. This seasonal anomaly inspired Merit Milla Vaahtera to use the surprising form of a sled as lounger. The concept of out-of-season sunbathing may have inspired the design of this generously proportioned lounge chair, but its use is clearly flexible.

Chair
Birch, plywood
Location > Finland
In production
By > www.adessin.fi

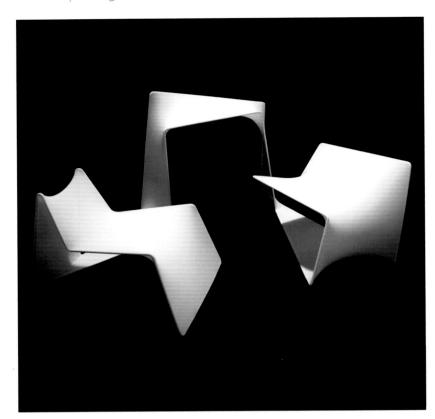

LIINA chair
Saana Rönkönharju – Swedish
Maria Ljungsten – Finnish

This chair invites users to explore different seating configurations. The structure consists of a light steel frame with a textile surface stretched across it to form one continuous line. The intended seating areas of the installation are not immediately apparent. 'The freedom of form invites people to explore the furniture in new ways' say Rönkönharju and Ljungsten.

Chair
Steel, textile
Location > Denmark
In development

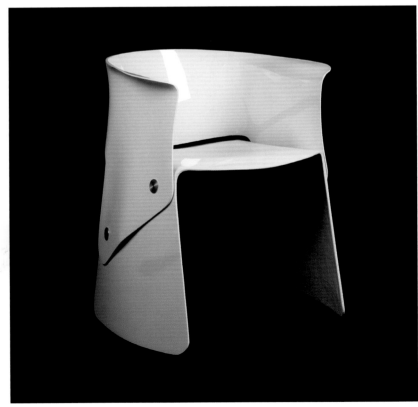

Wing Chair
Joa Herrenknecht
German/Canadian

The 'Wing Chair' has a uniform base and two possible back rests; low and high. The backs are interchangeable and can be attached by the two giant screws on either side of the base. Joa Herrenknecht tried to integrate the soft, elegant curves of a saddle into the design – the use of glass fibre reinforcement helped to achieve this ambition of fluidity.

Chair
Glass-reinforced plastic
www.yoma.de
Location > Germany
In development

Chair
Frida Jeppsson
Swedish

At first glance, this is an archetypal
chair with no outstanding features
to note. But on closer inspection,
from a certain angle, it is possible
to see the shadow of another chair
back within the semi-transparent
polyethylene. The hidden chair is a
'pinnstolen', a classic Swedish chair,
and it represents the hidden soul
of this new design, without which
'Chair' would be unremarkable.

Chair
Polyethylene
www.fridajeppsson.se
Location > Sweden
In development

One structural form has been designed
to absorb another, each representing
a different period in history; see also
'Ghost Chair' on p. 64.

Néo Noé
Philippe Riehling
French

The ambition to produce an ecologically sound product led Philippe Riehling to look at how little waste he might produce with a design cut from a single piece of beechwood ply. All materials were locally sourced and produced, and the chair has been assembled with wooden fixings and a reduced-solvent glue. These decisions make the chair a 'monomaterial' product, and so more easily recycled at the end of its life. Riehling is an industrial designer qualified in ecodesign, the process of which colours his work.

Chair
Beech ply
www.riehling.com
Location > France
Available to order

Mosquito
Michaël Bihain
Belgian

Michaël Bihain set out with the
ambition to humanize a furniture
design. He believes that in the near
future 'we will not need anymore
material stuff' and so decided that
he should create a product that
could exist independently with
a character of its own. Bihain
combines this theoretical approach
with experiments with both the
archetypal shape of a chair and
construction techniques. The
'Mosquito' chair uses a single
piece of bent plywood.

Chair
Plywood, paint or whitened
oak veneer
www.bihain.com
Location > Belgium
Available to order

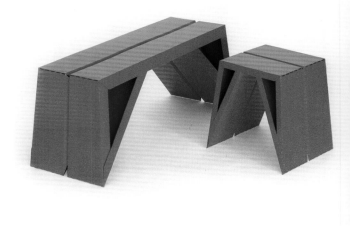

Bullet
Mikael Mantila
Finnish

Mikael Mantila most usually lets materials influence his designs, so the precut perforated steel used in 'Bullet' dictated the form of the chair. This design was created as an experiment to force the material into a 3D form. The result is an elegant chair that can, thanks to its durable material, be used both indoors and outdoors.

Chair
Steel sheet, steel rod, paint
www.coolcorporation.fi
Location > Finland
Available to order

My Truss
Arno Mathies
Swiss

No welding or other costly or tricky methods of manufacture are needed in the construction of 'My Truss', which is made from a single folded sheet of aluminium. The furniture is strong and durable despite this simple manufacture and the lightweight material.

Chair
Aluminium, double-sided tape, powder-coated finish
Location > Switzerland
Available to order

RU Chair
Shane Schneck
American

Shane Schneck produced this pragmatic and utilitarian design for Promosedia in Italy. The chair explores the function of supporting a person with the removal of the two front legs, and Schneck says 'the feeling is similar to how one may feel seated on a wood dock hanging over the edge of water'. Iconic Eames moulded plywood chairs inspired the choice of the material and the manufacturing process used.

Chair
Plywood, paint
www.shaneschneck.com
Location > Sweden
In production
By > www.ncmobler.se

Bastard
Els Woldhek/Whatels
Dutch

The 'Bastard' chair is a product of the conventional furniture-making industry, albeit in an unusual way. It is constructed from the waste leather used by manufacturer Montis in the production of other designs. These leftovers dictate the final shape of the chair, as stitching the pieces together creates a deformed, irregular and awkward shape. The 'Bastard' is born half from the mass-production process and half from a craft production.

Chair
Leather, beech, foam
www.whatels.net
Location > the Netherlands
In production
By > designer

Waste from the design industry is also the primary material in Christian Kocx design 'Non-woven' on p. 79. Néo Noé on p. 52 seeks to reduce manufacturing waste.

Ply-Ply
Jani Koivula
Finnish

Jani Koivula wanted to design a
chair that made use of existing
and cost-effective manufacturing
techniques. The result, 'Ply-Ply',
illustrates the possibilities of form
that can be achieved by widely
practised techniques. Compressed
plywood and turned solid wood
are the deliberately limited
components chosen.

Chair
Solid wood, plywood
www.mutu.tv
Location > Finland
Available to order

P'tite Lulu
Bernard Moïse
French

This deep and svelte wooden chair series is built around the trestle form. Constructed from a sycamore frame and moulded plywood body, the series includes several variations of seating, each designed to encourage a different kind of interaction and posture. For example, 'Lulu la généreuse' is a 'three-buttock chair' designed for one person to sit and another to perch to one side.

Chair
Sycamore, plywood, varnish
www.bernardmoise.com
Location > France
Available to order

Providing for modern ways of sitting is one way in which the chair continues to evolve. See also 'The Shuffle Chair' on p. 42.

Buitenbeentje
Anna Ter Haar
Dutch

The fourth leg of each
'Buitenbeentje' chair is made
from a casting of layer upon layer
of polyurethane. The newly created
leg is strong enough to take the
same weight as the other legs,
despite appearing fluid and as
though in motion. Buitenbeentje
means 'odd man out' and refers
to the freakish nature of this
Frankenstein design.

Chair
Wood, polyurethane
www.annaterhaar.nl
Location > the Netherlands
Available to order

Re-love project 1
Maezm
South Korean

The team at Maezm have established a project to give new purpose to unloved objects. Unwanted clothes, although infused with memories and sentiment, are no longer desired for their original function. In this example, Maezm have applied them as upholstery to a batch of discarded chairs to produce another product; a sofa. Although new, this retains the memories and sentiments of its sum of older parts.

Sofa
Found textiles
www.maezm.com
Location > South Korea
In production
By > designer

Issues of waste and sentimentality are dealt with in tandem here and in the Meterware series on p. 150 and p. 279.

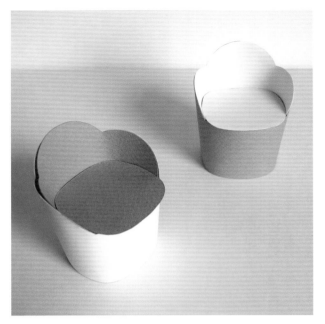

mme
Takesui Mori
Japanese

The plum blossom is a motif
often used in Japanese design,
from traditional illustrations to
contemporary confectionary.
Here, Takesui Mori has taken
this popular icon in its most simple
form and applied it to a seat. The
finished 'mme' chair is constructed
from foam and covered in fabric.

Chair
Polyurethane foam, upholstery,
textile or leather
Location > Denmark
Available to order

Ladycross Sandstone Chair
Max Lamb
British

The Quarry Series sees Max Lamb
collecting stone from various
quarries around the UK. The
original form of the quarried stone
then dictates the form of the final
design. Each piece of furniture is
laboriously carved using hand tools
and the nature of the strenuous
work has tempered Lamb's attitude
towards the design accordingly –
he must focus on the areas that
demand attention and limit work
on those that do not. Patience and
physical strength are required –
attributes not commonly associated
with contemporary design.

Chair
Sandstone
www.maxlamb.org
Location > UK
Available to order

See more of Max Lamb's work in 'Bronze Poly Chair' on p. 46.

Pulp Everyday
Demelza Hill
British

The chairs are produced from 100 per cent household paper waste, and each chair uses a specific type of paper, such as newspaper, white paper, or cardboard, which is clearly revealed in its final colour. Hill believes that the chairs can be a learning crutch to teach people, especially children, about the processes and benefits of recycling their waste, and the chairs could be the end product in a motivational programme for schools.

Chair
Paper pulp
www.demelzahill.com
Location > UK
In development

Paper pulp is a popular material with sound eco-credentials. It appeals to the designer-maker generation because it is inexpensive and avoids industrial investment. See also 'Packaging Lamp' on p. 189 and 'Pulp' on p. 239.

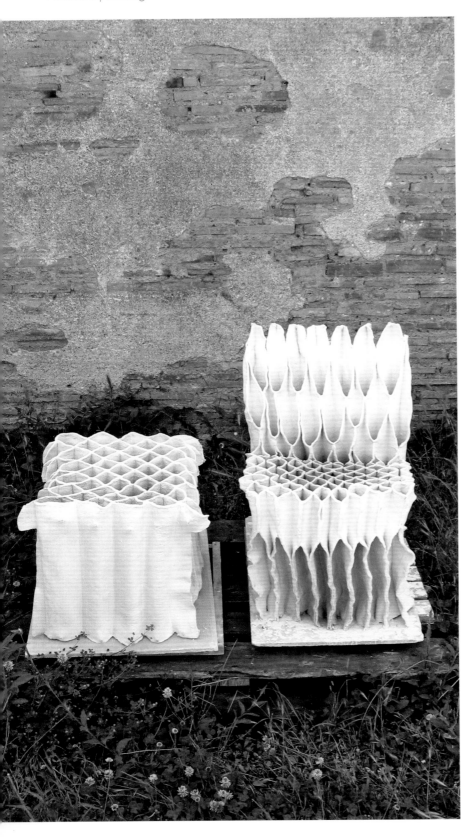

Pétrifié en porcelaine
César Canet
French

This experimental process enables the creation of ceramic shapes without the use of moulds. A felt skeleton is built and then covered in porcelain. When the object is placed in a highly heated kiln the felt burns away. Canet's interest in this technique lies in the void created by the disintegration of the felt and the subsequent lightness of the final object.

Chair
Porcelain
Location > France
In development

Sissi
Tété Knecht
Swiss/Brazilian

This is a simple chair that 'does not have the pretension of being minimal', says Tété Knecht, a Brazilian designer who works from Lausanne. The strength of the design comes from two directions; the archetypal chair shape and the layer of woven Viennese straw. The economical form is born out of Knecht's observations of the most practical contemporary designs, and the unusual material use is a reflection on the Austrian armchairs that have been in Knecht's family for generations.

Chair
Wood, straw
www.teteknecht.com
Location > Switzerland
In development

Teddy Bag
Andrew Millar
British

The 'Teddy Bag' is a chair that is stuffed by the user, who is invited to fill the empty vessel with unwanted toys or clothes. The idea, says Andrew Millar, is that 'people are taking responsibility for their own waste'. This is a product borne out of observation of the fashions of reuse and recycling and the increasing amount of disposable goods around us.

Chair
Industrial wool felt
www.andrew-millar.com
Location > UK
Limited edition

Ghost Chair
Lonneke Gordijn,
Ralph Nauta
Dutch

The form glimpsed inside the chair
represents the possibilities of
computer-generated design; it is
free-flowing, organic and complex.
This 'Ghost Chair' can only exist
within its plexiglass 'host'.
Designers Lonneke Gordijn and
Ralph Nauta (or Design Drift) say
that this method represents freeing
themselves from old styles and
moving towards futuristic design.

Chair
Plexiglass
www.designdrift.nl
Location > the Netherlands
In production
By > designer

Elbow Room, Dog Bowl,
Double Backed
David Irwin
British

Each of the chairs from the Dining
Chairs Series addresses a common
dining problem. One prevents a
dog from begging for food at the
table by the addition of a bowl on
its underside, and a separate rail
on the back of another chair offers
a dedicated space to hang a jacket.
On a third, a change in the angle
of one leg buys more personal
space for the sitter by forcing the
neighbouring chair further away.

Chair series
Ash, plywood
www.davidjirwin.co.uk
Location > UK
Available to order

Tre di Una
Hunn Wai
Singaporean

Joinery is often overlooked as a
method of construction in favour
of seemingly seamless objects.
Hunn Wai is more interested in
what he calls the 'honest
exploitation of materials', as seen
in pre-industrial-revolution design.
With the 'Tre di Una' (Three from
One) chairs he has experimented
with epoxy clay, applying it in place
of the joints of an everyday wooden
chair to create these 'hybrid
creatures'.

Chair series
Beech, steel, pigmented epoxy clay
www.hunnwai.com
Location > Singapore
Available to order

Preoccupation with process and making can
manifest itself as an emphasis on a particular
area of construction. 'Brace Angle Furniture'
on p. 131 also makes a feature of the joint.

Hairy Chair
Charles Kaisin
Belgian

The 'Hairy Chair' has definite
anthropological characteristics.
An old chair is completely covered
with layers of finely shredded
paper, concealing the structure
of the original chair. This creates
a brand new object and causes
the viewer to speculate over its
function; is this sculpture or design?

Chair
Wood, paper
www.charleskaisin.com
Location > Belgium
Limited edition

Spool Chair THONET #14
Keisuke Fujiwara
Japanese

Thonet chairs were among the first furniture designs to be mass-produced in the 19th century. Keisuke Fujiwara plays with the idea of the 'industrial' heritage of the chair by applying his own layer of craft to its surface. The 'unnecessary' intervention is the point on which Fujiwara invites the viewer to ponder. Each chair in the series ('Water' and 'Fire' are shown here) has been wrapped with 6 km (3.73 miles) of fine thread in a process that takes two months.

Chair
Wood, thread
www.keisukefujiwara.com
Location > Japan
Limited edition

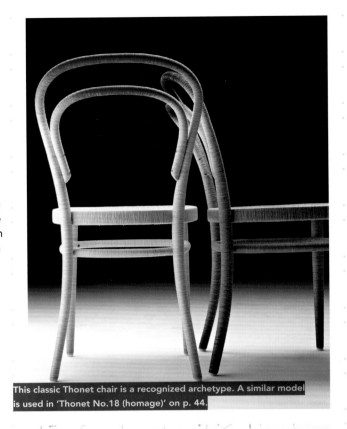

This classic Thonet chair is a recognized archetype. A similar model is used in 'Thonet No.18 (homage)' on p. 44.

Butterfly
Kerem Küçükgürel
Turkish

The 'Butterfly' chair was developed for a site-specific project; a Turkish patisserie in Istanbul, which industrial designer and stylist Kerem Küçükgürel was redesigning. The skilfully manufactured solid wood chair has an elementary form with just one subtle detail; an interestingly angled backrest, from which the chair takes its name.

Chair
Wood, plywood
www.keremkucukgurel.com
Location > Turkey
Available to order

Silent Chair
Linus Berglund, Mats Seitz
Swedish

The 'Silent Chair' is from a collection called Reticent Figures. Each design was conceived, against popular design convention, to deter rather than attract attention. The 'Silent Chair' is stackable, made from birch and bears no distinctive characteristics or ostentatious features; instead it is a deliberately archetypal, anonymous piece of furniture. Seitz and Berglund say 'we left out all extravagances and put our effort in the proportions of the chair'.

Chair
Birch, birch ply, stain or lacquer
www.matsseitz.com
www.linusberglund.se
Location > Sweden
In production
By > www.ekdahls-mobler.se

Deliberately quiet chairs are produced by some designers as an antidote to ostentatious design. For another example, see the 'Ash and Corian Chair' on p. 43.

Easel Chair
Lisa Widén, Anna Irinarchos
Swedish

In the back support of this chair there is a soft frame of polyurethane. Lisa Widén and Anna Irinarchos of WIS Design were inspired by antique, formal portraits of family members; they selected representative elements of the portraits and applied them to a series of objects. In the 'Easel Chair', the frame allows the room beyond the otherwise solid and strict chair to be viewed and celebrated. Adaptations in the construction of the chair become its features; the legs that support the backrest take on the appearance of an easel, while the soft frame offers the sitter cushioned comfort.

Chair
Beech, polyurethane, paint
www.wisdesign.se
Location > Sweden
In development

Thin Chair Version 2
Jun Hashimoto
Japanese

That Hashimoto wanted to create a 'simple' and 'delicate' design is instantly apparent – the 'Thin Chair' is an ethereal and considered reinterpretation of the archetypal chair. Hashimoto's aim was to rid the design of any decorative elements and instead concentrate on an elementary but new manufacturing process. The 'Thin Chair' is therefore constructed from a series of thin steel plates that have been bent, cut and bonded.

Chair
Steel sheet, powder-coated finish
www.juniodesign.com
Location > Japan
Available to order

Maneki Chair
Yuki Abe
Japanese

Considering how mutation and genetic manipulation might change furniture led designer Yuki Abe to create pieces with 'superpowers'. The 'Maneki Chair' has an added, waving arm, just like the welcoming traditional Oriental Maneki-neko or beckoning cat. This additional function (or power) gives the chair an associated value as an object of luck – and also offers a place to hang a jacket or hat.

Chair
Birch, paint, lacquer, or stain
www.howaboutviktor.com
Location > Finland
In production
By > www.vow.fi

See also Yuki Abe's 'Hanabi' on p. 86.

Rubber Up
Richard Megson
British

Granulated rubber enveloping a
simple steel subframe gives this
chair an unusual, uneven texture.
The hardwearing rubber is perfectly
suited to outdoor use, since its
most common application is as
playground flooring. Megson
recognized that the same qualities
that made the granulated rubber
applicable for this use – strength,
flexibility and cushioning – would
also make it appealing as an
upholstery choice.

Chair
Steel, bonding agent, rubber
Location > UK
Limited edition

Plastic Back Chair
Raphaël von Allmen
Swiss

The 'Plastic Back Chair' is made
in just three parts. Each of those
three parts is produced using cost-
effective methods like welding,
laser-cutting and CNC machining,
which means the chair does not
require expensive investment in its
manufacture and can be produced
in small quantities. Welded
aluminium profiles form the legs,
a polypropylene back is folded
around them and riveted in place,
while an aluminium seat adds
tension and pressure to the back.

Chair
Polypropylene, aluminium
www.raphaelvonallmen.com
Location > Switzerland
In development

Cut 'n' Paste
Huib Muilwijk
Dutch

This chair is not a complete whole but a group of individual units. They come with packaging tape and the instruction to bind them together to create a new piece of furniture; several chair or table forms are possible. The idea is to force adults to engage and 'play' with their furniture as children might.

Chair
Expanded polystyrene, plywood, coating
www.madebymidas.com
Location > the Netherlands
Available to order

800mm Chair Series
Laura Perryman
British

This series is made from vacuum-formed seats with storage beneath. The basic form can be mass-produced, with a different print from Perryman's catalogue of designs applied each time. Bespoke prints can be used, and the two elements that make up the seat can be exchanged or adapted to create new combinations.

Chair
Polyethylene terphthalate modified with glycol (PETG) plastic, textile
www.lauraperryman.org.uk
Location > UK
Limited edition

Chip Chair
Jason Wech
American

Samples of laminate cover the 'Chip Chair' – no surprise once it is understood that the chair was designed as an advertisement for the Wilsonart laminate manufacturing company. 'The inspiration for this particular piece came from a scene in Walt Disney's animated movie 'Finding Nemo' where a school of fish impersonate objects,' reveals Wech. The chips appear to be floating, having chosen to take on the shape of a chair. In reality, they are individually attached to a steel frame.

Chair
Laminate, steel
www.jasonwech.com
Location > USA
Available to order

Witte Non
Bram Boo
Belgian

Developed for an art and design
centre in Belgium, this stackable
chair was influenced by the
building's past use as a 'béguinage',
home to Catholic lay sisters. Bram
Boo took the crisp, structured form
of the beguine cape as a starting
point for the sculptural folds of the
aluminium chair. The name 'Witte
Non' means 'White Nun'.

Chair
Aluminium, steel,
powder-coated finish
www.bramboo.be
Location > Belgium
In production
By > www.unicdesign.be

See also Bram Boo's 'Backstage' on p. 107.

Loop Chair Series
Wen-Ting Tseng,
Wei-Cheng Wu
Taiwanese

Although these modern chairs are
constructed from a combination
of aluminium, wood and plastic, the
shadow cast when light hits them is
reminiscent of an ancient furniture
design: the iconic image of a Ming
Dynasty chair.

Chair
Aluminium, wood
home1.usc.edu.tw/m9594105/
Location > Taiwan
Available to order

Iconic furniture design is referenced but
not replicated here, just as it is in the
'Drückeberger' cabinet on p. 105.

Do Re Mi
Joe Nunn
British

The Do Re Mi collection of chairs and stools was developed as part of a project to create furniture for amateur musicians. Produced in sycamore and brass, the pieces reflect vernacular furniture construction as well as evoking the traditions of instrument production. Pieces such as this chair were designed with the ergonomic needs of musicians in mind.

Chair
Sycamore, brass
www.tobeofuse.org
Location > UK
Available to order

5pm in the Spring
Keisuke Fujiwara
Japanese

The possibilities of an under-utilized anodizing process led Keisuke Fujiwara to design the Titanium Series and this design; the '5pm in the Spring' chair. The process creates delicate colouring on these simply formed chairs, and means each displays an individual, graduating palette. Process and material are everything, so the structural design is conceived merely as a platform on which to display them.

Chair
Titanium
www.keisukefujiwara.com
Location > Japan
Limited edition

Stitched Chair
Henny van Nistelrooy
Dutch

Kevlar® textile has been stitched together and covered in epoxy resin. The result is a strong and solid form with unusual detailing that originates in the sewing and weaving. Henny van Nistelrooy was attempting to confront issues around the production and transportation of furniture with this design. His solution removes the need for high tooling costs and avoids issues of space and weight that arise in the transportation of conventional furniture.

Chair
Aromatic polyamide textile, resin
www.hennyvannistelrooy.com
Location > UK
Available to order

The invention of new methods of craft manufacturing produces contemporary aesthetics and allows young designers to bypass industrial manufacture. See also Yael Mer's 'Volume' on p. 93 and 'Flexible Ceramics' by Bas Kools on p. 256.

Victorian Grandfather Chair
Adam Rowe
British

Classic designs are reinterpreted with new methods of construction. See also Philipp Scholz 'Digital Dishes' on p. 237.

Wingback Chair
Frank Flavell
British

Adam Rowe is currently creating a series of furniture that challenges what he sees as the common misconceptions of value placed on certain materials. The 'Victorian Grandfather Chair' makes much of the unlikely mix of oriented stand board (OSB), an inexpensive contemporary material, and leather, a high quality, traditional material. To emphasize the point, the leather is manipulated in a suitably traditional manner, while the OSB is used to its full capacity and is daringly angular. This modern interpretation of a classic type loses none of the impact, detail or craftsmanship of the original.

Easy chair
OSB, leather
www.adamrowedesign.com
Location > UK
In development

The 'Wingback Chair' is intended as a product to be used in public spaces like bars and restaurants. It offers the sitter an element of privacy and intimacy against a crowd, a function that is especially effective when a pair of chairs is placed opposite one another. The specific needs and desires of the modern consumer within public areas were the starting point for this and a further series of designs by Flavell. The chairs, Flavell imagines, would also be highly coveted within a public area due to their suggestion of exclusivity and detachment, so thrones and cardinal's seats were further sources of inspiration.

Chair
Beech, beech ply
www.frankflavell.com
Location > UK
In development

itti & ette
Marieke Gast
German

The wooden surface of these easy
chairs echoes the construction
inside sofas and chairs that is
normally obscured by upholstery.
The flock patterns on the surface in
turn represent upholstery. The flock
provides a degree of cushioning
as well as applied decoration; its
pattern represents woven textile
or the outline of someone sitting
in the chair.

Easy chair
Plywood, oak veneer, flock
www.mareikegast.de
Location > Germany
Available to order

Non-woven
Christian Kocx
Dutch

Christian Kocx visited a company
that uses the injection-moulding
process to make mass-produced
plastic parts and gathered the
remnant pieces of plastic. The
'Non-woven' chairs make use of
these, and in its new context this
scrap material reveals surprising
aesthetic qualities.

Easy chair
Thermoplastic remnants
www.kocxontwerpen.nl
Location > Belgium
In development

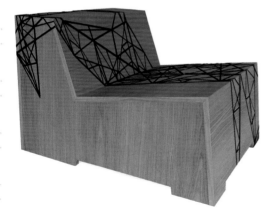

Hardwood Wingback
**James Kinmond,
James Harrison**
British

James Kinmond and James
Harrison, of James Design UK,
have updated the classic wing chair.
Subtle reworkings of the iconic
elements of the chair have been
made to create a design that would
appeal to the modern consumer.
Particular attention was paid to
the deep buttoning of Chesterfield
upholstery, retaining the overall
effect while replacing the process
with a simplified contemporary
upholstery technique.

Easy chair
Oak, textile
www.jamesdesignuk.co.uk
Location > UK
In production
By > designer

Kate Chair
Sebastian Herkner
German

The application of new materials
and the exaggeration of famous
features creates an altogether
new look for the classic wing chair.
The various elements of the 'Kate
Chair' are constructed from a 3D
knitting technique, new wool, steel,
walnut and leather. Each element
is designed to offer comfort and
stability within this generously
scaled design.

Easy chair
Textiles, steel, wood, leather
www.sebastianherkner.com
Location > Germany
Limited edition

Upholstered Chair
StokkeAustad
Swedish

The design of the 'Upholstered Chair' re-evaluates the relationship between product and user through a range of devices. The seat is shortened and dragged into the structure, so that the user is forced to step into the frame of the chair to sit. The whole chair is covered in fabric, making it feel as though its construction is a single unbroken form, from which the legs are dragged out. The chair is 'untypical' say StokkeAustad, and therein lies its considerable character.

Easy chair
Foam, steel, textile
www.stokkeaustad.com
Location > Sweden
In development

Plus de Madam Rubens
Frank Willems
Dutch

Pieces of discarded mattress are used for the plump seat of this chair. These are strapped to antique wooden frames and the whole object is covered with a foam coating. This chair has voluptuous qualities – hence the reference to Rubens's ladies.

Chair
Latex, wood, foam coating
www.frankwillems.eu
Location > the Netherlands
Available to order

Pouf de Paille
Tété Knecht
Swiss/Brazilian

Knecht experimented with many mixes of wet and dry components in the search for a new material. She settled on a combination of straw and latex, applied in many layers for 'Pouf de Paille', because 'straw evocates our collective memories; it is connected to comfort, warmth, nature'. She found the mixture was both resistant and flexible, and that the straw remained effectively visible.

Chaise
Straw, latex
www.teteknecht.com
Location > Switzerland
In development

For more new composite designs see 'Eternit' on p. 36 and 'One Day Paper Waste' on p. 101.

Octopus
Atelier Blink
Belgian

The idea of recycling jeans led to the weird form of the 'Octopus' chair. Emilie Lecouturier and Céline Poncelet of Atelier Blink discovered that this clothing type could be given an altogether unexpected function when stitched together and stuffed to make an adaptable, comfortable seating solution.

Easy chair
Textile, polystyrene beads
www.atelierblink.com
Location > Belgium
Available to order

Old clothes make a thrifty upholstery solution, also used in 'Re-love project 1' on p. 59.

Meltdown Series
Tom Price
British

Tom Price has devised an ingenious method of construction for his Meltdown Series. The chairs are created by heating a seat-shaped form and pressing it into a giant coil of polypropylene rope, or plumbing pipes, tubing, hose or any other thermoplastic material. The material fuses together the rope and forms a comfortable surface. The series stems from Price's interest in the possibilities of using chance as a tool for design products – here the simple application of heat turns a product into furniture.

Easy chair
Polypropylene rope, rigid and flexible plastic tubing
www.tom-price.com
Location > UK
Available to order

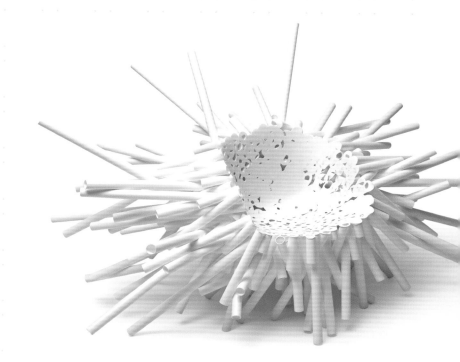

Cushion
Matthew Harding
Australian

This cushion is glass-reinforced plastic rather than upholstery. It is intended as an outdoor seat and was first developed as an art installation for Canberra, commissioned from designer Matthew Harding. This production version of 'Cushion' plays on the idea of archetypical casual, comfortable seating but offers durability and resilience.

Easy chair
Glass-reinforced plastic
www.matthewharding.com.au
Location > Denmark
In development

Pump it up
Nacho Carbonell
Spanish

'Pump it up' is more than a piece of furniture; it is a means to create an emotional attachment between consumer and object. Sitting on the chair displaces air into the attached animals, breathing life into them as the chair adapts to fit your shape. Carbonell suggests that this action will force an emotional connection between the sitter and the animals; 'they are your creations, your new friends, and they will exist only as long as you stay in the chair'.

Easy chair
Foam, rubber
www.nachocarbonell.com
Location > the Netherlands
Available to order

Some designers promote the benefit of an emotional connection between product and person, and giving designs animalistic characteristics is one route to this. For other examples, see the 'Branch Stools' on p. 27 and 'Je m'appelle Moustache' on p. 174.

Hanabi
Yuki Abe
Japanese

This is casual seating at its most elementary. The 'Hanabi' is made up of 12 arms, each one a pillow stuffed with lightweight polystyrene beads, making this seat lightweight and portable. The 'Hanabi' can be used individually, or can be positioned en masse to create seating for many, in place of a sofa.

Easy chair
Textile, polystyrene beads
www.howaboutviktor.com
Location > Finland
In production
By > www.vow.fi

Sandbank
Christiane Hoegner
German

Sandbank arrives at your door as a ready-to-make kit complete with bags, instructions and shovel. This is an 'outdoor seat of variable dimensions and basic comfort' says Hoegner. Josef Hoffmann's gridded 'Kubus' sofa inspired the block design, which Hoegner chose to reinterpret with individual bags. Allowing each owner to create their own design depending on location and desire makes this an interactive product that Hoegner concedes is more installation than furniture.

Sofa
Polypropylene, sand
www.christianehoegner.com
Location > Belgium
In development

With concept-led design, often the consumer is given little more than an idea; the realization of the product is left to them. See Peter Marigold's 'Prop' on p. 319.

KuKunochi
Leif.designpark
Japanese

Leif.designpark have created
an evolving design community
by working alongside a number
of skilled craftsmen. Their work
is a sensitive reinterpretation
of traditional craft, the influence
of which is easy to see in pieces
like the 'KuKunochi' sofa. Here,
the iconography of a forest is
represented by a rustic, hand-
carved backrest in white ash and
a dense, heavy, upholstered base.
While the essential elements of a
traditional sofa are respected, new
ideas on scale, shape and materials
have been introduced.

Sofa
Wood, polyurethane foam, textile,
polyurethane finish
www.leif-designpark.com
Location > Japan
Available to order

See more modern Japanese craft in 'Hat
Plate' by Emiko Oki on p. 239.

Hunting Lines
Daniel Becker
German

'Hunting Lines' is part sofa and part chaise longue. It has generous proportions, but designer Daniel Becker says it is the antithesis of a cosy piece of furniture. Rather he describes the strong lines of the sofa as 'brutal' and 'disharmonic'. This piece of soft upholstery is, it seems, anything but soft. The yellow line exaggerates the 3D nature of the design.

Sofa
Steel, wood, foam, textile
www.danielbecker.eu
Location > Germany
In development

Cup
Eric Degenhardt
German

Degenhardt's ambition was to create a light and svelte sofa and armchair series that could happily sit in the centre of a room rather than against an interior wall. The sofa owes its angled form to a slender wooden structure beneath the Kvadrat textile upholstery.

Sofa
Wood, elastic, latex foam, textile
www.eric-degenhardt.com
Location > Germany
Manufacturer >
www.richard-lampert.de

Snowbench
Duncan Wilson
Scottish

The 'Snowbench' uses visco-elastic
memory foam and diaphragm
valves to retain the imprint of
the user, thereby documenting
the physical interaction between
person and object. The design was
inspired by a snow-covered park
bench and the experiences of
disturbing the snow's surface by
leaving a mark or discovering the
trace of a previous presence.

Sofa
Ash, visco-elastic polyurethane
foam, cotton textile
www.duncan-wilson.com
Location > UK
In development

A4
Sofia Grew
Finnish

This seat is so named because it borrows its form from a folded piece of A4 paper. The sofa invites people to lounge informally and breaks the conventions of traditional sofa forms. The 'folded' effect is created by a moulded core reinforced with glass fibre.

Chaise
Glass-reinforced plastic, foam, wool textile
www.sofiagrew.com
Location > Finland
In development

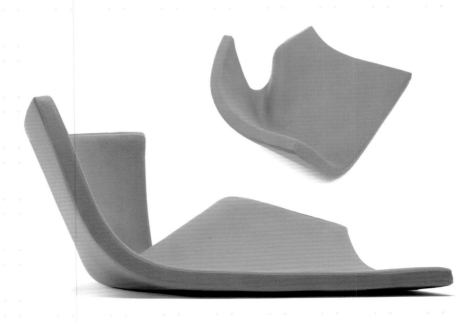

The simple folds of paper were also inspiration enough for the 'Teo Stool' on p. 29.

Intersection
Philippe Nigro
French

This sofa series is a reflection on what happens when forms collide. 'Intersection' is made up of a puzzle of upholstered sections, in direct contrast to the fluid, singular forms that are popular in sofa models. The different sections vary in colour, size, height of backrest and depth of seat.

Sofa
Wood, polyurethane foam, wool textile
www.philippenigro.com
Location > France / Italy
In production
By > www.ligne-roset.com

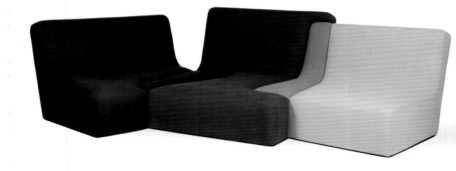

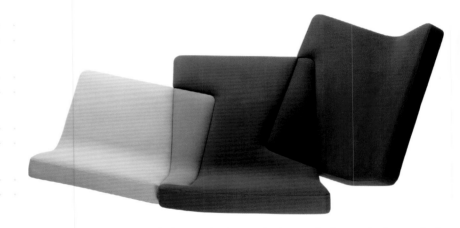

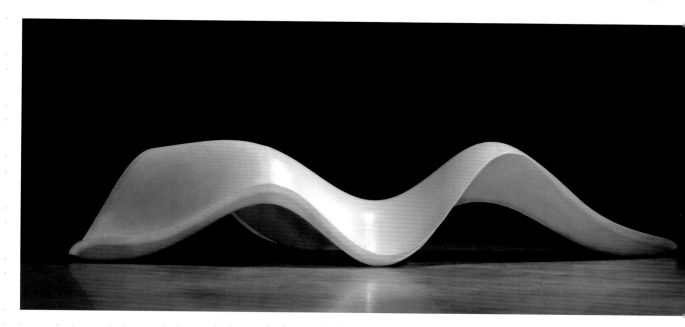

Lounge Landscape
Nicola Burggraf, Susanne Hoffmann, Steffen Reichert, Nico Reinhardt, Yanbo Xu
German

A group of students at Staatliche Hochschule für Gestaltung (HFG) in Offenbach invented a new composite material that is light and durable for this specific application. 'Lounge Landscape' is made from a polyester-based fabric reinforced with glass fibre. The seating units are cut from a single master mould with CNC machining, and each unit is designed to offer the user freedom to change position and sit and lie as they please. The semi-transparent nature and curvaceous form of the material reinforce the physical lightness of the seat.

Chaise
Glass-reinforced plastic,
3D polyester mesh
www.form-finding.org
Location > Germany
In development

Mugroso
Liliana Ovalle
Mexican

For the poverty-stricken inhabitants of Mexico City's suburbs, necessity dictates the recycling of objects and materials into random and absurd functional compositions. Ovalle studied the improvised method of construction and noted the resulting collages of material and form. She adopted a similarly ad hoc, but ultimately functional, construction method for this sofa.

Sofa
Steel and walnut structure
www.lilianaovalle.com
Location > Mexico
Available to order

See more freeform design, using individual elements positioned by the user, in 'Nix' and 'Clutter Shelf' on p. 123.

Dream of sand
Nacho Carbonell
Spanish

Nothing could be further from regular outdoor furniture constructed from metal and concrete than Carbonell's rubber coated, sand-filled seating. His method of encasing sand within a pliable, colour-saturated rubber casing means furniture can be constructed on the spot. It also creates a remarkably tactile object whose shape can be playfully manipulated. Carbonell notes that this method of construction could offer opportunities for the furniture to be directly integrated into an existing environment.

Sofa
Sand, latex
www.nachocarbonell.com
Location > the Netherlands
Available to order

Volume
Yael Mer
Israeli

The ingenious construction method developed by Yael Mer is a new craft, and a unique approach to batch production. The 'Volume' chair is made by filling empty shells, constructed from wallpaper, with expanded polyurethane foam. The two-dimensional patterns are hand-assembled and the results are charmingly misshapen. This product celebrates the hand of the maker and positions itself as an alternative to mass-produced furniture.

Sofa
Wallpaper, patterned paper, polyurethane foam
www.raw-edges.com
Location > UK
Available to order

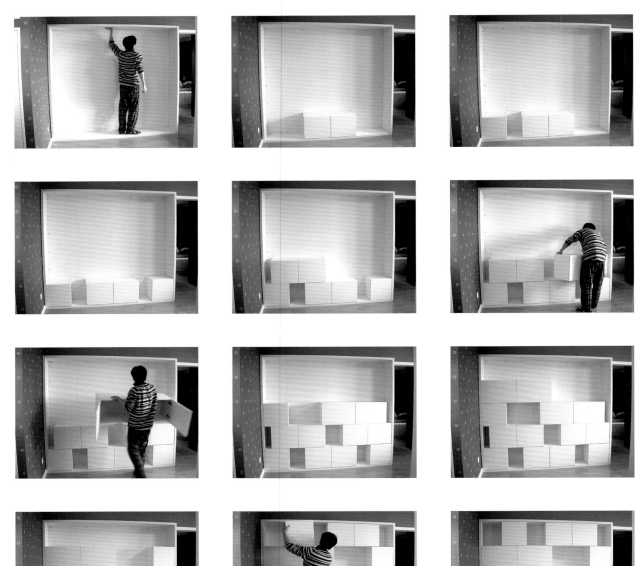

Boox
Han Li, Yan Hu
Chinese

When you get bored with the configuration of your Boox bookshelf, you can change it. This is because Boox is a stackable combination of individual units in three different sizes, designed to be endlessly reconfigured. The Boox boxes were inspired by the packaging used to move furniture, but here the boxes are transformed from container to furniture and reappointed in veneered wood fibreboard to make them sturdier.

Shelving
Fibreboard, melamine veneer
Location > China
Available to order

Magazine Mixte
Floris Hovers
Dutch

An inspiring journey around Romania by designer Floris Hovers led to this design. 'Magazine Mixte' is what Romanians call the small shops that are found everywhere and stocked with everything. The same spirit of unpretentious and eclectic function is mirrored in this cabinet, through a combination of four different types of wood and a strong, basic form that also evokes the 1950s and 1960s design prevalent in Romania.

Cabinet
Birch, meranti, deal, plywood, medium density fibreboard (MDF)
www.florishovers.nl
Location > the Netherlands
Available to order

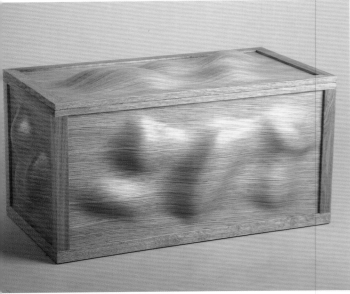

Bulging Box
Ashley Price
British

The 'Bulging Box' looks as if its contents are about to burst free at any minute. Price has cleverly brought this static piece of storage furniture to life by utilizing the susceptibility of 3D veneer to manipulation and moulding. The undulating form creates the illusion of an over-filled container, while references to traditional cabinetry in the oak frame are nicely retained.

Storage
Solid oak, 3D oak veneer
www.ashleypricedesign.co.uk
Location > UK
Available to order

Drawer
Makoto Yamaguchi
Japanese

Makoto Yamaguchi was among a group of five architects invited by manufacturer Deroll to design a product under the theme 'box'. The idea was to produce a box that was precious and craft-intensive, and which possessed charm. Yamaguchi produced his design in oiled white oak. The box has various sections, each with a drawer, extending the principal use of a box into something far more substantial.

Drawers
White oak
www.ymgci.net
Location > Japan
In production
By > www.deroll.com

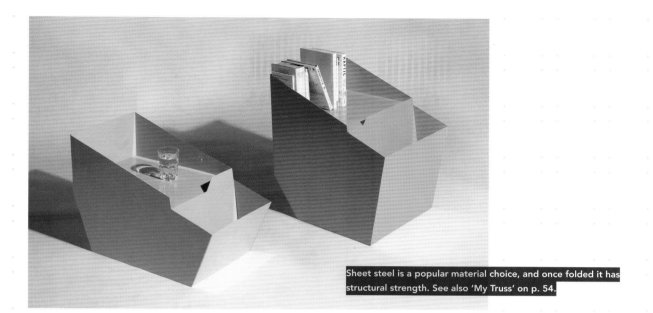

Sheet steel is a popular material choice, and once folded it has structural strength. See also 'My Truss' on p. 54.

Oona
Cordula Kehrer
German

'Oona' was created because designer Cordula Kehrer was in the market for a bedside table and found herself dissatisfied with what was available. This bent sheet metal unit offers plenty of areas to store books and magazines and ample tabletop space for the essential bedside accoutrements.

Storage
Sheet steel, powder-coated finish
www.cordulakehrer.de
Location > Germany
In development

Möbelette
Katrin Sonnleitner
German

'Behind its tidy façade,' says Katrin Sonnleitner, this curious storage unit 'embodies chaos.' Disorder is given a presentable face – that of a regular cupboard – but behind the frontage is a textile sack into which clothing disappears. 'Möbelette' is a reaction to the amorphous piles of clothing that litter living spaces, and its function is to offer a tentative illusion of order.

Storage
Wood, textile
www.katrin-sonnleitner.com
Location > Germany
Available to order

To be continued
Julien Carretero
French

Layers of polyurethane composite are cast one on top of another, with each trying to follow the form of the layer below. This process is flawed, and so each layer is slightly different, creating a slowly mutating form. Carretero uses different coloured composites to draw attention to the multiple layers, exaggerating the oddity of the resulting shape. The final form is cut to create storage units.

Storage
Polyurethane composite, pigments
www.juliencarretero.com
Location > the Netherlands
Available to order

Shed
Studio Gorm
Korean/American

Like a giant dollshouse, 'Shed' requires the humans using it to change their perspective. This storage system is an exercise in space-saving design, intended to be used in one-room apartments. By containing elements that are familiar and expected of each room, the 'Shed' unit allows a studio apartment to remain uncluttered and ultimately free of a defining function.

Storage
Medium density fibreboard (MDF), birch veneer
www.studiogorm.com
Location > USA
Available to order

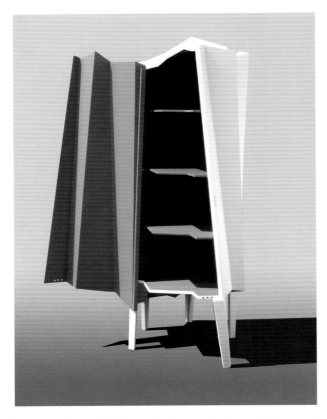

Dazzle 003
IAFR
Dutch

Harry Koopman and Bruno van Hooijdonk of Interior Adventures For Real (IAFR) say the idea for their Dazzle 003 series 'originates from the wish to make something dynamic and arbitrary at the same time'. The cabinets feature complex folded and twisted elements while retaining the functions and scale of traditional pieces of furniture. They are contemporary versions of familiar furniture types, made with the skill of traditional craft.

Cabinet
Medium density fibreboard (MDF), beech, lacquered finish
www.iafr.nl
Location > the Netherlands
Available to order

Ninho
Herme Ciscar, Mónica García
Spanish

The potential of hardwood as a design material has long been celebrated; Portuguese designers Herme Ciscar and Mónica García want to inspire the same reverence for its more humble cousins, like plywood and oriented strand board (OSB). This series of office storage makes use of both these materials: rather than disguise them, it uses their textural and patterned surfaces as conspicuous decoration.

Cabinet
Plywood, OSB, beech
www.hermeymonica.com
Location > Spain
In production
By > www.aicmartinezmedina.com

OSB is no longer just a cheap material; see also 'Victorian Grandfather Chair' on p. 78.

One Day Paper Waste
Jens Praet
Belgian

Making the abstract concept of recycling waste a reality inspired Jens Praet to find a new function for a 'disused object'. This series is constructed from shredded confidential papers that have been mixed with resin and compressed into a new form. The process appealed to Praet because it offered a visual solution in which the new object clearly belies its past function. Praet says 'we can still recognize part of its previous mysterious information … It gives to the material from which it is made of a new function, dignity and timeless importance.'

Cabinet
Paper, resin, aluminium handles
www.jenspraet.com
Location > Italy/the Netherlands
Available to order

Save
Katarina Häll
Swedish

Häll found inspiration for this series of storage units in abandoned and forgotten houses in her home country. 'With their barred and bolted doors and windows, they reveal nothing about the stories and treasures that are inside.' The 'Save' cabinet appears to be closed and inaccessible, like an abandoned house, with wooden boards nailed across the doors. The seemingly hastily applied boards are in reality the point of entry to the cabinets; their handles. Their addition also provides graphic decoration.

Cabinet
Fibreboard, pine
www.katarinahall.se
Location > Sweden
In development

Jewellery Drawer
Malin Lundmark
Swedish

The process of intarsia, which uses inlaid wood as a decorative surface feature, inspired Malin Lundmark to use pieces of jewelry as decoration on this series of storage furniture. Instead of hiding jewelry away, Lundmark suggests that what decorates the human body can just as easily ornament an inanimate piece of furniture. 'In most cases people store jewelry in cases but this becomes storage in a new way.'

Drawers
Medium density fibreboard (MDF), lacquer
www.malinlundmark.com
Location > Sweden
Available to order

Stack
Shay Alkalay
Israeli

The principle of 'Stack' is elementary: individual drawer units can be built up to a desired height. But the plywood drawers can be made in a variety of depths; together with the ability to access them from front or back, this creates a unique and engaging form. This imposing design openly invites curiosity to its engineering. Shay Alkalay produced two versions of the drawers, one for mass-production and the limited edition shown here.

Drawers
Plywood
www.raw-edges.com
Location > UK
In production
By > www.establishedandsons.com

Shay Alkalay is part of Raw Edges Design Group; other works from the studio include 'Volume' on p. 93.

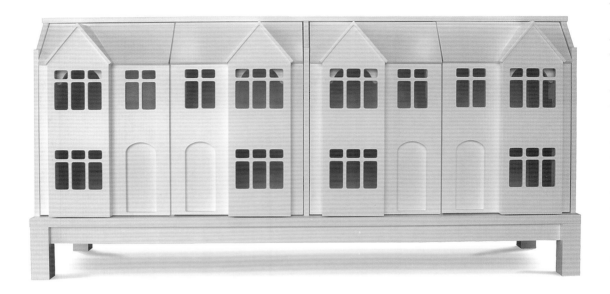

Terrace Sideboard
William Warren
British

Our homes are a place of storage and they say as much about our personality as anything else we own, comments William Warren. This sentiment reveals the reasoning behind the 'Terrace Sideboard', an architectural replica of the type of home where Warren grew up. The sideboard provides effective storage while also creating a nostalgic, miniature cityscape within a room.

Sideboard
Medium density fibreboard (MDF), painted finish
www.williamwarren.co.uk
Location > UK
In production
By > www.bytrico.com

Sentiment and nostalgia are commonly communicated by many young designers. See also 'Pearl' on p. 218 and Tina Roeder's 'Happy Porcelain' on p. 254.

2D-Furniture
Wouter Nieuwendijk,
Suzanne van Oirschot
Dutch

Wouter Nieuwendijk and Suzanne van Oirschot borrow the character of furniture, objects and household items for this collection. Without their borrowed iconography, the furniture would be little more than storage boxes, but with their applied images they take on characters other than their own.

Cabinets
Medium density fibreboard (MDF),
Formica® laminate
www.checkhuh.nl
Location > the Netherlands
Available to order

Drückeberger
Silvia Knüppel
German

Rather than conform to the usual characteristics of storage furniture, this piece projects 'a new chaotic order'. A foam block in the shape of more traditional furniture, it is cut to create openings that hold objects placed in them. Knüppel compares the knife to a key – vital to access the cupboard's potential. She says Drückeberger 'stores things which normally don't fit and make no sense inside a cupboard, like chairs, mirrors etc'.

Cabinet
Foam
www.silviaknueppel.de
Location > Germany
Available to order

This design is a celebration of disorder and chaos. See also 'La Désinvolture' on p. 327.

Around
Joachim Jirou-Najou
French

'Around' presents an unusual application of textiles in furniture design. The principle is of a textile envelope made rigid by armatures. This external, seemingly soft, skin hides the wooden and steel structure within, to which it is attached by a system of magnets.

Cabinet
Wood, steel, polypropylene, wool, lacquer
www.joachimjirounajou.com
Location > France
In development

Pivot
Shay Alkalay
Israeli

These drawers are carried on spiky legs rather than traditional runners, allowing each of the drawers to open at an unexpected angle in a single, fan-like movement. This innovation offers a brand new aesthetic and original engineering solution. Practically, it also lets the drawers extend fully, so the user can search through each thoroughly for lost items.

Drawers
Hardwood, painted finish
www.raw-edges.com
Location > UK
In production
By > www.arcomeubel.nl

Backstage
Bram Boo
Belgian

This storage unit, described as a bookcase or cupboard by designer Bram Boo, has doors on two sides and external storage bins. These features allow the user many configurations and encourage them to store and display items on the outside of the furniture as well as within. 'Usually, what I want to reach when I'm working on furniture or other projects is a kind of flexibility in the use of it, so that the object can adapt itself to your needs and to the space where it will be used.' Boo by his own admission creates 'surprising things' although these exist within a formal language despite their playfulness.

Cabinet
Medium density fibreboard (MDF), steel, plywood, lacquer
www.bramboo.be
Location > Belgium
In production
By > designer

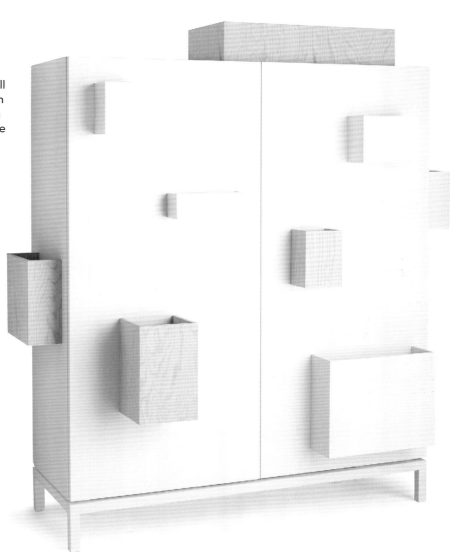

Using recognizable design motifs on novel products creates a humorous dialogue between designer and consumer. See also '2D-Furniture' on p. 105 and 'Flat Light' on p. 221.

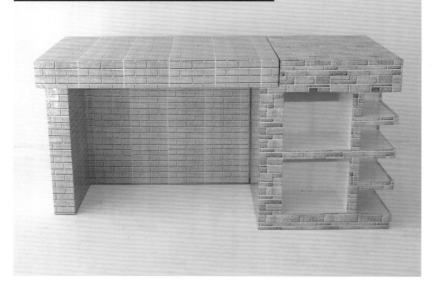

Office
Productlove
Marlie Mul – Dutch
Elina Kellermann – German

When Mul and Kellermann were faced with the problem of making improvised spaces for their exhibitions they began 'building' units from polystyrene. The potential of this quick and easy way to create volume was recognized by the design duo, who went on to develop lightweight furniture objects that could temporarily define and alter interior spaces. Illustrations of brickwork suggest building material that 'stands for solidity, reliability, security and domesticity' and are attached to the polystyrene as a façade.

Storage
Extruded polystyrene, magnets, metal, plastic coating, paper, lacquer
www.productlove.org
Location > the Netherlands/ Germany
Available to order

PointOfView Cabinet
Sjoerd Sies
Dutch

Perspective and visual illusion play an important role in this design. 'Looking at an archetypical cabinet, I captured one specific point' says designer Sjoerd Sies, who has a background in graphic design. From there, Sies took the 'view lines' between his position and the cabinet and made them physical. This gives the cabinet its curious shape and means that from a certain perspective, only the expected cabinet is seen.

Cabinet
Medium density fibreboard (MDF), paint
www.sjoerdsies.com
Location > the Netherlands
In development

Le Coffre
Sealac
French

'Le Coffre' is a storage container that has evolved from a familiar item into a rare object. The form of the bin is that of an inexpensive stacking plastic container. Matthieu Blancher and Gael Nys of Sealac have sheathed it in soft, purple goat leather – instantly upgrading it to a luxury accessory.

Storage
Plastic, goat leather
www.sealac.com
Location > France
Available to order

See more from Sealac in 'Le Cercle Lumineux' on p. 209.

Grace Duo
Todo Design
Lebanese/American

'Grace Duo' continues an exploration of silhouettes and voids that Silva Ajemian and Jorge Prado of Todo Design had begun with an earlier design. 'As we looked at the object from different angles, we began to think about the space that contains the object and how that object defines the space around it.' 'Grace Duo' occupies these zones. The design is meant to prompt interaction between two users and their surroundings.

Storage
Plywood, automotive paint
www.tododesign.com
Location > USA
Available to order

Adam Wardrobe
Joscha Brose
German

Joscha Brose of StudioHausen has designed a wardrobe that he admits is 'not practical' and was not created out of a desire to make a functional design. The use of the 'Adam Wardrobe', says Brose, is to 'amplify a pragmatic object'. The design was developed as something of a creative release following an intense period working on a separate commission involving practical wardrobe designs.

Wardrobe
Steel, powder-coated finish
www.studiohausen.com
Location > Germany
Available to order

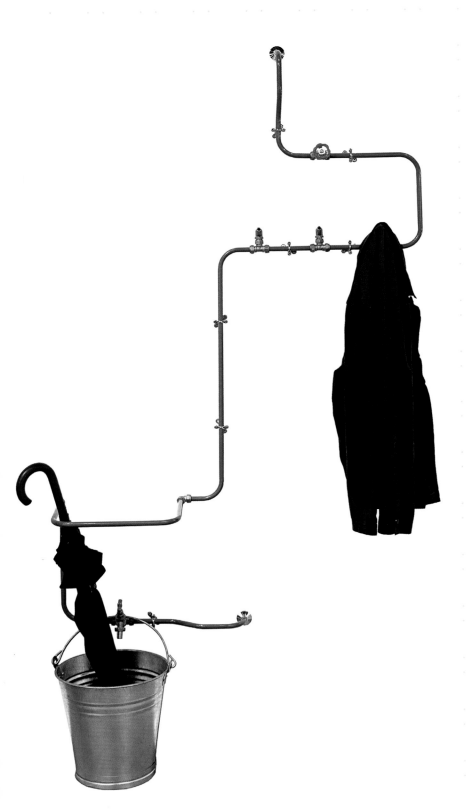

Hall Stand
Nick Fraser
British

Nick Fraser saw the aesthetic potential in copper piping and plumbing fittings and applied these industrial materials in a new use. These elements are familiar domestic objects and not usually afforded any attention. By reappropriating them, Fraser simply shifted the viewer's perception and created a unit that combines humour and purpose.

Hall stand
Copper, brass, steel
www.nickfraser.co.uk
Location > UK
Available to order

Hoist
Oscar Magnus Narud
Norwegian

'Hoist' is a floating, expandable
coat-hanger system. One end
is anchored to the ground by a
concrete base, and a bungee cord
is then fed through a pulley on the
ceiling and tightened. The system
takes up minimal space and is a
new, adaptable storage solution.

Coat hanger
Wood, concrete, rope,
bungee cord
www.oscarnarud.com
Location > UK
Available to order

Hallstand
Oliver Tilbury
British

A hat stand, umbrella stand and seat are all brought together in one piece of hallway furniture. Tilbury aims to bring the traditional workshop and computer-assisted design closer in his work, in order to produce creative designs that are more easily manufactured. The elements of this design are created from a combination of CNC routing, individual turnings and forms generated by 3D modelling.

Hall stand
English oak, felt, plywood, steel
www.olivertilbury.com
Location > UK
Available to order

Max
Rainer Subic –
German/Croatian
Admir Jukanovic –
German/Bosnian

'Max' is a flexible hanger designed
to be attached anywhere, thereby
avoiding the need for a traditional
wardrobe. The idea for 'Max' came
from a sailing trip when Subic and
Jukanovic were inspired by the
possibilities of using nautical rope
in a domestic environment.

Hanging rail
Polyester rope, polyvinylchloride
(PVC), stainless steel
www.pinkpinguin.com
www.jukanovic.de
Location > the Netherlands/UK
Limited edition

A study of modern lifestyles informs this and many other designs. See also Demelza Hill's 'Snap and Dine' on p. 254.

All About Hanging
Tatsuhiro Sekisaka
Japanese

This is a collection of several different coat stands for different places. They may be more closely integrated into daily use than regular coat stands, and offer an opportunity for an interim resting place for clothes that is between the bedroom floor and the closet. 'Bloom' is a slim pole when closed and can lean against the wall in any space, but opens out into a three-legged coat stand when it is needed. 'Mirror Mirror' provides hanging points and rails to allow clothes to be hung after trying them on, but then folds flat and can be leant against a wall. 'My Favourite Launderette' combines a laundry tub with a coat stand.

Storage series
Plastic, maple, polystyrene, aluminium
www.hitsujiame.com
Location > Japan
Available to order

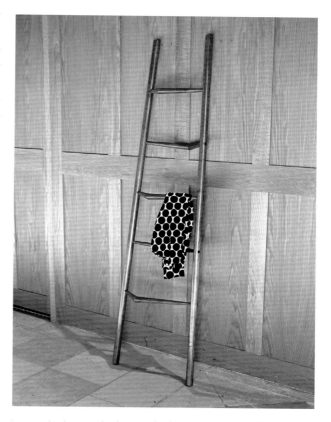

Unintended Ladder
Tomohiko Sato
Japanese

Although this object has the appearance of a ladder, the rungs have been bent, rendering them unfit for their regular use. Tomohiko Sato has determined another use for this familiar object: a clothes stand. 'A ladder usually has the appearance of being cheap or dirty but this work sweeps away those initial images with its elegant and sophisticated design,' says Sato.

Storage
Walnut
www.tomohikosato.com
Location > UK
In development

Brickshelf
Paul Kogelnig – Austrian
Gabriel Heusser – Swiss

'Brickshelf' is the simplest form of shelving; individual bricks and wooden shelves supporting each other. The single detail of interpreting the bricks as abstracted books provides the design with character but does so, importantly to Kogelnig and Heusser, without complicating the elementary approach to engineering in any way.

Shelving
Brick, wood
www.pervisioni.it
Location > Italy
Available to order

Tilt
Peter Marigold
British

'The series is based on the simple geometric principle that the total angles of a split form will always total 360 degrees.' Using this as his starting point, Peter Marigold took found pieces of timber and split each into four pieces. These sections then dictated the angles of the shelves in units constructed from plywood. The 'Tilt' series includes several variations of shelving based around this principle. 'The pieces are very dynamic and seem to have some humanoid qualities.'

Shelving
Beech, plywood
www.petermarigold.com
Location > UK
Limited edition

Seemingly awkward and unstable designs can belie clever engineering solutions. See 'Skinterior' on p. 21.

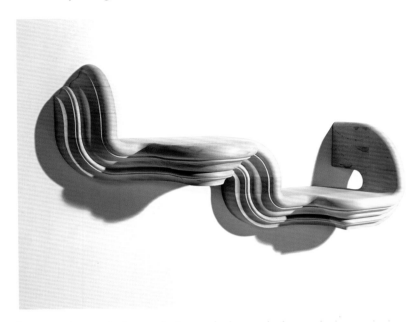

Shelf Space
Paul Loebach
American

The result of a collaboration with an aerospace machinery manufacturer, this shelf from Paul Loebach is a winning example of what can be achieved through the marrying of traditional materials and cutting-edge technology. The fluid form pushes the limits of wood engineering and cuts an unusual profile that meanders off the wall, twisting and turning as it goes.

Shelving
Basswood
www.paulloebach.com
Location > USA
Available to order

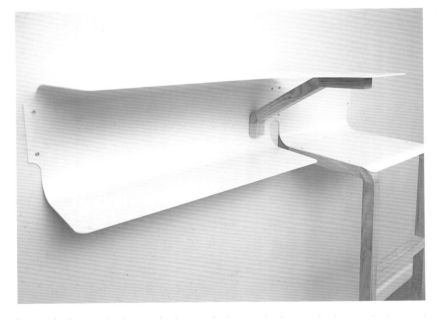

Tree House My House
Hyock Kwon
Korean

This shelf, ladder and seat collection explores the emotional effects of removing oneself. The elevated seating offers a personal space without relying on enclosing walls and is meant to provide a sense of detachment. 'The change in height gives you a different view point which removes most ordinary objects and people from your direct sight' says Kwon.

Shelving/seating
Aluminium, maple, powder-coated finish
www.hyock.com
Location > UK
Available to order

Shelving Chair
Jun Murakoshi
Japanese

Once a stacking chair is stacked, it inevitably loses its function and aesthetic appeal. Noticing this, Japanese designer Jun Murakoshi, went on to design a chair that was able to maintain a functional value while stacked. 'This product is usually a modular shelving unit but will become a chair when you need extra chairs.'

Chair/shelving
Beech, birch plywood, medium density fibreboard (MDF), felt and paper honeycomb panel
www.junmurakoshi.com
Location > Japan
Available to order

Designs with a dual function have added value. See also 'Two Lamps' on p. 196.

Fossile
Mostapha El Oulhani,
Jérôme Garzon, Fred Sionis
French

The external grooves on each
of these egg-shaped terracotta
modules allow them to be
interlocked securely and stacked.
The unlikely use of terracotta as
a material for an interior product
adds an unusual dimension to the
unit, as does the irregular shape
of the modules. The environmental
credentials of terracotta, which can
easily be recycled, were a deciding
factor in its use here.

Shelving
Extruded terracotta
www.machin-machin.com
Location > France
In production
By > www.rairies.com

Clutter Shelf
Chris Kirby
Canadian

Chris Kirby would like to design objects 'that adapt to the cluttered nature of the way we live, rather than force us to keep our lives neatly arranged in tidy square boxes'. The 'Clutter Shelf' is inspired by the beauty found in untidiness and, in fact, encourages it. Slightly skewed boxes defuse the tension created by misaligned papers and books. The set of boxes that makes up the shelving system nests together for compact shipping and storage.

Shelving
Plywood
www.chriskirbydesign.com
Location > Japan
In production
By > www.gnr8.jp

Nix
Christopher Brueckner
German

'Nix' is a shelving system that builds up easily using two parts generated from a 2D pattern. Although at first it looks chaotic, it is built on very simple principles. Ease of manufacturing was on Brueckner's mind when he put this design together: sheet material of almost any kind is used optimally, minimizing waste, and construction is simple, not to mention inexpensive. 'Nix' can be employed as a huge installation or a more functional domestic system.

Shelving/seating
Press board
Location > Germany
Available to order

Stackbox
Martin Born
German

Thinking through all the possible storage applications we might need and paying attention to notions of mobility led Martin Born to develop a new furniture form. 'Stackbox' can exist as a static composition or disassembled to act as independent shelves and storage. The central construction element is the leg that lends a regular pattern to the stacked elements. The intention is to produce the units using injection-moulded polypropylene.

Shelving
Polystyrene, polyurethane, foam, steel
www.mborn.com
Location > Finland /the Netherlands
In development

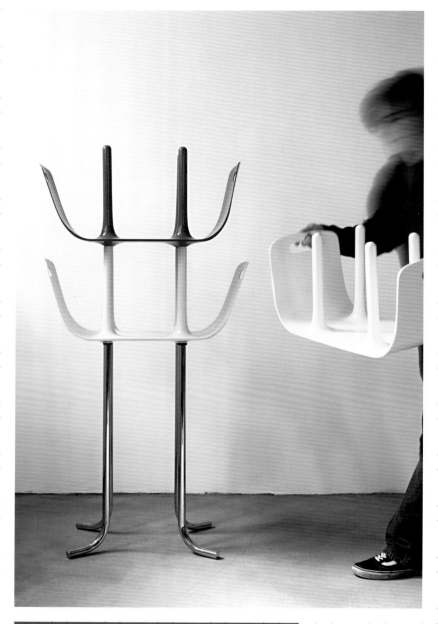

See Martin Born's solution to dividing space, 'Shades', on p. 331.

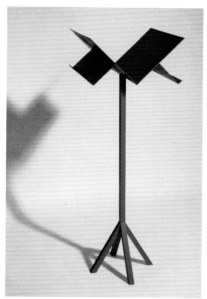

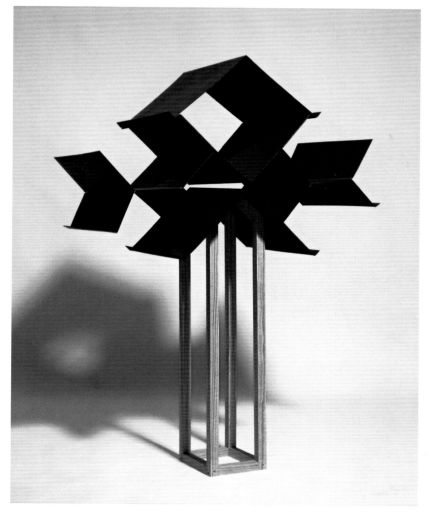

Profile Shelves
Maria Jeglinska
Polish

The graphic forms of these shelves were taken from geometric shapes found in industrial applications. The sculptural element is metal while the second element, the support, is constructed from wood.

Shelving
Wood, steel, paint
www.mariajeglinska.com
Location > France
Available to order

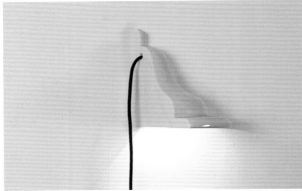

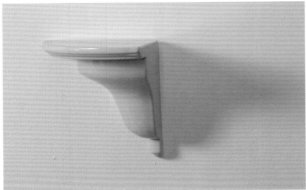

Interior Furniture
Katy West
Irish

Katy West's series of china
accessories includes a light and
shelves whose form is derived from
a generic wooden shelf found in
stores across the UK. She has taken
the basic form and manipulated it,
'stretched, rotated and sliced' it to
serve a number of functions, adding
value by creating them from
slipcast vitrified china.

Shelving
Ceramic
www.katywest.co.uk
Location > UK
Available to order

Here is a familiar archetype with added
value and a new perspective. See also
Sealac's 'Le Coffre', p. 110.

Fairy/tale
**Gudrun Lilja
Gunnlaughsdóttir**
Icelandic

The sentimentality of daily life –
memories, emotional encounters,
childhood nostalgia – sparks
Gudrun Lilja Gunnlaughsdóttir's
imagination. In an attempt to
visualize this, the collection of
shelves called 'Fairy/tale' is all
about reflection and shadow.
Stainless steel, cut by water jets
into a delicate filigree pattern,
casts elaborate shadows across
the wall and, in doing so, visually
extends the physical surface area
occupied by each shelf.

Shelving
Stainless steel
www.bility.is
Location > Iceland
In production
By > www.saltfelagid.is

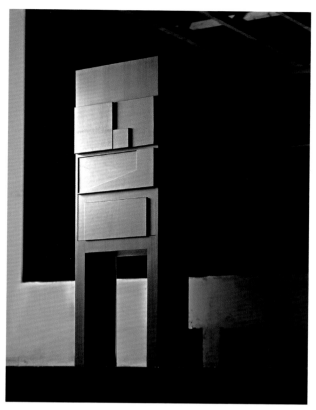

Boxed Body
Björn Rooijackers
Dutch

Björn Rooijackers suggests that this cupboard can be likened to the human body, because internal boxes and compartments are like organs. The 'Boxed Body' is made from medium density fibreboard (MDF) and is finished with a combination of hardwood veneer and grey leather.

Storage
MDF, wood veneer, leather
www.bjornr.com
Location > the Netherlands
Available to order

Adapt
Max Frommeld
German

This versatile product can take on the shape of its environment to eliminate dead spaces and allow the owner to use it as they see fit. The slats do not contribute to the structure's rigidity. They sit within a metal frame and can be slid back and forth, even meeting to produce a tidy corner that makes full use of all available space or negotiates alcoves. Bookends and hooks increase the system's adaptability.

Shelving
Wood, metal frame
www.ma-fro.com
Location > UK
In development

Max Frommeld's design seeks a new functionality. Samuel Accoceberry's 'Infinity' installation aims to do the same, see p. 332.

Foldable
Isabel Quiroga
German

With the idea of space-saving
furniture in mind, Isabel Quiroga
gave her dining table a second
function – or at least the capacity
to be stored decoratively. When
not in use, the table is intended to
be wall-mounted. The silk-screen
print on the tabletop then functions
as an interior feature while saving
floorspace too.

Table
Medium density fibreboard (MDF),
plywood, varnish, screen-print ink
www.isabelquiroga.com
Location > the Netherlands
Available to order

Brodie Table
Bernabeifreeman
Australian

The delicate craft of broderie anglaise and the industrialized process of metal punching are not usually linked, but the aesthetic of one and the possibility of recreating it with another appealed to Australian designers Rina Bernabei and Kelly Freeman. Thin, perforated aluminium sheet is used to its full potential in this decorative but nonetheless sturdy and easily manufactured table.

Table
Aluminium, stainless steel, powder-coated finish
www.bernabeifreeman.com.au
Location > Australia
Available to order

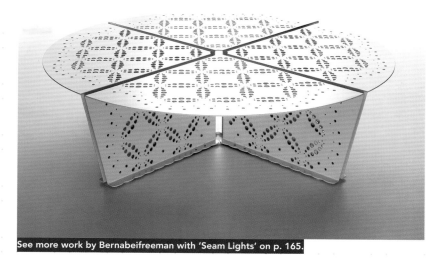

See more work by Bernabeifreeman with 'Seam Lights' on p. 165.

Nymphéas
Benoît Deneufbourg
Belgian

Just like a traditional 'nest', these three tables can be used individually or as a composition. The table adapts 'according to the desire of the consumer and the mood of the moment' says designer Benoît Deneufbourg.

Occasional table
Laminate, steel, powder-coated finish
www.benoitdnb.com
Location > Belgium
In production
By > www.unicdesign.be

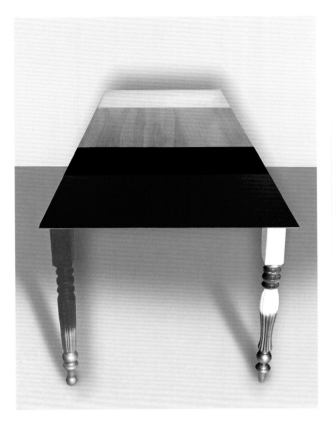

Coulure
Antoine Laymond
French

Old-style table legs are given
a new identity through a chaotic
application of coloured paint. The
legs' rustic charm and the obvious
marks of hastily applied paint are
in direct opposition to the slick
and perfectly finished aluminium
tabletop. Different colours are
applied again here, but this time
in neat, graphic panels.

Table
Aluminium, wood, paint
www.ldv-design.com
Location > France
Available to order

Using unwanted objects as raw material is
popular with young designers. See, among
many others, Laura de Monchy's 'To Handle,
To Pour, To Contain' on p. 207.

Pro-injection-table
Hannes Gumpp
German

Obsessed with the possibility of
construction techniques involving
sewing, German designer Hannes
Gumpp invested in canvas and
a sewing machine and set about
experimenting. The idea of
polyurethane foam within a textile
skin captured Gumpp's imagination.
Using computer-aided design he
created templates in textile into
which expanding polyurethane
foam is injected. Gumpp has begun
batch manufacturing several
designs in this manner.

Table
Canvas, polyurethane
www.hannesgumpp.com
Location > Germany
Available to order

Brace Angle Furniture
Valerian Gagnaire
French

If you thought this design was all about the angle joints you would be correct. Gagnaire has designed a steel brace angle that can be mass-produced cheaply and easily; his plan is that this angle be bought by consumers who wish to make their own piece of furniture. To complete a table, all else that is required is a screwdriver and some wooden sections of appropriate size. Industrial production and common DIY knowledge combine in the manufacture of this utilitarian item.

Table
Glass, steel angles, wood
www.valerian-gagnaire.com
Location > Switzerland
Available to order

For another design that invents a new method of construction, see the 'Clamp-a-leg' project on p. 318.

Ebb Table
Jarl Fernaeus
Swedish

Some objects that reveal their construction may feel cheap, but Jarl Fernaeus wanted to inject an atmosphere of exclusivity and elegance into his design, and to do so he employed Corian® and precision-cut pieces of wood. The name 'Ebb' is a reference to low tide, and Fernaeus likens the elements of his design to 'the naked and clean objects found on the sea bed at low tide'.

Table
Corian®, aluminium, wood
www.jarlfernaeus.se
Location > Sweden
In development

Subconscious
Daniel Rybakken
Norwegian

Intrigued by the effect of daylight on human perceptions, Rybakken notes that daylight in an interior gives a subconscious signal that there is space and activity beyond. If daylight is removed 'the feeling of space decreases, and the contrast between outdoor and indoor increases' resulting in feelings of isolation or loneliness. This design recreates the effect of direct sunshine by projecting a pattern from beneath the tabletop. Artificial shadows are cast onto the floor, creating the illusion of the sun shining through a nearby window.

Table
Birch
www.danielrybakken.com
Location > Sweden
In development

Frank Desk
John Slater
British

This piece of furniture is a reworking of the traditional, and now widely defunct, bureau or writing desk. John Slater has attempted to bring the writing desk up-to-date by adapting it for the modern form of correspondence: e-mail. Though details remain from the traditional bureau, making this a recognizable homage, the 'Frank Desk' is intended for use with a laptop. An additional detail is the conversion of the edge into a wraparound desk lamp.

Desk
Medium density fibreboard (MDF), tubular steel, steel sheet
www.john-slater.com
Location > UK
Available to order

The wing chair is another favourite archetype that is frequently reinvented. See 'Kate Chair' on p. 80.

Patches
Judith Seng
German

Each of these four tables functions
individually, but they find their
worth when placed together.
This 'constellation' of tables is
ever changing and designed to
offer a variety of informal situations.
The use of different woods –
pear, maple, walnut and olive –
emphasizes the individual units.

Table
Hardwoods
www.judithseng.de
Location > Germany
Available to order

Borrowing engineering or building solutions from another industry is a means of reaching new construction solutions. See also the 'Bronze Poly Chair' on p. 46.

Grace Table
Philippe Malouin
Canadian

'Grand furniture pieces are marvellous, although rather tricky to transport, handle or store,' says Philippe Malouin. His response to this logistical dilemma was to borrow from the ambition of inflatable furniture and the science and expertise of Eurocraft, a leading manufacturer of inflatable structures. Traditionally, inflatable furniture has many disadvantages, such as a lack of stability or rigidity and little control over its shape. These problems have been solved by Malouin, who has created an inflatable table that can be deflated, significantly increasing its storability and transportability, but still has great strength and rigidity. This is a grand table, big enough to accommodate ten guests when inflated, and small enough to fit in a duffel bag when deflated.

Table
Rubber, beech, polyurethane resin, polypropylene rope
www.philippemalouin.com
Location > UK
In production
By > designer

Serie
Lifegoods
Swiss

Each element of this series can be easily moved and assembled; the plywood construction does not call for screws or expertise in its making. The storage is intended to be multifunctional and accessible, and this series is completed by a large table that can be used in an office or dining room and which incorporates a slit in the centre to insert cords and cables.

Storage, table
Plywood
www.lifegoods.ch
Location > Switzerland
Available to order

Solid Honey-comb System
Kazuyuki Kawase
Japanese

The structure of this cardboard table is based upon basic origami techniques. The traditional shapes 'Yamaori' and 'Taniori' appear as 'A' and 'V' forms. Kazuyuki Kawase of the Link design group has combined these to make the main body of the table. The structure is pushed out of a folded, flat piece of corrugated cardboard and needs only glue to complete its assembly.

Table
Cardboard
www.link-design.org
Location > Japan
Available to order

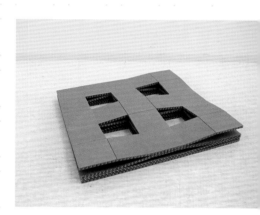

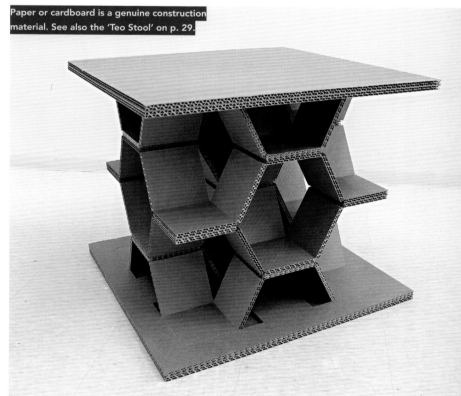

Paper or cardboard is a genuine construction material. See also the 'Teo Stool' on p. 29.

Bureau
Marina Bautier
Belgian

Marina Bautier creates gentle designs from oak. The 'Bureau' desk is a spare wooden table that is 'visually and materially light'. Bautier wanted to produce a piece of furniture that could adapt to all living spaces. 'The construction is such as not to corrupt the geometric simplicity of the structure', says Bautier.

Desk
Oak, steel
www.lamaisondemarina.com
Location > Belgium
In production
By > www.delaespada.com

Tafel Tafel
Mareanne Bosch
Dutch

Mareanne Bosch's skills as a silversmith are clearly reflected in her product designs. The shape of an 18th-century French table has been chiselled by hand into the surface of an industrially manufactured, sheet aluminium table. The use of a traditional craft and familiar archetype fused with a contemporary material and form creates an interesting tension.

Table
Aluminium
www.mareannebosch.nl
Location > the Netherlands
Available to order

Borrod
Line Depping
Danish

'Borrod' was designed as part of a graduation project on the theme of the irrational and chaotic human being. The table is designed to negate the need to tidy: the owner can slide the two halves of the tabletop apart, fill the material hammock with whatever had been littering the tabletop, slide the sections together and continue working or dining.

Table/desk
Ash, metal, fabric
www.linedepping.dk
Location > Denmark
In development

For another design that offers a quick remedy to the chaos of contemporary life see 'Möbelette' on p. 98.

Creep
Susan Bradley
British

This series of powder-coated steel
furniture is a celebration of nature.
Designer Susan Bradley uses flower
and leaf motifs and applies them
to basic forms, allowing the filigree
details to extend beyond the edges
of shelves and tables, thereby
mirroring the natural growth
patterns of plants.

Occasional table
Steel, powder-coated finish
www.susanbradley.co.uk
Location > UK
In production
By > designer

Craft techniques are increasingly given new applications, resulting in unexpected aesthetics. See the 'Flower Vases' on p. 224.

Grandma's Revenge
Mikael Heikkilä
Finnish

By applying a combination of cross-stitching, weaving and knotted pile techniques, Heikkilä has created a unique form of textile decoration for this glass-topped occasional table. The inspiration was retro craft, but the result is gothic and dramatic. Finnish designer Heikkilä claims the table has 'rock spirit'.

Occasional table
Metal, glass, cotton
www.mikaelheikkila.com
Location > Finland
Available to order

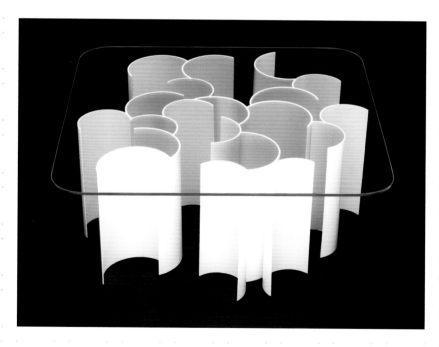

Splinter
Mia Cullin
Swedish

Irregularity inspired Cullin's low table design 'Splinter'. The frame of curved steel, which Cullin likens to fragments of broken porcelain or shells, creates an irregular pattern. The decorative table base is the key feature, with a simple glass top adding function. 'An unexpected detail or a distortion makes the object exciting,' says Cullin.

Occasional table
Steel, glass
www.miacullin.com
Location > Sweden
In development

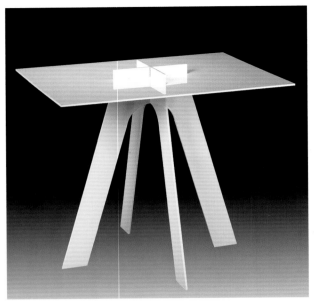

Bureau
Martin Holzapfel
German

The 'Bureau' combines two functions
in one; a desk and a shelf. The shelf
is unattached and rests on the
desktop, allowing its owner the
freedom to position it wherever
they wish. This is both a functional,
hardworking design by Martin
Holzapfel, who notes the increased
desire for office furniture at home,
and an experiment in creating a
pleasing abstract form. The piece is
'a small cosmos for your homework',
says Holzapfel.

Desk/shelf
Medium density fibreboard (MDF)
www.holzapfel-moebel.de
Location > Germany
Available to order

Plus Collection
Pinar Yar, Tugrul Gövsa
Turkish

The 'Plus' tables were designed
with efficiency in mind. The metal
parts can be flat-packed, easily
shipped and effortlessly assembled
by their new owner. The collection
of varying sizes and functions
of tables makes good use of
existing and cost-efficient metal
manufacturing processes.

Table
Stainless steel,
powder-coated finish
www.pinaryar.com
Location > Turkey
In production
By > www.gaeaforms.com

The problem of how to transport furniture
efficiently and cost effectively prompts new
solutions. See also 'U Form' on p. 167.

Heavy Metal Table
Siggi Anton
Icelandic

Sit on it or by it, indoors or
outdoors, use it as a bench or a
television table, or however you
want – Siggi Anton's 'Heavy Metal
Table' is nothing if not functional
and hardwearing. Anton admits to
a predilection for wanting to create
objects for glamorous spaces, but
in this case the table design was
born out of a more earthy pursuit;
working raw steel. Anton has
balanced the heavy, welded steel
base with something smoother; a
sleek teak tabletop, inspired by his
admiration for all things Eames and
the 1960s villa where he grew up.

Table
Steel, powder-coated polyester
finish, medium density fibreboard
(MDF), teak veneer
www.siggianton.com
Location > Iceland
In development

Le bureau cube
Eric Foussat
French

Foussat notes that the desk is
a serious piece of furniture not
often awarded consideration.
In response, 'Le bureau cube'
is part sculpture, part toy and
designed to inflict inspiration.
This playful spirit and love of bold
form is key to Foussat's work.

Desk
Aluminium, medium density
fibreboard (MDF), paint, gel coat
www.georgesdeprovidence.com
Location > France
In production
By > designer

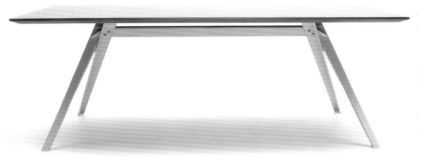

Discu
Dirk Winkel
German

This table's design is all about geometric symmetry. Its build is 'a new take on the principles of L-profile steel construction', says Winkel, whose ambition has been to manufacture an extremely stable, straightforward table. He started experiments for the construction using 2 square metres (22 square feet) of steel, but his exceptionally solid design meant he was able to reduce this to just a quarter of the amount for the final table base, which supports a solid wooden top.

Table
Sheet steel, wood
www.dirkwinkel.com
Location > Germany
In development

See more from Dirk Winkel in 'A Stacking Homage' on p. 39.

Table-Chair
Made By Midas
Dutch

The 'Table-Chair' is a multifunctional, elementary unit. Its form is naïve, a reflection of the simple functions it promises and the almost fairytale story of its inception. Made By Midas say 'The story behind the "Table-Chair" is of romance. The table and the chair are so in love they are as one.' The low structure can function easily as a seat or a table depending upon the whim of its owner.

Table/chair
Medium density fibreboard (MDF)
www.madebymidas.com
Location > the Netherlands
Available to order

Suppenkaspar
Nina Farsen, Isabel Schöllhammer
German

The idea that imperfections or
'deviations from the conventional'
can act as a springboard for
creativity led to the development
of the 'Suppenkaspar' series.
The 'defective' table has only two
legs, but weights held on plumb
lines compensate for their absence.
The legs of the table taper, and
the weights hardly touch the floor;
and yet, despite appearances,
the table is stable and secure.

Table
Birch ply, nylon, steel, iron, lead
www.ninafarsen.de
Location > Germany
Available to order

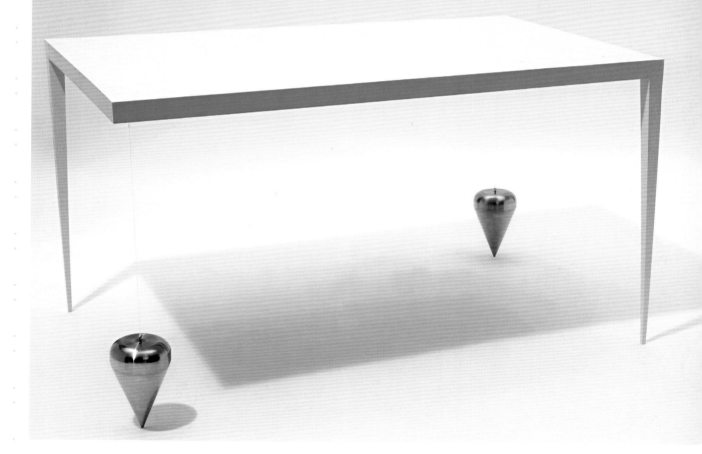

Soft dressing table
Kiki van Eijk
Dutch

This dressing table appears to be made of fabric but is, even more spectacularly, constructed from ceramic. Kiki van Eijk wanted to add a feeling of fragility as well as tactility to her design. The dressing table is, after all 'a very feminine and emotional piece'. The complex manufacturing process includes first making the design from textile, then creating plaster moulds and casting the whole piece from ceramic. The application of a matt glaze adds to the deception.

Dressing table
Ceramic, birch ply
www.kikiworld.nl
Location > the Netherlands
Available to order

Visual illusions are a common means of engagement. See also 'Public Garden' on p. 232.

Worktop
Normal Studio
French

Three major methods of shaping materials – crushing, extrusion and thermoforming – have been applied to the different elements of the 'Worktop' table. Jean-François Dingjian and Eloi Chafaï of Normal Studio have approached each of the different functions of the office desk separately and created an individual graphic element from each. Normal Studio 'questions the possibilities within everyday objects, daily rituals and the ways of life which are attached to them' in a process intended to stretch from research to production.

Table
Oak, Corian®, plastics
www.normalstudio.fr
Location > France
Available to order

£250 Million Topless Table
Tiago Da Fonseca
Portuguese

Tiago Da Fonseca has always admired the scale and elegance of London's Battersea Power Station. The undetermined future of this iconic building led Fonseca to reflect on issues of expectation and potential. This building is a well-loved, though essentially unusable, object in its current incomplete state. Just like the Power Station, the '£250 Million Topless Table' exhibits potential; all it needs is a top to make it functional. Fonseca is leaving the decision whether to complete it or not to the consumer.

Table
Beech
www.tiagodafonseca.com
Location > UK
In development

Keyboard
Susanne Philippson
German

This one-legged entrance table seems to defy gravity and have no apparent function. But the table holds keys thrown onto its leather surface, because magnets are concealed beneath. The polished stainless steel table was produced in a limited edition for the exhibition 'Burning Chrome'.

Occasional table
Stainless steel, leather, magnets
www.philippson.org
Location > Germany
Limited edition

Apparently unfunctional designs add an element of surrealism.
See 'This Is (Not)' on p. 257.

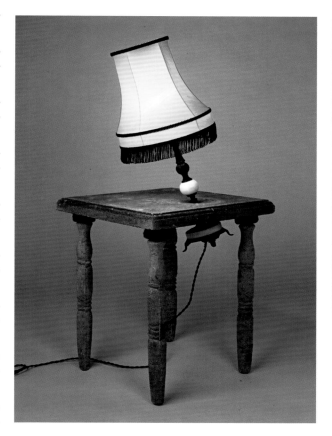

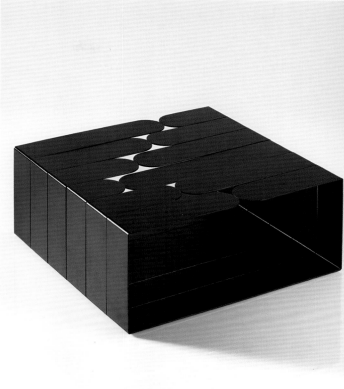

Embedded Meanings
Side Table
Scott Garcia
British

Scott Garcia says that his work
tends to focus on ideas and
concepts rather than traditional
form and function. This is apparent
in this collection of tables, where
Garcia has used concrete to create
decorative designs inspired by
Surrealism. The side table subverts
the ordinary; a fully functioning
vintage lamp has been caught
in the middle of the table.

Occasional table
Concrete, stainless steel,
brass, viscose
www.scottgarcia.moonfruit.com
Location > UK
Limited edition

Lia
LauberDeAllegri
Swiss

Swiss design platform INOUT
curated an exhibition for which
they invited young designers to
construct a piece of furniture from
a single A0 (841 × 1189 mm or
33.1 × 46.8 in.) sheet of aluminium.
Laeitita de Allegri and Livia Lauber
chose to optimize the material by
cutting six identical strips and
assembling them in parallel.

Table
Aluminium, powder-coated finish
www.lauberdeallegri.com
www.inoutdesigners.ch
Location > UK
Available to order

Meterware Table
Volksware
German

Discarded wooden tables have been attached together, one after another, to form one infinitely long table. On request Silke Wawro (who works under the name Volksware) will saw off a section of the table at the length required by a customer. This creates an individual product each time. Wawro is continuing to develop this original method of producing and selling furniture.

Table
Various woods
www.volksware.nl
Location > the Netherlands
In production
By > designer

Times Table
Mike Murphy,
Anton Nemme
Australian

The 'Times Table' was developed for a specific commission: office workers required large working areas and a piece of furniture that was easy to disassemble and move. The table is therefore assembled without the need for glue or fastenings, and is self-bracing. It arrives and can be stored flat-packed, and is the sum of just nine plywood parts.

Table
Plywood
www.formular.com.au/timestable/
Location > Australia
Available to order

Few parts and no fastenings make a piece of furniture attractive to construct and transport. See also 'Plastic Back Chair' on p. 72.

Walking Table
Wouter Scheublin
Dutch

To give a lifeless piece of furniture human qualities is to strengthen our emotional attachment to it. This is the theory Wouter Scheublin has set out to investigate with his astonishing 'Walking Table'. The table is carried by two sets of mechanical legs, and starts to walk when it is pushed. The distinction between lifeless and living becomes just a little more grey with this unexpected design.

Desk/dining table
Ash, steel
www.wouterscheublin.com
Location > the Netherlands
Available to order

Some designs are more machines than objects. For another example, see 'Sleeping Beauty' on p. 179.

Patchwork Pieces
Eliz Erdal
British

Eliz Erdal was interested in making a piece of furniture of value from nothing. 'I began by looking at patchwork quilts and shanty towns and from this I took the idea of using off-cuts and the mixing of different surface textures.' Erdal collects pieces of wood left over from regular furniture manufacture and pieces them together, allowing the shape and form of the pieces to dictate the final pattern.

Occasional table
Various woods
Location > UK
Available to order

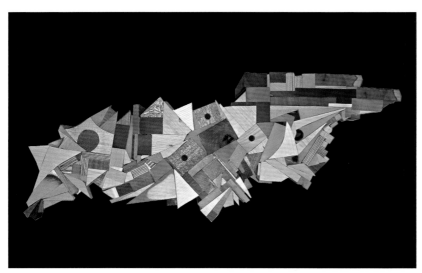

Budak
Ünal & Böler Studio
Turkish

This system of seating and shelving is composed of single units that can be stacked together to form an organic, architectural unit without the use of fixtures or screws. Structural strength increases as the built form grows. 'Budak' means 'tree knot' and the seemingly random (but actually repetitive) patterns found in natural forms have clearly influenced this structure's design.

Table/shelving
Aluminium
www.unalboler.com
Location > Turkey
In development

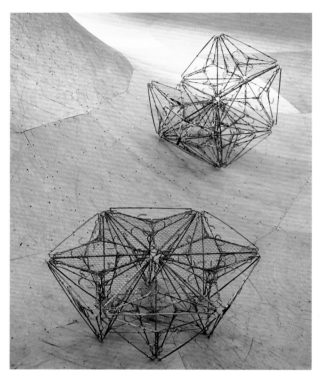

Hanging Out
Jesse Fokkink
Dutch

Dutch designer Jesse Fokkink observes that our living spaces are becoming more like showrooms, while shops are recreating the cosiness and warmth of private living spaces; these two areas play an increasingly important role and are yet increasingly separate. The desire to combine shop and living space led to the development of a furniture that uses the coat hanger as its principle material.

Table, chair
Metal, galvanized metal wire
www.jessefokkink.nl
Location > the Netherlands
Available to order

Ty-bihan
Gaël Horsfall
French/British

Ty-bihan means 'little house' in Breton, and it is an old Breton kitchen that inspired the form of this design. Seating, lighting, storage and dining table are all incorporated in one furniture form. The design is intended for an open-plan living space, and aims to facilitate the ritual of dining together as a group or family.

Table, seating, storage
Oak
www.gaelhorsfall.com
Location > UK
Available to order

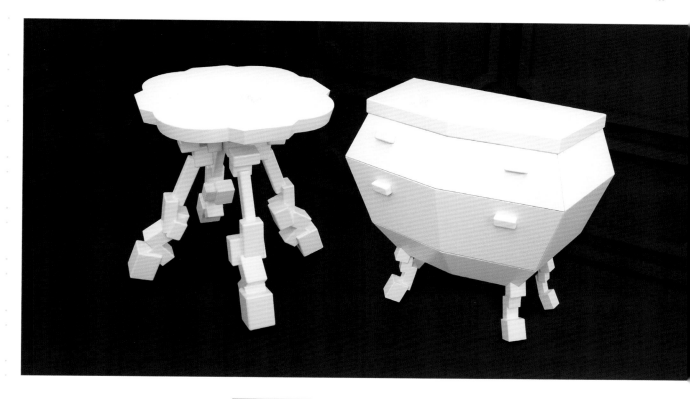

Neo Rococo
Smånsk Design Studio
Swedish

While there are many examples of the Rococo and Baroque styles being replicated with a new motivation and for a new market, Smånsk Design Studio have taken such homage a step further. They have updated the ornamentation of these styles by reducing them to their most basic forms, which they discovered through lowering the resolution at which they viewed images of period furniture.

Table, storage
Wood, paint
www.smansk.com
Location > Sweden
In production
By > designer

Pixellated forms are a popular modern aesthetic, offering digital interpretations of older forms. See the 'Materialized Vase' on p. 233.

Plakbanterie
Johan Bruninx
Belgian

Old furniture is given a new lease of life by an unusual application of brown paper. The paper is cut into pieces and applied to well-worn furniture to form a new protective skin that conceals cracks, scratches and dents. The finished result takes on the surprisingly convincing appearance of marquetry, because it is carefully applied in geometric patterns on the surface.

Tables, cabinets
Wood, brown paper tape
myspace.com/bruninx
Location > Belgium
Available to order

Covering old objects with a new skin offers them an extended life. See also 'Tea Set Noir' on p. 258.

Mu
Min Chen
Chinese

Young Chinese designer, Min Chen, questions the plausibility of an original design industry in contemporary China. Her response is to take traditional Chinese calligraphy as a model for genuine and important Chinese style. The resulting Stereo Calligraphy Series is a translation of these characters from 2D to 3D. Chinese Calligraphy represents key philosophical and value concepts and so, Chen believes, does this exploratory series of new furniture forms using the unique linear forms of calligraphy as their starting point.

Table, seating, storage
Maple, plywood
www.chenmindesign.com
Location > Italy
Available to order

The PlasticNature
Alexander Pelikan/
PeLi Design
German

The final form of this hybrid design combines the kind of production techniques usually found in the production of crafted vernacular furniture with those of injection-moulded plastic furniture. Cavities are cut into wooden parts, which are then placed in a mould. Plastic resin is injected into the mould and fills the spaces to complete the forms. 'The PlasticNature' is a comment on the similarity between these two methods of manufacture. Although apparently different, Pelikan points out that each was developed in order to further the progress of mass-production.

Chair, stool, table
Pine, walnut, plastic
www.pelidesign.com
Location > the Netherlands
Available to order

Informal Dining Range
Lucy Kurrein
British

The lack of inhibitions that we associate with childhood led Lucy Kurrein to reappropriate the naïve, simple and sturdy forms of children's furniture, in a hope that the same feelings of 'inhabition' would somehow be translated to the adult users. Casual dining is, Kurrein notes, the most popular way of dining today, and she has designed this series to reflect and further the trend. Kurrein has taken the exact proportions of a child's chair and rescaled them to accommodate her casual adults.

Table, chairs
Solid oak, lacquer
www.lucykurrein.com
Location > UK
In production
By > www.ercol.com

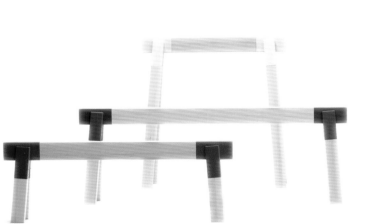

Trestle
TAF
Swedish

The design of this series of furniture is about durability and longevity. Lacquered steel fittings support a structure built from pine. The wooden elements can be replaced over time and can also be cut to different heights, facilitating various uses. The basic use of the trestle elements can be adapted throughout the owners' lifetime and they are able to function as supports for varying heights and widths of tables or even beds.

Trestle
Lacquered steel, wood
www.tafarkitektkontor.se
Location > Sweden
In development

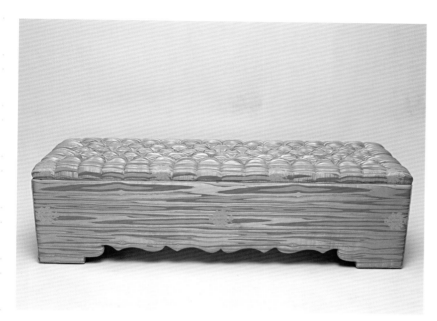

Survival Furniture
Minale-Maeda
Minale – Italian/German
Maeda – Japanese

These designs recall the development of furniture in the medieval period. The pieces are each covered in fabric but this is not, say Kuniko Maeda and Mario Minale, intended as ornament. Rather the heavy, woodgrain-patterned custom brocade is meant to represent another form of functionality, as wood might once have done. The designers also wanted to magnify the art of upholstery through this collection.

Table, bench, mirror, chandelier
Textile, plywood
www.minale-maeda.com
Location > the Netherlands
Available to order

Trends in sustainable design often feature previously undesirable materials. See also Heath Nash's 'Fullcolourball' on p. 248.

1 X 1
Nina Tolstrup
Danish

Nina Tolstrup developed these designs for a project concerned with sustainability. She took old scaffold boards and cut them into 2.5 × 2.5 cm (1 × 1 in.) sections, hence the name. Inspired by the simplicity and rawness of this basic material, she then made a variety of functional furniture objects, including floor and suspended lights and a series of trestles.

Storage, lights, trestle
Pine
www.studiomama.com
Location > UK
In development

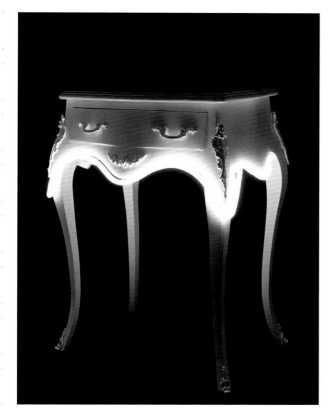

NeoNeon
Lee Broom
British

Each piece from this series is
first hand-carved in mahogany,
then given a high gloss finish and
finally dressed with neon tubing.
The juxtaposition of traditional
furniture archetypes and bold
industrial lighting is used to
dramatic effect. The harsh neon
light casts deep shadows in the
reflective, richly lacquered surfaces.

Chair, mirror, storage
Mahogany, lacquer, neon
www.leebroom.com
Location > UK
Limited edition

Lighting

SpringRain
Nosigner
Japanese

The use of bean-starch vermicelli, which the Japanese call 'spring rain', as a light shade is a peculiar, but perhaps inspired, choice. Not only is the lampshade completely biodegradable, or indeed edible, it also offers a dramatic, effective and pliable construction material. The vermicelli is boiled before being wrapped around the light source and fixed in place by a hair-dryer.

Hanging lamp
Bean-starch vermicelli
www.nosigner.com
Location > Japan
In development

Seam Lights
Bernabeifreeman
Australian

Rina Bernabei and Kelly Freeman
reinterpreted the language of
pleating, gathering and stretching
fabric over frames, as found in
archetypal cloth lampshades,
with perforated sheet aluminium.
The light, thin metal lends the
lamps a paper-like quality, and the
fine perforations assist the complex
folding during manufacture.

Hanging lamp
Aluminium, stainless steel,
powder-coated finish
www.bernabeifreeman.com.au
Location > Australia
Available to order

Just as craft is employed to create contemporary forms, the
latest methods of manufacture can be employed to replicate
craft processes. See also the 'Hadji Bowl' on p. 235 and
'PuzzlePerser' on p. 281.

Mold Lamp
Michel Charlot
Swiss

This pendant lamp celebrates the
moulding process, keeping defects
that occur during the process
and visual signs of the mould
and making them key features.
The properties of thin Eternit fibre
cement were explored in detail
by Charlot – the 'Mold Lamp' is
therefore exceptionally strong yet
light, it can be used both indoors
and out.

Hanging lamp
Eternit fibre cement
Location > Switzerland
In production
By > www.eternit.ch

Stella
Nathalie Dewez
Belgian

The 'Stella' lights are made using
welded steel rods. Their graphic
form was developed from
exercises in creating 3D shapes
from triangular forms. Dewez hit
upon a method of arrangement
that was aesthetically pleasing
and which offered the opportunity
for numerous variations.

Hanging lamp
Steel, paint, borosilicate glass
www.n-d.be
Location > Belgium
In production
By > www.habitat.com

Anomalies can ensure individuality and add worth.
See also 'To be continued' on p. 98 and 'Accidentels' on p. 187.

U Form
Elisabeth Henriksson
Swedish

'U Form' lights can be built in any number of configurations; anything from a small shade to a large installation is possible from a kit of parts, and this flexible form and size make it useful in any kind of space. 'I have been working with the same themes for some years; change, versatility and repetition,' says Henriksson. The light, she adds, is an exercise in economical design, because it is both inexpensive and easy to produce and ship and produces very little waste in its manufacture.

Hanging lamp
Acrylic or metal
www.elisabethhenriksson.se
Location > Sweden
In production
By > www.orsjo.se

Allowing the user to alter the form of their product helps to extend its longevity. See also 'Boox' on p. 95.

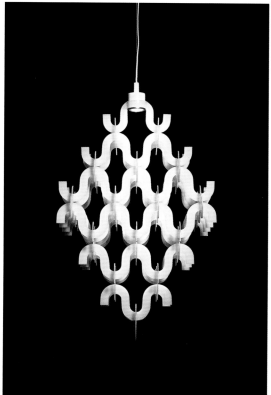

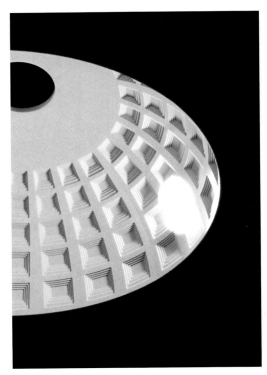

Pantheon Light
Naoki Terada
Japanese

The desire to recreate a poignant and personal experience led Naoki Terada to create this pendant lamp. Artificial light illuminates the shade just as Terada witnessed daylight entering the dome of the Pantheon, mimicking the 'solemn and divine' atmosphere that he recalls experiencing. The ambitions of the design are shamelessly romantic, as Terada invites the public to share his experience.

Hanging lamp
Corian®
www.teradadesign.com
Location > Japan
Available to order

Nostalgia and shared experiences can be used to prompt empathy in the viewer. Daniel Rybakken uses similar techniques for 'Subconscious' on p. 132.

Urchin
Christopher Hardy
Australian

This sculptural light makes good use of the most contemporary manufacturing techniques. Rapid prototyping has been employed because it suits the low-volume production of the light, CNC milling shapes most of the light's parts, and white polyurethane paint, as used in the car industry, finishes the product. The design grew from a desire to harness these new and emerging production techniques and an interest in low-energy light emitting diodes (LEDs).

Hanging lamp
Acrylobutadiene styrene, polycarbonate, polyurethane, aluminium, polyurethane paint
Location > Australia
Available to order

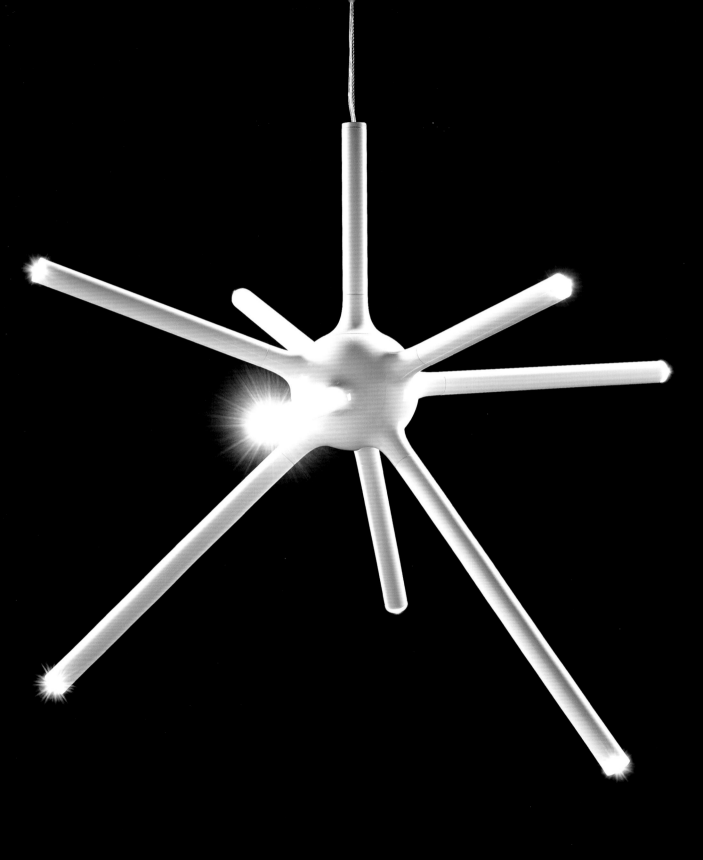

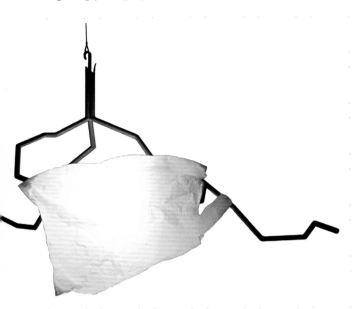

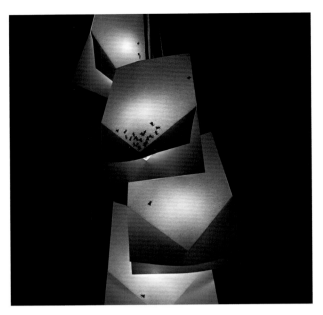

Bag stuck in a tree light
Edward Vince
British

Plastic bags stranded in the branches of trees are a common urban sight. Edward Vince has sought to capture this occurrence by recreating the bag as a suspended lamp, complete with branches. The bag itself can be replaced with different coloured or graphic-decorated variations of the everyday carrier bag.

Hanging lamp
Mild steel, silver, paint
www.edvince.co.uk
Location > UK
Available to order

A4 lamp shade
Chris Kirby
Canadian

'People become stressed when they live in a messy place,' observes Canadian designer Chris Kirby. 'We all strive to attain the clean living presented in design literature but so often fall short.' The 'A4 lamp shade' is part of a series of objects through which Kirby examines messiness as a state of conflict with the preconceived rules of modern living. The shade incorporates what we normally consider a blemish as a design feature: images of flies are stamped onto the shade's inside surface, transforming the negative association of a dead fly caught in a lamp into a playful accent.

Hanging lamp
Paper, ink
www.chriskirbydesign.com
Location > Japan
Available to order

See more of Chris Kirby's investigations into our environment in 'Clutter Shelf' on p. 123.

Ikarus
Aylin Kayser,
Christian Metzner
Germany

Although 'Ikarus' was developed as a means of visualizing electricity consumption, the beauty of the design almost eclipses that initial intention. This is a simple but highly effective idea: the warmth from a light bulb slowly melts a shade made from wax, causing it to deform into any number of exciting shapes. The speed and direction of the melting wax can be manipulated through the position and power of the light bulb. As 'Ikarus' melts away completely it serves as a dramatic and poetic symbol of energy dissipation.

Hanging lamp
Paraffin wax, stainless steel, steel
Location > Germany
Limited edition

Another design that exploits a natural process to create its form is 'The Honeycomb Vase' on p. 227.

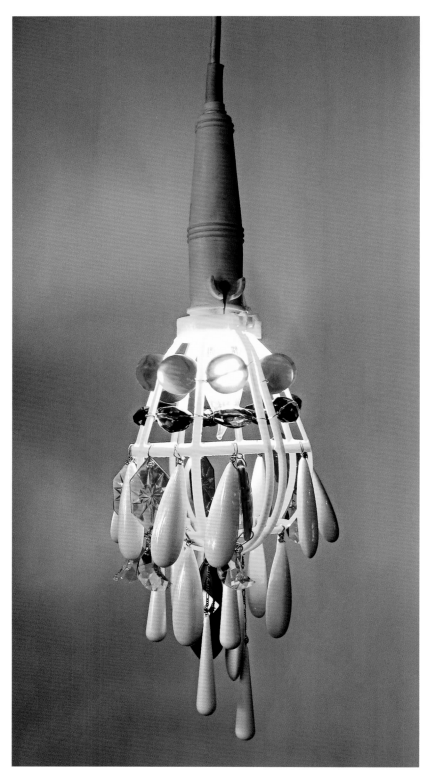

Construction Chandelier
Justin Giunta
American

This lamp is part of the Subversive Home Series, and designed to 'bridge the gap between antique and modern lighting'. Designer Justin Giunta takes crystals and salvaged pieces of antique chandeliers and applies them to an inspection lamp that is most often found on construction sites. Despite the decorative flourishes, the lamps remain reminiscent of that earlier process. Giunta acknowledges the common association between owning a chandelier and prosperity, and deliberately created his industrial version of a classic as an object of 'accessible decadence'.

Hanging lamp
Austrian crystal, Swarovski crystal, mixed secondhand items
www.justingiunta.com
Location > USA
Available to order

Calamare Light
Jan Tromp
Dutch

The formal language of the 'Calamare Light' refers to clothing rather than conventional lighting types. Tromp chose to disrupt the geometry of an archetypal lampshade by using 'sleeves' of Xorel® fabric. These can be rolled up in order to emit more light.

Hanging lamp
Xorel® textile
www.valvomo.com
Location > Finland
Available to order

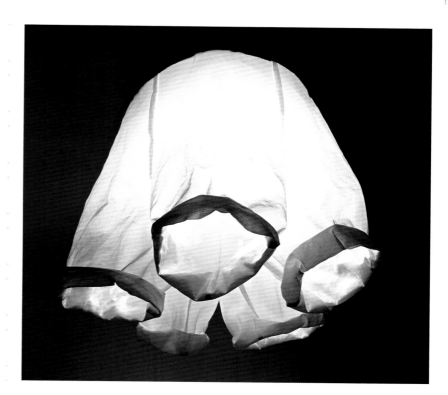

Sunda
Tom Pawlofsky
German

'With Sunda I started to question: what happens if a designer becomes deeply involved in programming skills, and uses the full power of computer-controlled manufacturing?' says German designer Tom Pawlofsky. Investigating new approaches to computer-based design led to the creation of a strip pattern and this range of lights, which are made from CNC-cut polycarbonate with interlocking joins.

Hanging lamp
Polycarbonate foil
www.pawlofsky.de
Location > Germany
Available to order

Je m'appelle Moustache
Katrin Greiling
German

Verging on the threshold of anti-design, 'Je m'appelle Moustache' is barely describable as a product. Designer Katrin Greiling has added a human feature, a moustache, to a bare light bulb, injecting personality and character into an otherwise inanimate object. The effect is surreal, while the concept is minimal. Achieving this emotive quality is Greiling's ambition: 'I tell stories with products. Functional in one way but I also want to stimulate the consumer.'

Hanging lamp
Leather, silicone
www.katringreiling.com
Location > Sweden
In production
By > designer

Glassbulb Light
Studio Oooms
Dutch

Guido Ooms and Karin van Lieshout of Studio Oooms have given an everyday object a new dimension through a simple addition; a wine glass is used to replace the regular glass bulb that surrounds the filament. The bulb functions as well as before, but is now promoted to an interior feature rather than a disregarded everyday accessory.

Hanging lamp
Glass
www.oooms.nl
Location > the Netherlands
In production
By > designer

Lingor
Mark Braun
German/Swedish

Mark Braun revisits an infrequently
used material and manufacturing
technique with the 'Lingor' lamps.
Phosphorescent enamelled steel
is compressed to form these
utilitarian shapes; the simple forms
were chosen because they show
off the classic finish especially well.

Hanging lamps
Sheet steel, enamel
www.markbraun.org
Location > Germany
Available to order

For more work by Mark Braun see 'Fusion'
on p. 261.

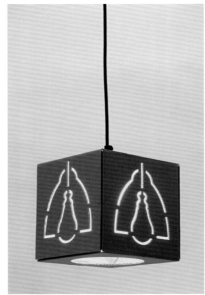

Not A Box
David Graas
Dutch

Here, packaging and product are integrated into one object. All the functioning parts of the lamp are inside the box, which carries a graphic, cut out, image of a lampshade and bulb. At first glance this may be taken to represent a shade within the box, but in fact the box itself is the shade. Graas is dealing here with issues of waste and disposability in design.

Hanging lamp
Cardboard
www.davidgraas.com
Location > the Netherlands
Limited edition

Packaging and product in one is a sustainable solution. See also 'Packaging Lamp' on p. 189.

Lighting Bug
Studio Gorm
Dutch

When switched on, the 'Lighting Bug' swings around energetically at the end of its cable. The animated light owes its motion to a built-in motor and propellers. The movement of the light resembles that of an insect carving irregular arcs through a room, casting shadows and animating the space as it moves. Among Studio Gorm's inspirations for the charming 'Lighting Bug' were old nautical films: 'I remembered old movies where the lamps swing around as the ship moves on the sea, casting strange shadows.'

Hanging lamp
Metal, plastic
www.studiogorm.com
Location > USA
Available to order

Lamp/Lamp
Hironao Tsuboi
Japanese

'We never pay attention to light bulbs but take more interest in the equipment that surrounds them' says Hironao Tsuboi. He has decided that the iconic form of the light bulb is decoration itself and developed an interesting product to show it off. 'Lamp/Lamp' requires hand-blown glass and has two fittings – the first functions, and the second allows the light to show off the form of a classic bulb.

Light bulb
Glass, metal
www.100per.com
Location > Japan
In production
By > designer

Swirl Light
Luiza Milewicz
Australian

These chandeliers are constructed
from masses of optical fibres,
woven through polypropylene
rings and lit by changing colours
of halide lighting. The chandeliers
were originally conceived as
a jewelry project for a dance
performance and were then
evolved into these theatrical
installations. They are transparent
sculptures by day and dramatic
sources of light at night.

Hanging lamp
Optical fibres, polypropylene,
rotating colour wheel
www.luminadesign.net
Location > Australia
Available to order

Sleeping Beauty
Nadine Sterk
Dutch

This remarkable design turns a normally facile domestic object into a living machine. When supplied with energy, 'Sleeping Beauty' knits its own lampshade, only ceasing when the light is switched off. Feeding the lamp energy encourages it to grow – just like a living organism. It was Nadine Sterk's ambition to build a machine that would become an animated part of a space, with an existence apart from human contact.

Hanging lamp
Steel, wool
www.ateliernl.com
Location > the Netherlands
Limited edition

The process of construction is the key feature of this design, which is an industrial take on craft production. The 'Big Dipper' is an invention with a similar intent, see p. 251.

Campanula
Marko Nenonen
Finnish

The 'Campanula' suspended light represents a bell. Bells would be used to call people to the dinner table, and it was once believed that the bell was capable of warding off evil spirits, so Finnish designer Nenonen concluded that it might be reassuring to have the symbol of a bell hanging over a dinner table. The coloured interior of the aluminium lamp is intended to combat the inferior quality of light from energy-efficient bulbs.

Hanging lamp
Aluminium, steel,
powder-coated finish
www.howaboutviktor.com
Location > Finland
Available to order

Marko Nenonen is a member of Finnish design group How About Viktor. So is Yuki Abe, whose 'Maneki Chair' is on p. 71.

Flowers
Mirjam Hüttner,
Claude Muller
German

Six different-shaped lampshades
hang together like a bouquet of
flowers. But just as two bouquets
can never be identical, each
chandelier also differs from any
other depending on the positioning
and selection of the individual
shades by the designer.

Hanging lamp
Aluminium, powder-coated
or anodized finish
www.huettners.com
Location > Germany/Luxembourg
Available to order

Weave Your Lighting
Kwangho Lee
Korean

'Weave Your Lighting' is a series
of works where Kwangho Lee
uses the electric cable of a light
as an expressive, creative material.
Lee believes in the 'boundless
capabilities' of ordinary objects
and has set out to prove, in this
ever-expanding and increasingly
theatrical series of works, how a
simple object can transcend its
everyday use. He cites his mother's
hobby of knitting as an early trigger
for the series. The cables replace
yarn as a raw material, from which
Lee weaves and constructs form.

Hanging lamp
Electric cable
www.kwangholee.com
Location > Korea
Available to order

Amorphous Lamps
Annie Adams
American

These lamps are part of a body
of work titled 'Manufacturing the
Absurd'. The aim was to produce
unexpected products by following
a process of nonsensical design
decisions. The lights are made
from 'crystal glaze', a silicone sheet
material embedded with Swarovski
crystals. They are completely
pliable and only reveal their shape
when hung.

Hanging lamp
Silicone, Swarovski crystals
Location > USA
Available to order

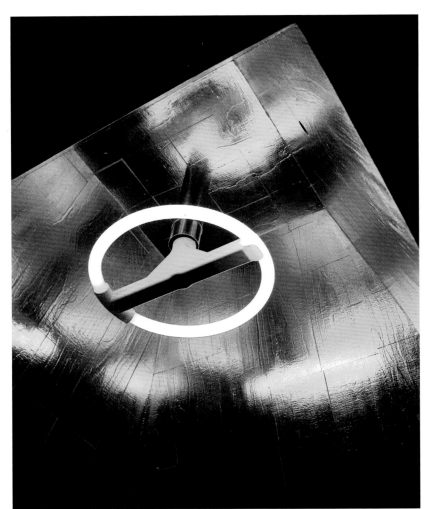

Hotspot
Niels van Eijk, Miriam van der Lubbe
Dutch

The gold foil applied to the interior of the 'Hotspot' is in direct contrast to the rough plywood exterior of the lamp and lends the emitted light a diffused, warm glow. The suspended plywood construction includes an arm that allows the user to direct the light where desired.

Hanging lamp
Plywood, gold foil
post@ons-adres.nl
Location > the Netherlands
In production
By > www.quasar.nl

See more of Niels van Eijk and Miriam van der Lubbe's work together in 'Public Garden' on p. 232.

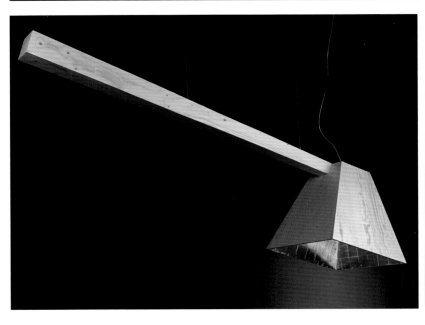

InnerTube
Sylvain Willenz
Belgian

The shape of this soft and flexible
rubber shade is maintained by
the circular TL fluorescent tube
against which it sits, and came
about through the designer's
interest in experimenting with
rubber manufacturing processes.
The finished design, says Willenz,
was not so much about the
application of an unusual material
but about designing an object with
the fewest possible components,
and so an exercise in reductionism.

Hanging lamp
Latex
www.sylvainwillenz.com
Location > Belgium
In production
By > designer

Torch
Sylvain Willenz
Belgian

'Torch' recalls the archetypal lines
of a common handheld torch and
mixes this imagery with that of a
car headlight, referenced through
the addition of a diffuser made
from textured sheet polycarbonate.
The light can be hung from the
ceiling, laid on the floor, on a
tabletop in groups or singularly.

Hanging/table lamp
Moulded plastic, polycarbonate
www.sylvainwillenz.com
Location > Belgium
In production
By > www.establishedandsons.co.uk

Archetypes of everyday forms are regularly given new, but familiar roles. See also the 'B45' light on p. 213.

Twinlampshade
Aude Genton
Swiss

What could have been a regular technical detail became the key decorative element in this design. Genton chose to secure plastic sheeting into the form of the lampshade with a decorative edge and hand stitching.

Table lampshade
Polypropylene
www.audegenton.com
Location > Switzerland
In development

Whatels Accidentels
Els Woldhek/Whatels
Dutch

Woldhek used industrial methods that usually produce identical items to create an object with individual character, letting 'the process itself influence and develop the product'. The light is plastic, electroplated without intervention, which gives a unique, unpredictable outcome; uneven electric current produces layered, jewelled edges ordinarily considered a defect. Woldhek likens it to a 'naturally grown unique object'.

Table lamp
Polypropylene, copper finish
www.whatels.net
Location > the Netherlands
Available to order

See also Whatels's 'Bastard' chair on p. 55.

Fono Light
Klauser & Carpenter
German/British

The 'Fono Light' is one of several products that designers André Klauser and Ed Carpenter have come together to produce. Both its name and and its form reference the megaphone. The shape aptly allows the control of light, and 'Fono' is most useful where glare-free, indirect light is required, such as on a bedside table. Its simple form is made from rolled steel.

Table lamp
Steel, powder-coated finish
www.klauserandcarpenter.com
Location > UK
In production
By > www.thorstenvanelten.com

La Liseuse
Benoît Deneufbourg
Belgian

Because table lamps are often positioned against a wall, Benoît Deneufbourg has created a 'half lamp'. Deneufbourg imagined a classic table lamp and then divided it down the middle to suit this observation. The form is made of two pieces of folded steel 'combined to create a form as simple as possible'.

Table lamp
Steel, lacquer
www.benoitdnb.com
Location > Belgium
In production
By > www.macrolux.net

Mary Joe 2
Leslie Hildebrandt
German

Designer Leslie Hildebrandt describes 'Mary Joe 2' as a 'very friendly light'. A traditional gas-lamp base is juxtaposed with a cartoon-like shade. The shade is made from soft foam, which produces a warm light and lends the piece a curious and charming character, like a 'piece of a drawing that broke out of a picture'.

Table lamp
Foam, metal
www.lesliehildebrandt.com
Location > Germany
Available to order

Lost Model
Fabien Cappello
Swiss

Cappello uses evaporative pattern sandcasting, a technique most often used for prototyping, in which a polystyrene model melts away during the casting process. To create individual rather than identical designs, Cappello chooses fragments of polystyrene packaging from household appliances to use as models. In doing this, he borrows their formal character and reforms them into an unfinished, irregular and raw series of lights.

Table lamp
Aluminium
www.fabiencappello.com
Location > France/UK
In production
By > designer

Packaging Lamp
David Gardener
British

An ambition to eliminate waste led designer David Gardener to incorporate packaging and product into one. After studying different types of packaging, Gardener quickly decided that paper pulp would be a good material to use, because it is durable, shock absorbent and easily mass produced. The ability to mould the pulp gave Gardener the freedom to create one light in the form of another. The components of the light are placed within the outer case for transport to be pieced together by the consumer; the middle section of the lamp looks like a turned wood section, but its shape is determined by the electronic components that are packaged within it.

Table lamp
Paper pulp
www.davidgardener.co.uk
Location > UK
In development

Coma
**Buchegger, Denoth,
Feichtner**
Austrian

This Austrian design group argue
that industrial design has no real
function any longer in Europe.
Thomas Feichtner says that to
remain valid, industrial design
must be capable of producing
in large quantities for a willing
mass audience, and that this
condition does not currently exist.
Therefore, the design group are
currently committed to returning
to traditional craft practices.
'Coma' is a geometric table lamp
constructed from folded aluminium.

Table lamp
Aluminium
www.bdf-ad.com
Location > Austria
In production
By >
www.designwerkstaette-schatzl.at

Clipping Rod
Tomas Kral
Slovakian

This lamp can be clipped onto
the side of a desk or a shelf, and
a simple lock system means that
the spotlight can be moved along
the length of the wire stem. The
weight of the spot and its position
on the flexible stem change the
direction of the light and enable
the illumination of different zones.

Task lamp
Stainless steel
www.tomaskral.ch
Location > Switzerland
Available to order

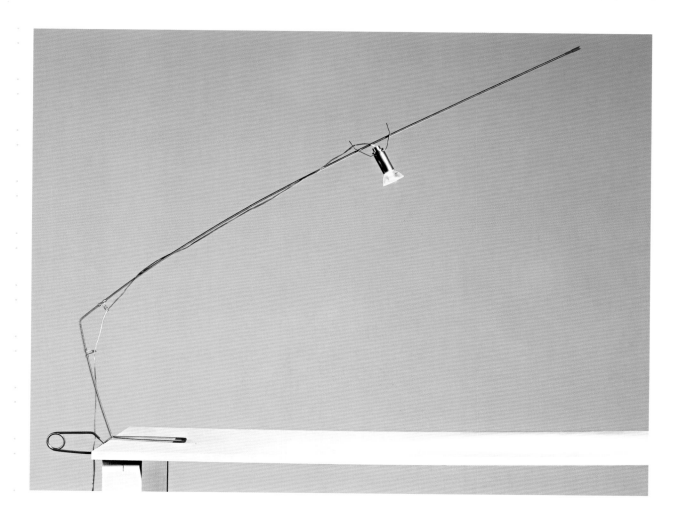

Fortuna
Patrick Rampelotto
Italian/Austrian

In these small lamps, a light sits beneath an upturned trophy cup. Trophies are personal, emotionally charged objects that represent sentimentality – this is their principal function. The minimal intervention of turning over the cups immediately changes our perception of the object. Although the basic form of a trophy is repetitive, each is in some way different, which adds to the originality of the pieces.

Table lamp
Various metals, various stones, plastic, wood
www.patrickrampelotto.com
Location > Austria
Available to order

Gold Toy Lamp
Ryan McElhinney
Irish

When Ryan McElhinney lived in Arizona he would buy bags of secondhand toys for a couple of dollars from local thrift stores. This unusual raw material has become the starting point for McElhinney's one-off designs. The lamp is made from recycled toys bonded to a base and then spray coated with a high-gloss polyurethane lacquer.

Table lamp
Plastic, wood, polyurethane lacquer
www.ryanmcelhinney.com
Location > UK
Limited edition

Obscure, everyday products can be reappointed to arresting effect. See the 'Glassbulb Light' on p. 174 and 'Jigsaw Wallpaper' on p. 277.

Skinny
Marcel Sigel
Australian

A shade usually surrounds the
source of light, but in 'Skinny'
the light is within the shade itself.
Because of its thin aluminium
frame, the lamp softens and
diffuses its light in every direction
from this interior source.

Table lamp
Aluminium
www.zuii.com
Location > UK
In production
By > designer

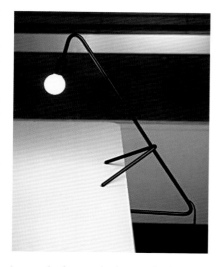

Giraffe
Rice Design
Japanese

Nobuhiko Arikawa of Rice Design
wanted to design a lamp that could
hang from a table and be moved
around easily, with a form that
had character and elegance.
After simplifying his design to
its most basic parts and minimal
shape, the form which gave
the design its name appeared;
a giraffe. The lightweight brass
frame balances securely on any
table edge.

Table lamp
Brass, paint
www.rice-design.com
Location > Japan
Available to order

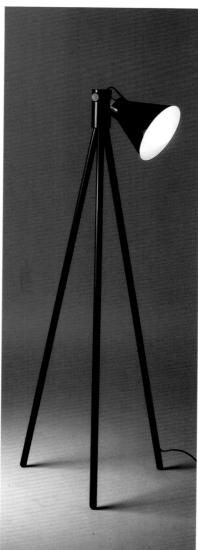

Tre1
Elina Järvinen
Finnish

The cone-shaped shade and
anthropomorphic qualities of this
lamp might look familiar. They were
borrowed from an unlikely source
of inspiration – a sick dog with a
cone collar. To keep the design
minimalistic and playful, Järvinen
reduced the construction to its
most basic elements: three legs,
shade, bulb and wiring.

Task lamp
Metal, paint
Location > Finland
In production
By > www.selki-asema.fi

Two Lamps
Rui Xavier
Swiss

Rui Xavier and the Lifegoods studio
in Switzerland have designed a
bedside lamp with dual functionality.
It works primarily as a simple table
lamp, but a second light source
allows the top to be detached to
become a flashlight.

Table lamp
Glass, aluminium
www.lifegoods.ch
Location > Switzerland
In development

Adding a second function can give new
meaning to a regular typology. This is
especially popular in lighting design.
See also 'Plug' on p. 217.

Softy
Laurens van Wieringen
Dutch

The unusually flexible form and
highly tactile surface of the 'Softy'
give the lamp an appealing quality
and invite interaction. It can be
used within a group, and adapted
to suit its owner. The lamp is made
from flexible vinyl and is produced
by dip moulding.

Table lamp
Vinyl
www.laurensvanwieringen.nl
Location > the Netherlands
In development

Flexibility, a new visual effect, is made possible by
the application of new materials and manufacturing
processes. See also Pepe Heykoop's 'A Restless
Chairacter' on p. 43.

Magnet Light
Jochem Faudet
Dutch

This lamp's innovation is to use neodymium magnets to join its components. The lack of permanent fixings means both the arm sections and the light source (direct or ambient) can be changed very simply to suit the task at hand. Faudet was seeking 'a solution to making a small articulating joint without having to use a spring or counterweight as most task lights do'. The result is a family of interchangeable, lightweight, and, ultimately, functional lights.

Lighting system
Stainless steel
www.jochemfaudet.com
Location > UK
In development

Soil Lamp
Marieke Staps
Dutch

The energy source for this lamp is an unusual one. Soil and water act as the electrolyte in cells containing copper and zinc – a basic battery. The more cells there are, the more electricity is generated. 'This technique offers a wealth of possibilities. The only thing that the lamp needs is a splash of water every now and then' says Staps. The casing for this process is glass, to show the curious and pioneering technique and to provide a visual reference to the classic light bulb.

Table lamp
Glass, copper, zinc, soil, water
www.mariekestaps.nl
Location > the Netherlands
In development

Using alternative energy sources especially relevant for this generation of designers, the low energy light bulb is afforded particular attention. See 'Flame Lamps' on p. 206 for an example.

Cage Lamps
Edouard Larmaraud
French

This family consists of a reading lamp, bedside lamp and ceiling lamp. The starting point for the project was the technical constraint of using the lampshade technique to create a lamp in itself. Larmaraud has inverted the expected structure of a lamp by placing a cylindrical lampshade on the interior of the object, with the metal structure forming a cage around it.

Lighting series
Steel, epoxy lacquer, cotton
www.larmaraud.com
Location > France
In production
By > www.matejewski.com

Light Box
George Pegasiou
British

'The light is an exploration into making lighting more emotionally engaging, interactive and intuitive to use,' says George Pegasiou, who feels that much contemporary lighting design is overstylized and impersonal. Pegasiou points out that a lamp's shade is simply a container for light, and he realizes this abstract idea with a literal interpretation. The handle of the drawer invites the user to open it, and then functions as a method of controlling the release of light.

Table light
Medium density fibreboard (MDF), wood
www.urban-shed.com
Location > UK
Available to order

See more from George Pegasiou in 'Pressing Matters' on p. 311.

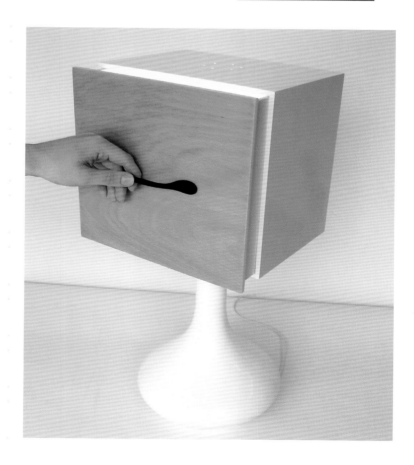

Lamp Adapted
Anna McConnell
British

Anna McConnell is attempting to increase a product's lifespan by adding materials to secondhand furniture. Inspired by a nostalgic memory of a recent past when furniture was bought to last through generations, McConnell has adapted a lamp to better suit a new lifestyle. The old standard lamp has been given a hinge and can now function as a task light, increasing and updating its use and therefore its value.

Floor lamp
Secondhand materials, steel hinges
www.annamcconnell.co.uk
Location > UK
In production
By > www.newbritishdesign.com

Extending the lifecycle of furniture objects offers a solution to excessive consumption. Maezm's 'Re-love project 1' on p. 59 achieves this, as does 'Plakbanterie' on p. 156.

Character Lamps
Jenny Beardshall
British

The uprights of these lamps are
made from flocked, turned wood
and support a voluptuous glass
balloon shade. The balloons
commonly feature in Beardshall's
designs, but here she has taken
the simple form and maximized its
decorative potential in a purposeful
pursuit of character. 'The key
to these designs has been
collaborations and influences
from street art, character design
and strong uses of colour and
contrasting textures.'

Standard lamp
Glass, wood
www.rawstudio.co.uk
Location > UK
Available to order

'itti & Ette' on p. 79 similarly uses the idea of an interior skeleton as ornament, as does 'Veins of the House' on p. 297.

Happy Lamp
Vaugh|Shannon
Irish

The design of this lamp came from the frustration of using existing lamps on which the controls are difficult to reach. The ergonomic location for the controls on 'Happy Lamp' dictated an unintended anthropomorphic form, which is sometimes perceived as a male body, say Vaugh and Shannon – hence the name of the lamp.

Floor lamp
Steel, powder-coated finish, textile
www.vaughshannon.com
Location > Ireland
In development

Shadow Lamp
Edouard Larmaraud
French

These lamps have an added dimension that emphasizes whether they are switched on or off. When switched off, they look like an archetypal lamp but when switched on the structure inside is silhouetted against the lampshade as a cast shadow, revealing either the lines of a traditional lampshade or the outline of a bulb.

Floor lamp
Steel, lacquer, cotton
www.larmaraud.com
Location > France
In production
By > www.matejewski.com

AWARE Laundry Lamp
Interactive Institute
Swedish

Interactive Institute are a Swedish collaboration of art, design and information technology. The AWARE project concerns energy awareness, and the 'Laundry Lamp' was devised as a problem-solving product, combining a light with the opportunity to dry clothes. Hanging clothes around the light source ensures energy is shared, and the owner, by default, creates their own personalized design incorporating their laundry as design material.

Floor lamp
Metal, powder-coated finish
www.tii.se
Location > Sweden
Available to order

This product not only maximizes energy use, it is also a physical reminder of the issue. A similar tactic is employed by 'Standby' on p. 291.

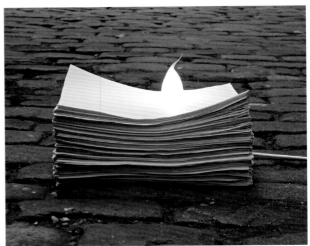

Flame Lamps
Gitta Gschwendtner
German

This collection of ten lights
showcases energy-efficient
candle bulbs. Each of the electric
'Flame Lamps' is a playful take on
traditional lighting types, designed
to mimic tradition. The oil lamp
sees a bulb embedded in an old
oil canister, while the burned log
lamp sees the bulbs surrounded by
firewood. We all ought to be using
energy-saving bulbs, but people
remain reluctant to switch and are
unaware that 'they are attractive in
their own right' says Gschwendtner.

Floor/table lamps
Wax, plastic, wood, coal, paper
www.gittagschwendtner.com
Location > UK
Limited edition

To Handle, To Pour,
To Contain
Laura de Monchy
Dutch

The lights in this series are made
up of an unlikely combination of
old plastic canisters and cut-glass
lampshades. Laura de Monchy is
trying to make something beautiful
out of seemingly worthless objects:
independently, neither element has
any significant design appeal but
together they are 'precious objects
with a new function'.

Floor/table lamps
Plastic, glass
www.laurademonchy.nl
Location > the Netherlands
Limited edition

Being Floorlamp
Rane Vaskivuori
Finnish

The 'Being Floorlamp' is an ambiguous object. Vaskivuori, of Valvomo Architects, has bestowed distinctly human qualities on this curious lamp, which has a textile body and a polycarbonate diffuser 'face'. Behind this face are light-emitting diode (LED) bulbs, while a fluorescent lamp sits within the body for ambient lighting. The 'wrinkled and glossy' texture of Xerol® textile in comparison to the hard LEDs, says Vaskivuori, led the design process.

Floor lamp
Xorel® textile, polycarbonate
www.valvomo.com
Location > Finland
In development

Product, creature or sculpture? Some designs keep the consumer guessing. See also 'Hairy Chair' on p. 67.

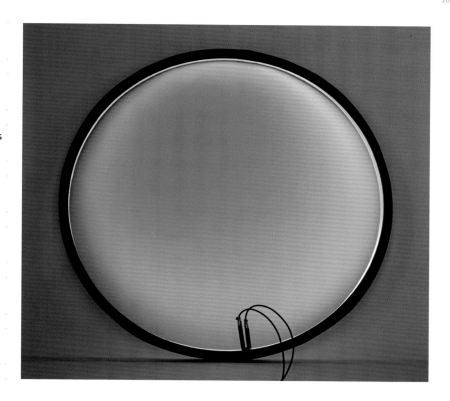

Le Cercle Lumineux
Sealac
French

Inspiration can come from the most unexpected quarters for designers Matthieu Blancher and Gael Nys. With 'Le Cercle Lumineux' they recognized intrinsic beauty in the scale and form of an old bicycle wheel, and so used it as a mould for a simple light produced in collaboration with leather craftsmen. The wheel is moulded leather and its interior is coated with yellow neon paint that casts a halo of colour around any object. Designed to be casually propped against the nearest wall, 'Le Cercle Lumineux' is as much an incidental installation as a functional object.

Floor lamp
Moulded leather, paint
www.sealac.com
Location > France
Available to order

Bespoke
Laura Evans
British

This site-specific design responded to the restrictions placed upon furnishing a listed Georgian building. A table with a built-in light was required by Laura Evans' commissioner, and the design also needed to bridge two distinct and different areas of a room. Evans employed an oversized shade to create maximum light and drama, and brought together the quirkiness and the geometry of the Georgian location in a piece that is both bold and functional.

Floor/lamp/table
Steel, enamel, walnut, silk
Location > UK
In production
By > www.listercarter.com

The Unexpected Visitor
Mathias Hahn
German

Minor social situations are what influence designer Mathias Hahn's work; the objects that are part of the ordinary day-to-day routine are often overlooked, he says. This combined coat stand and hall light creates an atmosphere of hospitality for guests; jackets are hung within the frame, suggesting protection, and the illuminated object is intended to mark the gateway to a home. This is intended as a humble addition to an interior, the only discernable decoration coming from the coloured cable simply pressed into a groove in the wooden leg.

Floor lamp
Ash, aluminium,
powder-coated finish
www.mathiashahn.com
Location > UK
Available to order

Left or Right BIG
Julian Appelius
German

Julian Appelius's intention was
'to produce a low-complexity
product that can be produced
easily and economically'. The
light is available in both left- and
right-hand versions and offers a
multitude of applications. A stack
of books is a necessary addition,
providing both stability and a
surface that can then double as
a side table. The lamp is perfectly
proportioned to be a bedside or
sofa reading light.

Floor lamp
Metal, powder-coated finish
www.julianappelius.de
Location > Germany
Available to order

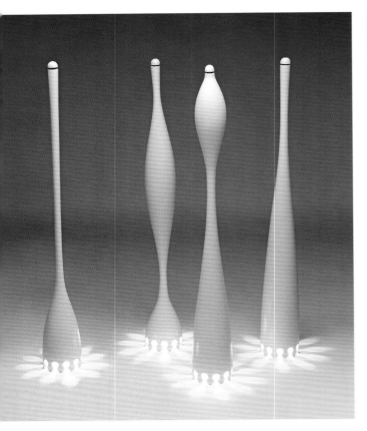

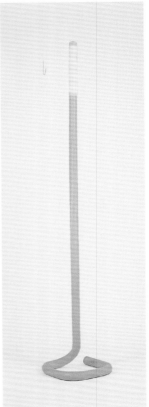

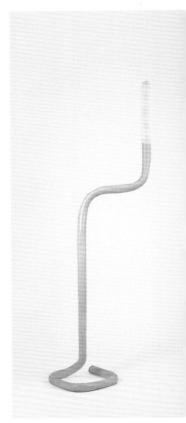

Floor Flower
Design Ship Tora
Japanese

The 'Floor Flower' is intended to
bring a smile to its owner's face.
The light source at the base of the
object casts a shadow pattern that
creates a flower shape across the
floor. This unusual light has a less
common design mission; to alter
the mood of its user through
interaction. The light's creators
are a collective of eight young
designers from Fukuoka City.

Floor lamp
Glass-reinforced plastic
www.designshiptora.com
Location > Japan
In development

Flexible Light
Shigeichiro Takeuchi
Japanese

The qualities of the 'Flexible Light'
are exactly as it name suggests;
silicone sponge pipe and flexible
tubing allow this floor lamp to be
manipulated in a variety of ways.
The light can be directed where
needed, and it can also work as a
coat stand when not illuminated.

Floor lamp
Steel, silicone
www.shigeichiro.com
Location > Japan
Limited edition

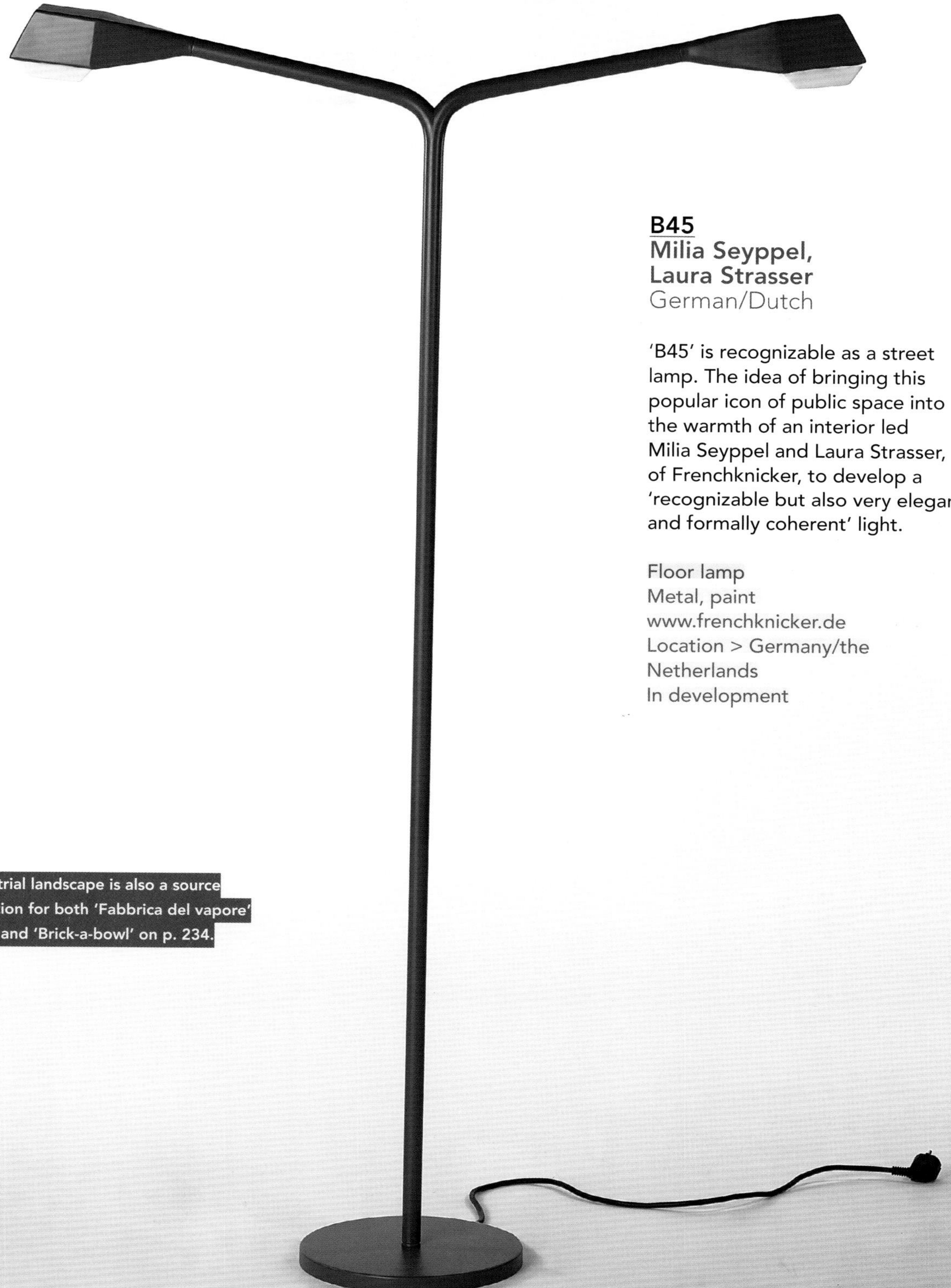

B45
Milia Seyppel,
Laura Strasser
German/Dutch

'B45' is recognizable as a street lamp. The idea of bringing this popular icon of public space into the warmth of an interior led Milia Seyppel and Laura Strasser, of Frenchknicker, to develop a 'recognizable but also very elegant and formally coherent' light.

Floor lamp
Metal, paint
www.frenchknicker.de
Location > Germany/the Netherlands
In development

The industrial landscape is also a source of inspiration for both 'Fabbrica del vapore' on p. 225 and 'Brick-a-bowl' on p. 234.

Tak Light
Khodi Feiz
Iranian/American

Feiz was looking at new formal typologies while creating this design. The 'Tak Light' is intended to be excessively functional, offering two light sources, one direct and another ambient, and using highly efficient light-emitting diode (LED) bulbs. Aesthetics have been overhauled too, with a dark high-gloss finish applied to a spun aluminium shell to give this large light increased presence and create a dramatic silhouette within the interior landscape.

Floor/table lamp
Aluminium, glass
www.feizdesign.com
Location > the Netherlands
In production
By > designer

3 Poäng
Isabelle Olsson – Swedish
Martin Meier – Swiss

This lamp invites the user to grab it, hold it and move it around. The name '3 Poäng' refers to the three points that are the minimum requirement to make an object stable. This lamp makes full use of them, because it can be positioned or propped just about anywhere. The '3 Poäng' design came easily to Olsson and Meier, who also work under the name Murge, in contrast to the rest of their work where there is an emphasis on long periods of research.

Floor lamp
Steel, powder-coated finish
www.macmeier.com/3poeng
Location > Sweden/Switzerland
Limited edition

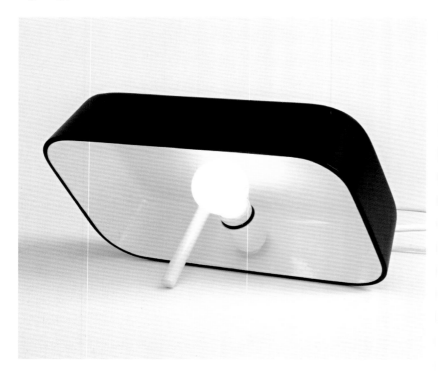

Vuoka
Mika Tolvanen
Finnish

While looking for a new typology for a simple object – a table lamp – Finnish designer Mika Tolvanen found this one. 'Vuoka' is Finnish for casserole, and there are obvious similarities with the rectangular cast aluminium dish that acts as a lampshade. A small arm props up the shade and allows the light out, making this seem like an impromptu act.

Floor/table lamp
Aluminium, powder-coated finish
www.mikatolvanen.com
Location > Finland
In development

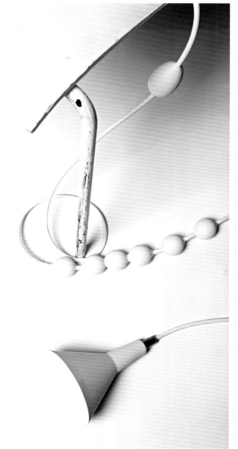

Boa-constrictor
Katarina Häll,
Karin Robling
Swedish

Katarina Häll and Karin Robling chose an unexpected inspiration for the visual identity of a lighting design; the effect of a snake whose lunch has been eaten, but not yet digested. The cable of the 'Boa-constrictor' light is reminiscent of the body of the snake, with small mounds interrupting its length. By indulging an engaging and playful visual simile, Häll and Robling break with the conventions of more familiar lighting design processes.

Floor/lamp
Woodcuts, aluminium,
soft-touch polyurethane
www.katarinahall.se
Location > Sweden
In development

See other work by Katarina Häll in 'Save' on p. 102.

Plug
Sebastian Herkner
German

Within the middle of this lampshade
sits an electrical socket. This
unusual addition enables electrical
equipment to be attached to the
light, therefore fully integrating it
into its surroundings and creating
usefulness for the light beyond its
usual function. The 'Plug' light can
be umbilically attached to a toaster,
laptop or other appliances, lending
both energy and light.

Floor/lamp
Steel, leather
www.sebastianherkner.com
Location > Germany
In development

Pearl
Hanna Brogård
Swedish

The 'Pearl' light is a nostalgic piece of work inspired by the jewelry collection belonging to the grandmother of the designer, Hanna Brogård of Jantze Brogård Asshoff design group. It channels heritage and tradition through its specific connection to a particular piece of jewelry, but also through an unashamedly decorative ambition. Brogård says 'I wanted to create a chandelier that went its own way but gives the room a soft and warm light.'

Wall lamp
Porcelain, opal glass
www.jba-design.se
Location > Sweden
In production
By > designer

1/4
Tetsuya Tsujimura
Japanese

Tetsuya Tsujimura calls his light
a 'compact chandelier'. When the
light is switched off, the object
appears to be a small, mirrored
box. When switched on, the
chandelier appears inexplicably
huge – too big to be contained
within its petite enclosure.
The magical effect is simply
produced: a single chandelier
arm is encased in a mirrored box
that offers infinite reflections.

Wall lamp
Aluminium, acrylic half mirror
www.t-products.jp
Location > Japan
In development

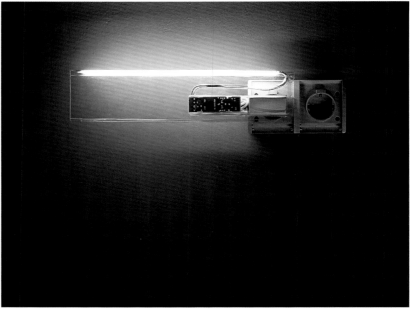

Daylight Comes Sideways
Daniel Rybakken
Norwegian

Rybakken's intention here is to create 'a feeling of expanded perceived space, through an illusion of natural daylight'. The wall-mounted light appears to be a semi-transparent window, and suggests an environment beyond the interior space in which it hangs. Rybakken artificially recreates the effect of daylight by using 1,100 light-emitting diodes (LEDs) behind a translucent surface and adding a motion that suggests shadows of objects outside of the room.

Wall lamp
Semi-transparent acrylic
www.danielrybakken.com
Location > Sweden
In development

See more of Daniel Rybakken's work with light in 'Subconscious' on p. 132.

Cheap Cheap
Hansandfranz
German

Konstantin Landuris and Horst Wittman have built up a collection of lighting designs, each illustrating a different approach to the possibilities of domestic lighting. 'Cheap Cheap' is a reductionist product that strips the function of lighting down to its bare essentials. It is a plastic holder for a single cold cathode fluorescent strip, which can be plugged directly into a socket and eschews the need for wires, cables or unnecessary decoration.

Wall lamp
Copolyester sheet
www.hansandfranz.de
Location > Germany
In development

For more reductionist design, see also the 'Silent Chair' on p. 69.

The Flat Light
Finn Magee
Irish

Irish designer Finn Magee placed a task light on his desk and was struck by the atmosphere of productivity and efficiency it lent the room. He wondered if an image of the lamp would be enough to create this same atmosphere. This then led to experiments to combine image and light using light-emitting diodes (LEDs). Magee is interested in investigating this area between object and imagery further.

Wall lamp
Laminated paper
www.finnmagee.com
Location > UK
In development

Accessories

Using traditional crafts to create new forms.
See also Max Lamb's work with carved stone
on p. 60.

Forest Vase
Liliana Ovalle
Mexican

When placed in quantity, these
vases create a surreal landscape
where the flowers seem out of
proportion to the trees that
surround them. A rapid prototyping
technique is employed to create
these delicate products.

Vase
Polyamide
www.lilianaovalle.com
Location > Mexico
Available to order

Flower Vases
StokkeAustad
Norwegian

By employing the time-honoured
craft skills of a local coppersmith
to realize this pair of elegant
vases, StokkeAustad have added
value to their contemporary
design. The forms result from an
exploration of how two individual
shapes can function together, and
have been designed to suit both
tall and short-stemmed flowers.

Vases
Copper
www.stokkeaustad.com
Location > Norway
In development

Fabbrica del vapore
**Guillaume Delvigne,
Ionna Vautrin**
French

This series of porcelain and
hand-blown glass vases combines
the achievable forms of these
two traditional disciplines in
contemporary, and surprisingly
graphic, forms. Delvigne
describes the vases as being
like micro-architecture. They are
inspired by industrial landscapes
and the image of coloured smoke
escaping from factory chimneys.

Vases
Porcelain, glass
www.guillaumedelvigne.com
www.ionnavautrin.com
Location > France
In production
By > www.industreal.com

Leather Vases
Simon Hasan
British

'Cuir bouilli' is leather hardened
by an ancient technique of soaking
and boiling. The heating alters the
tannin and collagen structures in
the skin, achieving an irreversible
hardness that gives the material a
strength more commonly found in
plastics or timber. Simon Hasan has
taken this obscure historical craft
and sought to make it relevant
to contemporary design and
manufacture. Each of this series
of vases is unique, combining
different moulds, hand-stitching
and brogueing with industrial
patent finishes. The result is a series
of brutal, industrial objects – far
away from the usual applications
of leather in contemporary design.

Vases
Leather, polyurethane resin,
acrylic, linen thread
www.simonhasan.com
Location > UK
In production
By > designer

Jungle Vase
Eelko Moorer
Dutch

The 'Jungle Vase' was created as
part of a larger installation, built
by Eelko Moorer in response to
his opinion that the domestic
landscape has become passive.
He proposed a new interior 'jungle',
which explored the values of
discomfort, danger and play.
The urethane rubber vase was
designed as part of that proposed
interactive space, but can be used
individually if the complete jungle
experience is to much for you.
It can be either attached to the
ceiling or other objects with the
attached silicone cords, or used on
the floor as a decorative element.

Vase
Urethane rubber, silicone
www.eelkomoorer.com
Location > UK
Available to order

The Honeycomb Vase
'Made by Bees'
Tomás Gabzdil Libertiny
Slovakian

Tomás Gabzdil Libertiny of Studio Libertiny bypassed all usual methods of construction and harnessed an existing, but untapped, method for this product. By inserting a mould into a bees hive, he took advantage of these industrious insects and their natural inclination to build. 'The Honeycomb Vase' is a comment on contemporary manufacturing processes; it is offered as a response and an alternative to the deluge of rapid-prototyping products currently on the market.

Decorative vase
Natural beeswax
www.studiolibertiny.com
Location > the Netherlands
Limited edition

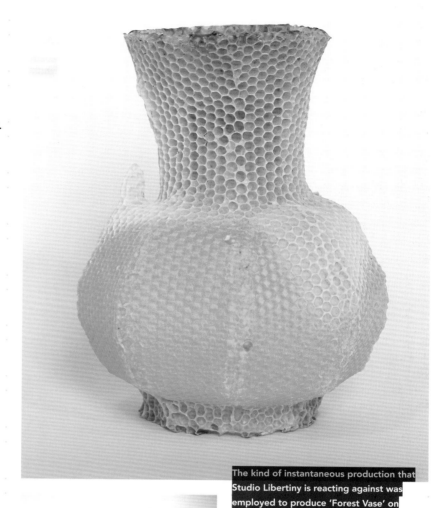

The kind of instantaneous production that Studio Libertiny is reacting against was employed to produce 'Forest Vase' on p. 224 and 'Barbaric Cut' on p. 266.

Grid Vases
Maria Jeglinska
Polish

The functions of a vase are to hold
flowers and contain water, functions
that are disassociated from each
other in these vases by Polish
designer Maria Jeglinska; the
grid structure that holds the flowers
is open and porous. The 'Grid Vase'
is part of a series of grid-based
works that began as complex-
versus-simple structural drawings,
initially without any specific function
in mind, which were later developed.

Vase
Aluminium, car paint
www.mariajeglinska.com
Location > France
Available to order

For more inventive materials and processes by Studio Libertiny see 'The Honeycomb Vase' on p. 227.

Paper Vases
Studio Libertiny
Slovakian

Tomás Gabzdil Libertiny placed a book on a table saw and cut through it. He was struck by the effect and the way in which every page edge showed a black-and-white pattern that indicated text printed upon it. His immediate response was to see what might happen if every page contained the same image. After using a computer program to predict the pattern caused by the print, he painstakingly glued together 700 sheets of paper. These were placed in a bench press before being carved by a professional woodturner.

Decorative vase
Paper
www.studiolibertiny.com
Location > the Netherlands
Limited edition

Vitra Virus
Pieke Bergmans
Dutch

Bergmans thinks that the next step in mass-production is to create 'controlled imperfect production' in order to create 'interesting, personal objects'. Designed to disrupt regularity, these crystal forms are blown directly onto pieces of furniture that imprint their own shape into the vase. Bergmans invites the user to be involved in her production process by bringing their own furniture to be 'infected' with the virus, and notes that it is 'the confrontation between the crystal and furniture that is key'.

Vase
Glass
www.piekebergmans.com
Location > the Netherlands
Limited edition

Pieke Bergmans pursues the idea of imperfection as valuable design detail. See 'Unlimited Edition' on p. 230.

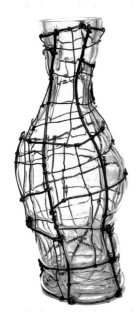

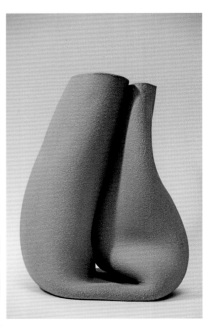

Image Collection
Vanessa Mitrani
French

Glass is hand-blown into cages
built from copper wire to create
the raw forms of this collection.
The outlines of the jugs, glasses
and bowls are deliberately
awkward, like hand-drawn sketches
of everyday objects. The glass
bulges from inside the wire frame
as a reminder of this material's
fluid and unpredictable properties.

Vases, decanters
Glass, copper
www.vanessamitrani.com
Location > France
In production
By > designer

Unlimited Edition
**Madieke Fleuren,
Pieke Bergmans**
Dutch

Madieke Fleuren and Pieke
Bergmans worked together at
the European Ceramic Work Centre
in Holland. Their ambition was
to develop a way of producing
individual objects within a formal
industrial process. 'Unlimited
Edition' is a series of vases made
using an extrusion machine.
The machine produces endless
tubes of clay that are forced into
awkward shapes and forms. These
are simply cut and placed onto a
drying table. 'We have managed
to develop a new product that is
always unique but can be mass-
produced: an "Unlimited Edition"'.

Vases
Ceramic, pigment
www.piekebergmans.com
www.madieke.com
Location > the Netherlands
In production
By > designer

Manipulating industrial manufacture to
create unique, one-off products is a reaction
to mass-produced design. See the 'Bastard'
chair on p. 55.

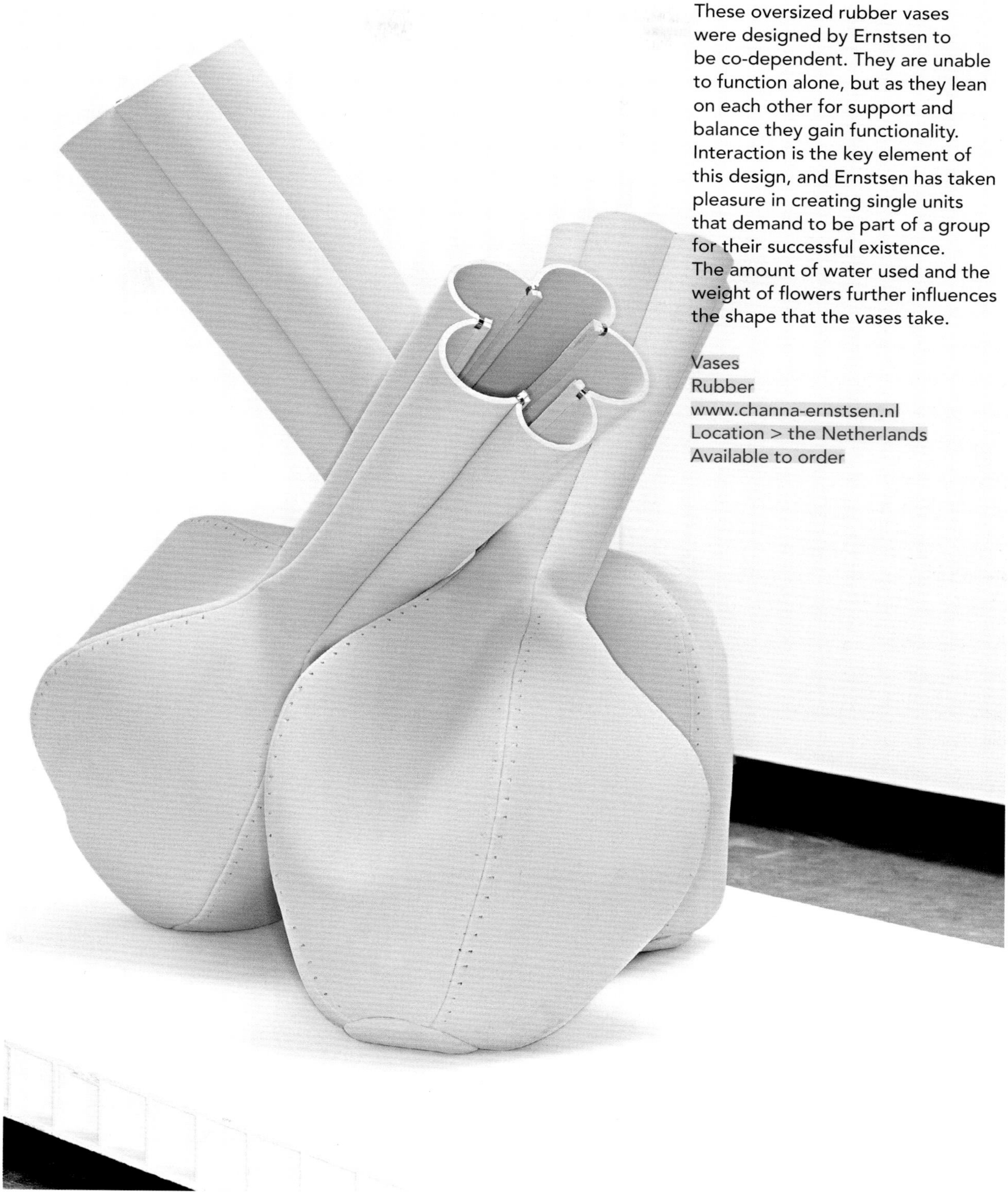

InterVases
Channa Ernstsen
Chinese

These oversized rubber vases were designed by Ernstsen to be co-dependent. They are unable to function alone, but as they lean on each other for support and balance they gain functionality. Interaction is the key element of this design, and Ernstsen has taken pleasure in creating single units that demand to be part of a group for their successful existence. The amount of water used and the weight of flowers further influences the shape that the vases take.

Vases
Rubber
www.channa-ernstsen.nl
Location > the Netherlands
Available to order

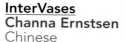

High Amphora/Jug/Pot
Nicolas Bovesse
Belgian

These glazed ceramic vases at first
appear to be archetypal, familiar
vessels elevated to a position of
prominence by being placed on top
of a pedestal. But Nicolas Bovesse
has added a more intriguing facet
to this design: when each piece is
turned on its head the hollow stand
turns into a cone-shaped vase for
long-stemmed flowers. Bovesse's
work is exploratory and inquisitive
and employs an eclectic mix of
manufacturing processes, forms
and materials. These pieces are
produced with the aid of skilled
artisan ceramicists in the town
of Vallauris, France.

Vases
Glazed earthenware
www.nicolasbovesse.com
Location > Belgium
In production
By > designer

Public Garden
**Niels van Eijk,
Miriam van der Lubbe**
Dutch

What looks like a quaint, floral motif
in fact incorporates unexpected
images of modern technology.
Headphones, ketchup bottles,
plugs and computer mice are
among the details that have been
arranged to mimic traditional Dutch
ceramic decoration. Technology
plays a more vital role in modern
life than nature does, suggest the
designers, who are also using their
optical illusion to make us aware
of our visual laziness.

Decorative bowl, jug
Ceramic, transfers
www.ons-adres.nl
Location > the Netherlands
Limited edition

Optical illusions and design riddles are also
the starting point for 'A4 Shade' on p. 170.

This digital reinterpretation of traditional craft forms was aided by computer software. See also 'Digital Dishes' on p. 237.

Materialized Vase
Erich Ginder
American

The 'Materialized' collection was designed by creating high-resolution laser scans of antique objects and then filtering them through digital software. This process broke the forms down into a simple geometry, which was then recreated in porcelain or glass. 'The process is somewhat random and makes unexpected changes to the original form,' says Ginder, adding 'My intent was to create objects that are shaped by a process free of the designer's hand.'

Vase
Porcelain
www.erichginder.com
Location > USA
Available to order

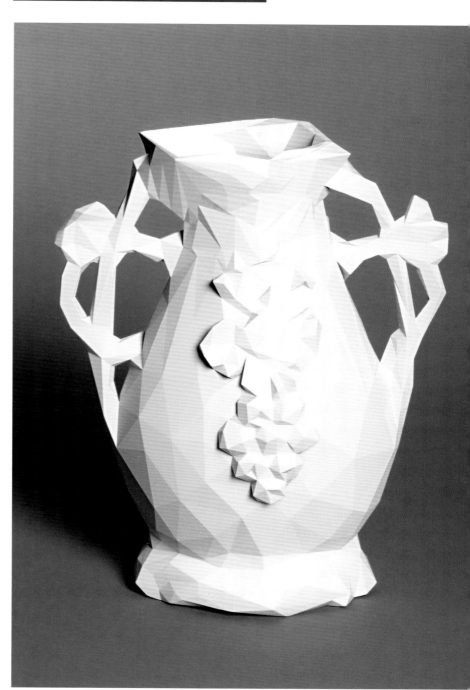

Brick-a-bowl
Lidewij Spitshuis
Dutch

These bowls are made up of small
terracotta bricks, arranged to
resemble the patterns seen in
the pavements of the Netherlands.
The influence of the Dutch streets
is direct and bold. Lidewij Spitshuis
completes the design by providing
a contrasting material for the
exterior of the bowl; smooth
and shiny lacquer.

Bowl
Terracotta, lacquer
www.lidewij.net
Location > the Netherlands
Limited edition

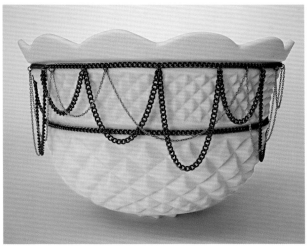

Hadji Bowl
Erdem Akan
Turkish

The traditional lace prayer cap has
been reappointed as a domestic
object by Erdem Akan. This
decorative bowl takes the familiar
form and pattern of the cap and
applies a manufacturing process
that enables Akan to recreate the
fragility of lace; rapid prototyping.

Bowl
Food-safe polyamide
www.erdemakan.com
Location > Turkey
In production
By > www.maybedesign.at

Chainwork Porcelain Bowl
Sarah Cihat, Michael Miller
American

Sarah Cihat works predominantly
in ceramics, while close friend and
collaborator Michael Miller works
mainly with metals. For this design,
Cihat concentrated on the form
of a cut-glass bowl. She cast the
bowl in porcelain to make the form
and shadows the principle feature,
rather than light travelling through
the glass. Miller then applied
antique brass chain to decorate
the bowl and enhance its texture.

Bowl
Porcelain, brass, copper
www.sarahcihat.com
Location > USA
In production
By > designer

Ceramic Paper
Akihiro Kumagaya
Japanese

The use of an exciting new process
dictates the fragile form of these
dishes. Ceramic powder and wood
pulp fibres are combined in a thin
'ceramic paper'. This behaves like
a regular sheet of paper and can
be folded and bent into shape,
but when it is exposed to a high
temperature, the wood pulp fibres
burn away leaving just the ceramic
behind. The result is a delicate
series of paper-thin vessels.

Bowls
Ceramic, wood pulp
http://ak.alekole.jp
Location > Japan
Available to order

See more manufacturing innovation with ceramic in 'Pétrifié en porcelaine' on p. 62.

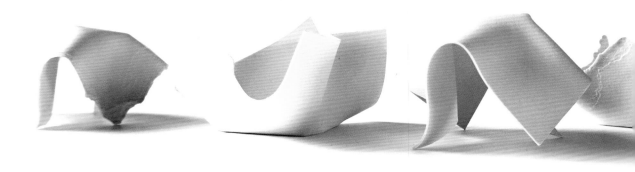

Digital Dishes
Philipp Scholz
German

These porcelain pieces were made as part of a collaborative project between the Staatliche Hochschule für Gestaltung (HFG) in Karlsruhe and Rosenthal. Philipp Scholz used a computer program to transform 2D pictures into 3D texture. 'Animal motifs have always been part of the standard repertoire of classic porcelain painting,' he says, and images of a toad, snail and stag beetle from Rosenthal's Medallion Series are reintroduced here as abstract impressions.

Tableware
Porcelain
Location > Germany
In development

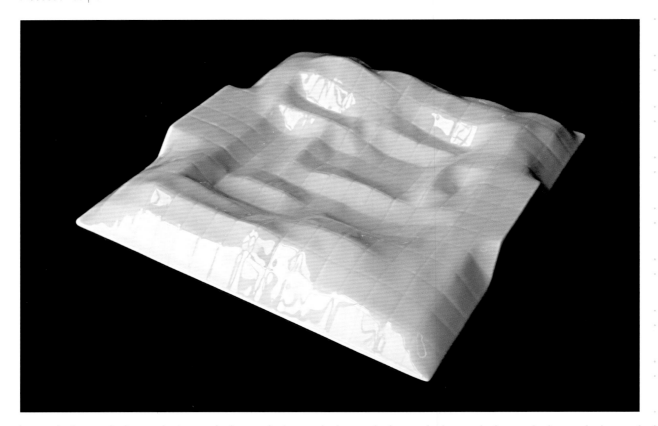

Topography
Thomas Antonietti
French

This ceramic bowl reproduces
a 3D topological grid on which
natural, organic curves are created.
The 'Topography' dish offers
different landscapes depending
on the point from which it is
viewed. This piece is intended
to sit among other products such
as a vase and lamp – together
Antonietti intends them to create
a new tabletop landscape.

Display dish
Glazed porcelain
www.thomasantonietti.com
Location > Japan
In production
By > www.raynaud.fr

Paper pulp is easily produced, malleable and with many applications. See, among many examples, 'Pulp Everyday' on p. 61.

Pulp
Jo Meesters
Dutch

'Pulp' is a collection of vessels made from paper pulp and using discarded vessels as moulds. Combining other materials with the paper pulp, such as epoxy and polyurethane, creates a new material with its own characteristics. This research into alternative materials led to the production of the watertight tabletop vessels shown here.

Tableware
Paper waste, glue, epoxy
www.jomeesters.nl
Location > the Netherlands
Available to order

Hat Plate
Emiko Oki
Japanese

The brim of these hats acts as a dinner plate and the crown becomes a cover that retains heat and keeps food warm. Emiko Oki created the plates through a desire to promote the qualities of ancient Japanese lacquerware, or urushi. Actual hats were taken as the core material for the designs, and lacquer was applied to the surface in many layers. The brim is removed and fixed to a hand-crafted wooden base that forms the plate.

Tableware
Felt, straw, lacquer
www.emikooki.com
Location > UK
In production
By > www.wajimaxkakitsubata.com

Fukidashi Box
Stefan Lie
Swiss/Australian

The materials and processes most typically used to produce traditional Japanese shoji screens were here applied to a new form. The 'Fukidashi Box', a small storage container, has been designed by Stefan Lie for a commission from Atelier Ishikawa in Japan. Lie wanted to produce a container that was light and strong, and turned to the time-honoured use of rice paper and slender lengths of wood to create this fluid shape.

Container
Rice paper, wood
www.stefan-lie.com
Location > Australia
In production
By > www.a-ishikawa.co.jp

Flock & Brass
Aude Genton
Swiss

The 'Flock & Brass' boxes were designed while Aude Genton was studying at Ecole cantonale d'art de Lausanne (ECAL) as a project with traditional silverware company Christofle. The graphic simplicity of the design contrasts with the luxury of the materials, and is intended to reveal the beauty of the polished brass and the flocked velvet. It also allows for free interpretation of the function of the boxes.

Containers
Brass, flock velvet
www.audegenton.com
Location > Switzerland
In development

Another product from the Atelier Ishikawa commission is 'Drawer' on p. 96.

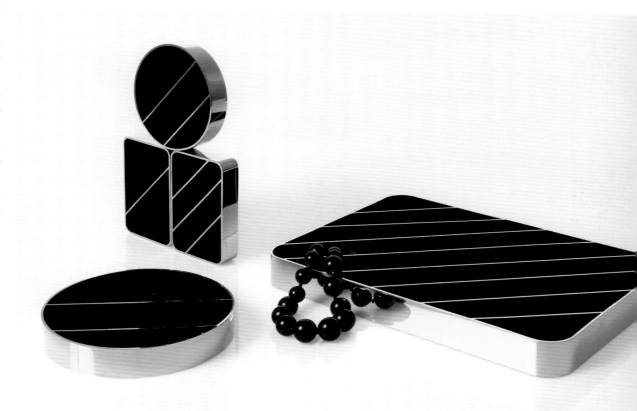

CMYK
Alexis Georgacopoulos
French/Greek

The four powder-coated steel trays
were inspired by the four basic
colours of the printing process
and the four basic geometric
shapes. Combining shape and
colours resulted in the Cyan Square,
Magenta Circle, Yellow Triangle
and Black Rectangle. An inclination
on the trays' surfaces adds a new
formal dimension and reveals the
applied colour.

Trays
Steel, powder-coated finish
www.georgacopoulos.com
Location > Switzerland
Available to order

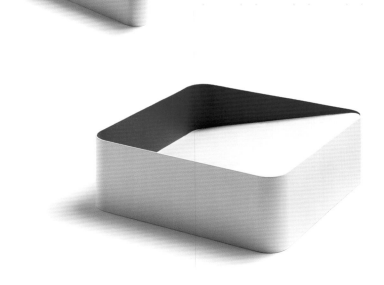

For another ceramic extrusion project see 'Unlimited Edition' on p. 230.

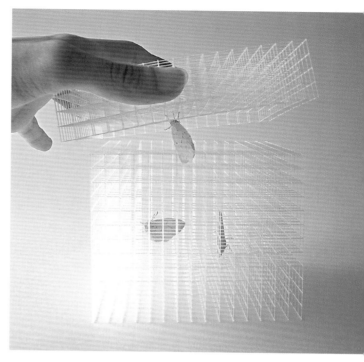

Rolling
Adrien Rovero
Swiss

Research into ceramic extrusion led to the development of this series of containers. Adrien Rovero rented a heavy-duty manufacturing machine and sought to use it as a means of producing objects in volume. Clay was passed through a nozzle and coiled around polygonal reels. Large and small, broad and narrow containers were produced, which Rovero then closed at the top and bottom with cork lids. Rovero has combined two materials seldom seen together in his design, and developed a new industrial method of ceramic manufacture.

Containers
Ceramics, cork
www.adrienrovero.com
Location > Switzerland
Limited edition

Insect Cage
Ryuji Nakamura
Japanese

The 'Insect Cage' was made as a result of a commission from Deroll to design a box. Ryuji Nakamura exploited the capabilities of stereo lithography machines to create this joint-free frame of repeated resin strands only 0.3 mm (0.012 in.) thick. The effect, which Ryuji Nakamura calls a 'fuzzy division', exaggerates perspective, while the delicate construction matches the intricacy of the creatures it contains. The box is a beautiful, curious interpretation of a traditional birdcage.

Container
Resin
www.ryujinakamura.com
Location > Japan
In production
By > www.deroll.com

Coat hanger
Eric Morel
French

The function of this hanger is a
matter of reflection for its owner.
Designer Eric Morel says that this
piece is about 'bringing a religious
image into the sphere of home
accessories', and that 'the Jesus
coat hanger is a reflective take
on the consumerism in our society'.
He adds that his design can be
seen as an icon or an iconoclastic
feature, depending on the viewer's
inclinations.

Decorative hanger
Plastic
www.ericmorel.com
Location > Germany
In production
By > designer

Monsieur DressUp
Anna Thomas
Canadian

This whimsical, wall-mounted storage system holds jackets, scarves, umbrellas and post. The individual units take the form of pieces of tailoring: a collar, cuff and pocket. Anna Thomas of Canadian design collective Loyal Loot says 'we strive to create designs with a natural quality by staying true to materials. The inherent value of these designs is meant to last a lifetime, ensuring they retain a non-disposable presence.'

Decorative hanger
Maple
www.loyalloot.com
Location > Canada
In production
By > designer

Flor
Gabriela Chicherio
Swiss

A support to aid the growth of houseplants is included as part of Chicherio's design. The support has been represented as a stylized plant, and so keeps this porcelain pot an interesting domestic object even without a plant inside.

Plant pot
Porcelain
www.chicherio.com
Location > Switzerland
Available to order

Window Story
Oh Kyung Eun
Korean

Two flowerpots communicate from either side of a window. On the inside is a houseplant or exotic flowers, and on the outside a hardy or wild plant. Each needs different temperatures and environments to survive, but Kyung Eun has imagined a dialogue between the two. The pots appear as two halves and support each other through the glass with strong magnets built into their structure.

Plant pots
Plastic, magnets
Location > Korea
Available to order

For more invented communication between the real and the fake, see Mareike Gast's 'Lockvogel' on p. 313.

Fullcolourball
Heath Nash
South African

The 'Fullcolourball' recycles
discarded plastic bottles using
local South African craft techniques.
The work is sustainable in many
ways, not least because it creates
a source of income for local
craftsmen. Nash takes the plastic
bottles from the normal plastics
recycling stream, returning excess
plastic to the same system, and
says of his intervention 'in essence
I'm at the mercy of the plastics
producers of South Africa – as the
makers of laundry detergents and
bleaches etc. change their palette,
so my palette has to change. It is
like an anthropological slice of
contemporary taste.'

Decorative ball
High-density polyethylene,
polypropylene, galvanized
steel wire, zip ties
www.heathnash.com
Location > South Africa
In production
By > designer

Nuoska
Kaisa Karvonen, Tiia Lepistö
Finnish

The 'Nuoska' chandelier is made
from 1,248 felted balls, strung
together on iron wires. Each is
made from recycled wool and
cotton, covered in layers of pure
new wool and felted in a washing
machine. 'Nuoska' is a Finnish name
for a certain kind of snow that
is perfect for construction, say
designers Kaisa and Tiia, and the
first snowballs of the winter, which
often contain both snow and dirt,
inspired the colour scheme of the
Nuoska chandelier.

Decorative hanging
Iron, wool, recycled textiles
Location > Finland
Available to order

Chorus
Daniel Jo
Korean

Daniel Jo observed that icons
are an important method of quick
and efficient communication in the
modern age. He took the idea of
a simplified and immediate visual
language and incorporated it into
his ceramic work. His work is,
by his own admission, popularist
and international, but also 'delivers
spiritual values symbolically'.
Jo is currently investigating the
possibilities of including additional
functional elements in his ceramics,
here incorporating a speaker.

Decorative range
Clay, glaze
www.danieljo.com
Location > Korea
Available to order

Speed Metal
Paul Loebach
American

The 'Speed Metal' candlestick
is a disturbed and surreal
version of a traditional form.
The 'beautifully distorted' object
is made in just a few minutes
using a rapid metal printing
process. Loebach says 'The form
of my designs come from my
drive to push the limits of what
a given material can do, and
to challenge what we are
conditioned to recognize
as "normal".'

Candle holder
Bronze alloy
www.paulloebach.com
Location > USA
Available to order

For another disturbed, surreal version
of a familiar object see 'Embedded
Meanings Side Table' on p. 149.

Big Dipper chandelier
Sarah van Gameren
Dutch

The 'Big Dipper' machine makes
use of an existing method of candle
manufacture in which a single wick
is repeatedly dipped into drums of
wax: here, however, multiple joined
wicks are dipped to form whole
chandeliers with eight arms.
Twenty-four chandeliers are
made every twelve hours. The
'Big Dipper' is a celebration of
manufacturing, with the machine
being the facilitator of innovation.
Van Gameren also points out that
the machine looks much like a giant
chandelier itself.

Candle chandelier
Aluminium, wax, wick
www.sarahvangameren.com
Location > UK
In development

Tea by candlelight
Helena Bancroft
British

Helena Bancroft is concerned with
giving new purpose to redundant
objects without disguising their
original function. Here, she gives
an old china teacup new life by
finding a second function for it.
Through the addition of a
candlestick, Bancroft invents
a modern interpretation of the
old-fashioned chambersticks that
would be carried to bedrooms
in the evening.

Candle holder
Reclaimed china, ceramic
Location > UK
In development

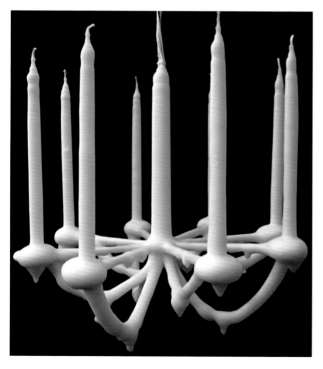

Lux it
Alex Estadieu
French

'Lux_it' is a comment on the history and tradition of dining habits, made through a reflection on the common practice of eating directly from packaging. Here, traditional glass, ceramic and metal dishes are fused with modern food containers, bringing together two different cultural experiences.

Tableware
Ceramic, glass, metal
Location > Finland
Available to order

ContemPlates
Freshwest Design
British

Marcus Beck and Simon Macro of Freshwest Design collected over 200 images of anonymous figures and produced various silhouetted scenes for their 'ContemPlates'. Along with the hand-printed originals, Freshwest also produce undecorated 'ContemPlates' together with a stencil under the collection name 'Karl Marx', allowing a wider selection of the public to own the designs by applying the image themselves.

Tableware
Bone china
www.freshwest.co.uk
Location > UK
In production
By > designer

The consumer is offered an opportunity to manufacture their own product. See also 'Cut 'n' Paste' on p. 73 and 'Brace Angle Furniture' on p.131.

Nabeshima Variations
Airconditioned
Multinational

The Variations Series are unique design variations using classic processes; here, Japanese Arita ceramics. Airconditioned (whose designers remain anonymous in order to focus attention on their designs) broke down the hand-painting process into five stages applying each one to an individual plate. The plates use Izumiyama clay, traditional dark navy paint and Nabeshima-style illustration.

Tableware
China
In production
By > www.bytrico.com
Limited edition

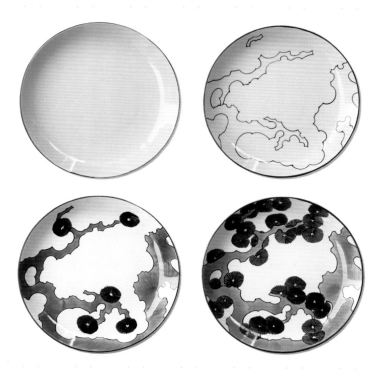

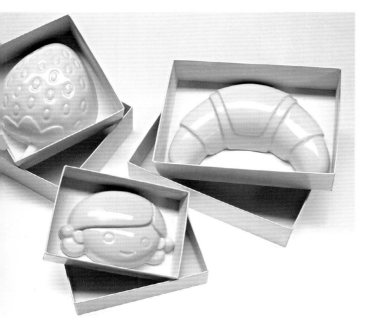

Happy Porcelain
Tina Roeder
German

Each of these small ceramic vessels is inspired by observations of friends' habits or a seemingly inconsequential story. German designer Tina Roeder has taken these personal stories as her starting point for a collection of charming dishes. Their childlike quality is no accident; Roeder admits that her admiration for a child's uninhibited imagination is a key influence in her work.

Tableware
Porcelain
www.tinaroeder.com
Location > Germany
Available to order

Young designers have the confidence to produce work that represents their own experiences or stories – much as artists do. See also 'Save' on p. 102.

Snap and Dine
Demelza Hill
British

The seemingly incompatible notions of 'eating on the go' and fine dining etiquette have been married in the 'Snap and Dine' disposable cutlery and crockery set. Although they are designed to be used just once (it is intended that they will be made from biodegradable resin), the set makes use of the pattern of a formal and traditional service. Hill hopes the user will be encouraged to eat outdoors without having to compromise their table manners.

Disposable tableware
Polystyrene
www.demelzahill.com
Location > UK
In development

See Demelza Hill's 'Pulp Everyday' on p. 61.

Uit de klei getrokken
Lonny van Rijswijck
Dutch

Rather than simply purchasing clay, Lonny van Rijswijck dug natural clay out of the earth in different areas of the Netherlands and used each specimen to produce a series of cups and saucers. The firing process reveals the comparative natural qualities of each type of clay and produces an amazing spectrum of colour and textures.

Tableware
Clay
www.ateliernl.com
Location > the Netherlands
Limited edition

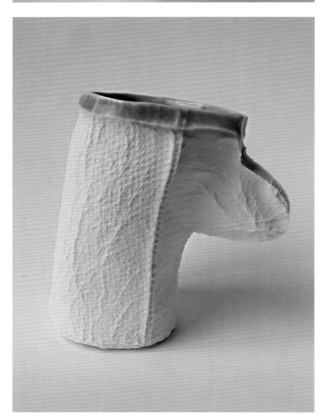

Flexible Ceramics
Bas Kools
Dutch

Although the product Kools wanted to make – a mug – is a simple form, the process of production was complex and time consuming, so Kools embarked on a project to dissect the usual methods of manufacture and create a quick and simple alternative. Experimenting with objects to hand, he found that an everyday kitchen cloth could be successfully used as a basic mould. Working with this flexible and immediate new method brought previously unconsidered characteristics to the finished ceramics, such as decoration in the form of imprinted texture from the sponge and stitching.

Mugs
Porcelain
www.baskools.com
Location > UK
Available to order

Invention of quick and efficient methods of manufacture is increasingly important to the independent maker. A DIY aesthetic with the potential to produce 'batches' of products has also been invented by Henny van Nistelrooy in 'Stitched Chair' on p. 77.

Stain
Bethan Laura Wood
British

This is a tea cup designed to improve through use, turning on its head the assumption that use damages or reduces the worth of an object. The interior of the cup has been treated so that some areas are more susceptible to staining by the tannin in tea than others. The more the cup is used, the more the pattern is revealed; its intensity will depend on the user's tea-drinking habits, therefore making a previously impersonal object an intimate one.

Tea cup
Bone china
www.woodlondon.co.uk
Location > UK
In production
By > designer

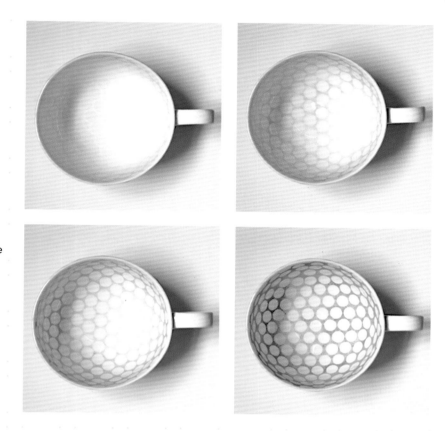

This Is (Not)
Jeremy Brown
British

The clue is in the name for this series, a phrase borrowed from Rene Magritte's iconic 'Ceci n'est pas une pipe'. Jeremy Brown's collection of mugs is inspired by the Surrealist works of Magritte and Duchamp. He has reconfigured the archetypal shape of a standard drinking mug and wineglass, playing around with individual elements until he reached objects with questionable functions. Brown states that he is trying 'to explore what makes an object an object'.

Mugs, glasses
Ceramic, glass
www.jeremybrowndesign.com
Location > Switzerland
Available to order

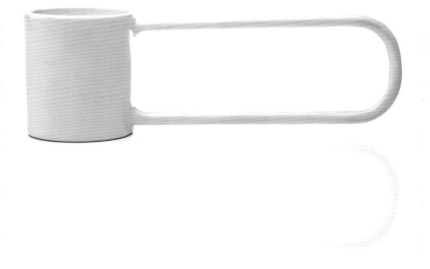

Tea Set Noir
Christine Misiak
British

Christine Misiak says her series
of reclaimed tea sets are much
more than just a worthy recycling
project. She takes forgotten or
unwanted tea sets and resurfaces
and restyles them to suit the
contemporary market, with the
intention of speaking out against
throwaway culture. Past and
present are celebrated in the mix
of modern customization and
traditional forms.

Tea set
Various metals
www.christinemisiak.co.uk
Location > UK
Available to order

Garav Teapot
Ronen Kro
Israeli

A woollen sock was stretched over
a teapot, and from this a ceramic
mould was taken. Applying the
texture of clothing to ceramics
visually emphasizes their function:
because the function of a teapot
is to keep drinks hot, Kro has given
the ceramic a new skin in the form
of clothing that would ordinarily
keep humans warm, and so
humanized its purpose.

Teapot
Ceramic
Location > Israel
Available to order

Avestruz
Daniel Marcelo Salvatore
Argentinian

Avestruz means 'ostrich' and it is easy to see why this is a fitting name for Daniel Marcelo Salvatore's tea set. It appears that a part of the body of the teapot and cups is submerged into the surface where they sit, reminding us of the ostrich's apocryphal reputation of sticking their head into the earth. The set was created for a 'Ceramic for Breakfast' competition organized by 'Macef' magazine.

Tea set
Porcelain
www.danielsalvatore.blogspot.com
Location > Argentina
Available to order

Apartment
Seongyong Lee
Korean

Korean designer Seongyong Lee's
hometown of Seoul is a place
where space is at a premium.
The 'Apartment' is a collection
of stackable trays that represents
the verticality of the Seoul
cityscape. Just as the city's
population grows and the
architecture grows to
accommodate it, the height
of 'Apartment' can be increased
through the addition of more levels
as more storage is demanded.

Trays
Glass-reinforced acrylonitrile
butadeine styrene
www.seongyonglee.com
Location > Korea
Available to order

Bowl
Alexa Lixfield
German

Concrete is a familiar material
in architecture and public spaces,
but its use in product design often
results in cumbersome objects.
Lixfeld acknowledges that her
concrete tableware boasts novel
aesthetics, but the streamlining
of the production process,
especially in comparison with
ceramics, appeals to her. These
experiments with methods and
ingredients show that her material
has the potential to be a legitimate
alternative.

Tableware
Creacrete™ concrete
www.alexalixfeld.com
Location > Germany
Available to order

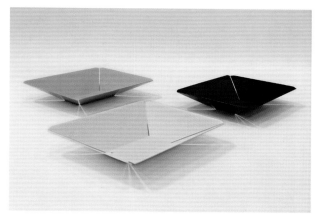

Fusion
Mark Braun
German/Swedish

'Fusion' tableware combines two glazes: smooth and shiny on the interior of the dishes and cups and matt on the exterior. Braun experimented with numerous materials and glazes before settling on this combination – the intention was to create a tactile product that engaged the senses and was soft to touch and yet was supremely functional too.

Tableware
Porcelain
www.markbraun.org
Location > Germany
In production
By > www.asa-selection.com

Lotus
Nick Smith
English

This simple fruit bowl was inspired by the technique of folding metal. Pared back to an absolute minimum, the low steel dishes have no decoration other than a powder-coated finish. Like most of Nick Smith's work, the 'Lotus' bowl is elementary, honest and, above all else, functional.

Bowl
Steel, powder-coated finish
www.nicksmithfurniture.co.uk
Location > UK
Available to order

Louise
Maarten Baptist
Dutch

Maarten Baptist produced the
'Louise' range of glassware as
a basic range of drinking glasses
that concedes just one irregular
feature; the addition of the kind
of feet more usually found on
furniture. These glasses were
designed when Baptist was part
of WAT Design with Jan Habraken,
before founding Joine Office for
Design.

Glasses
Dishwasher-safe glass
www.maarten-baptist.com
Location > the Netherlands
In production
By > www.umbra.com

Everyday Sunday
Niina Aalto
Finnish

The generic and ubiquitous
disposable plastic cup is offered
a new status via a decorative cast
resin cup holder. 'Everyday Sunday'
lends the plastic cup a new, more
glamorous identity, elevating it
from the mundane to the unique,
and 'customizes a plastic cup for
different situations by creating an
illusion of authenticity' says Aalto.
The potential for personalization
and the pleasure of expressing
individuality are exploited by Aalto,
who has farmed inspiration for
the decoration of the cups from
traditional 'Sunday best' crockery
and glassware.

Cup holder
Resin
www.aaltoniina.com
Location > Finland
In development

Upgrading humble, often disregarded, everyday objects is a popular pursuit and effective comment on consumption. It also suggests a designer's independent way of seeing. See also 'Lux_it' on p. 252 and 'Pint Glass Series' on p. 264.

Pint Glass Series
Emiko Oki
Japanese

As a foreigner in the UK, Japanese
designer Emiko Oki looked upon
the humble pint glass found in pubs
and bars across the country with a
fresh perspective. Oki admired the
functionality of the original design,
and chose to expand it in a
collection of tabletop accessories.
The series includes a goblet, a vase,
an ashtray and a candle holder.
The characteristics of the pint glass
– portability, stability and an easily
grasped shape – make it an ideal
basic form for these applications.

Series of accessories
Borosilicate glass
www.emikooki.com
Location > UK
In production
By > www.adriansistem.ro

Science Series Glassware
Tony Moxham – Australian
Mauricio – Guatemalan

The work of DFC Mexico City often
combines artisan techniques and
a modern sensibility. These vessels
are made from scientific-grade
borosilicate glass, and their forms
are based on DFC's impressions
of laboratory forms. The industrial-
style vessels are then decorated
using the pretty and traditional
Mexican technique of hand-etching
called 'arte en pepita'.

Tableware
Borosilicate glass
www.dfcasa.com
Location > Mexico
Available to order

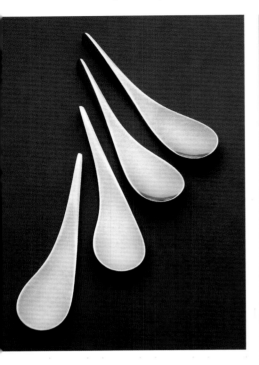

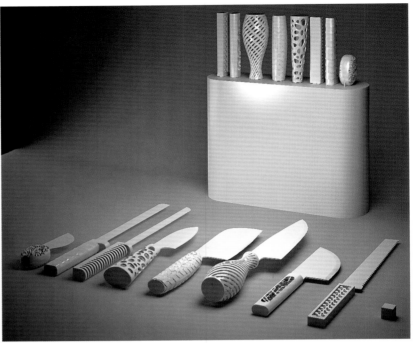

Petal Spoons
Oliver Smith
Australian

Tableware produced by Oliver Smith combines the best of both craft and industrial manufacturing. Smith, whose background is in jewelry design and silversmithing, seeks 'to combine the beauty and warmth of the handmade with the strengths of industrial production methods'. The 'Petal Spoons' are cast in stainless steel before being hand finished.

Cutlery
Stainless steel
www.oliversmith.com.au
Location > Australia
Limited edition

Barbaric Cut
Defne Koz
Turkish

This collection of kitchen knives combines white porcelain blades with ornate textured handles created by the rapid prototyping process of selective laser sintering. Koz took a 'barbaric' object, the knife, and attempted to civilize and refine it through delicate design. In some instances she looked to traditional Turkish crafts to inspire the complex and open patterns of the handles, while in others the ambition to push the possibilities of the process of 3D milling itself influenced the geometrical designs.

Kitchen knives
Polymer, porcelain
www.defnekoz.com
Location > Italy/USA/Turkey
Available to order

Rapid prototyping is often employed in the production of intricate graphic patterns. See also 'Speed Metal' on p. 250.

Stamp Cutlery
Tomás Alonso
Spanish

Alonso wanted to produce a cheap, lightweight, efficient cutlery range that was recyclable. After much research into existing plastic and wooden designs, Alonso settled on producing a series in aluminium. The familiar look and feel of the metal bears a closer resemblance to traditional cutlery, which we perceive as of better quality; as Alonso noted, all disposable cutlery tries in some way to emulate the real thing. In reducing the design to its most functional elements, the structure became the motif: stamping the pattern into sheeting adds strength while using the minimum possible material.

Disposable cutlery
Aluminium
www.tomas-alonso.com
Location > UK
In development

Jar Tops
Jorre van Ast
Dutch

'Jar Tops' turn readily available jars, of the kind that we all have in our cupboards, into vessels with a specific function; a sugar pot, milk jug, spice cellar, mug, water jug, or oil and vinegar set. The project began as a brief investigating the crossover between packaging and product. Glass jars are seen as disposable, but Ast noted their potential beyond this and made use of the standardized threads used on the top of almost all glass jars.

Dispenser attachments
Plastic
www.jorrevanast.com
Location > UK
In production
By > www.royalvkb.com

See other work by Jorre van Ast on p. 318.

Polka Pots
Marie Rahm, Monica Singer /Polka
German/Austrian

These enamelled pans boast strange, unexpected forms. Polka have played with our perceptions of what function is and the notion of the ordinary with this series of cookware. The familiar elements found on a kitchen pot have been rearranged, multiplied, and presented in a new arrangement intended to provoke thought on how and why we follow our usual domestic routines.

Pans
Steel, enamel
www.polkaproducts.com
Location > Austria
Available to order

Work Collection
Dick van Hoff
Dutch

When Dick van Hoff was asked
by esteemed Dutch manufacturers
Koninklijke Tichelaar Makkum to
design a collection of ceramic
objects, he chose to broaden the
traditional remit of the material.
Rather than add to their already
extensive collection of plates,
bowls and cups, van Hoff produced
hard-working products. The lamp,
vase, clock and box that make
up the 'Work Collection' are
each made from several parts
and combine ceramic and wood.
The designs, as van Hoff intended,
successfully illustrate the versatility
of ceramic as a contemporary
material.

Tabletop accessories
Ceramic, oak
www.vanhoffontwerpen.nl
Location > the Netherlands
In production
By > www.tichelaar.nl

Tablescape
Normal Studio
French

This table and the objects placed upon it were made at the same time as an installation, and the form and fabric of each is intended to complement the other. The table top is made from industrial silicon carbide, a ceramic most usually used for large-scale mirrors or observation satellites. The functional tabletop ceramics are described as 'modest' by J. F. Dingjian and Eloi Chafaï of Normal Studio. Together, the table and its decoration create a topographical landscape that draws upon comparative methods of ceramic production in their realization.

Tableware, table
Ceramic, silicon carbide, aluminium
www.normalstudio.fr
Location > France
In production
By > www.craft-limoges.org

Recycling Daily News
Greetje van Tiem
Dutch

Not so much a finished product
design as a new material, this is
a yarn made from old newspapers.
Van Tiem wanted to turn the
useless into the useful: 'I searched
for a material that was interesting
enough to work with and chose old
newspapers as they are full of
memories, facts, dates and figures.'
A single front page yields 20 m
(66 ft) of yarn, which can be woven
and used for many upholstery
applications. The yarn incorporates
a nostalgia for times past and an
atmosphere of sentimentality with
a practical invention.

Textile
Old newspapers
www.greetjevantiem.nl
Location > the Netherlands
In development

Invention of new materials is important in sustaining
design innovation. Paper is a popular raw material;
see also 'One Day Paper Waste' on p. 101.

Caba
Kwangho Lee
Korean

Kwangho Lee's 'Caba' breathes new life into secondhand and old furniture. Just as crocheted tablecloths or arm covers were once a homemade solution to cover ugly or worn furniture, the 'Caba' protects and decorates. Lee has updated the idea of crochet by creating a textile covering made from individual pieces of felt.

Chair cover
Felt
www.kwangholee.com
Location > Korea
Available to order

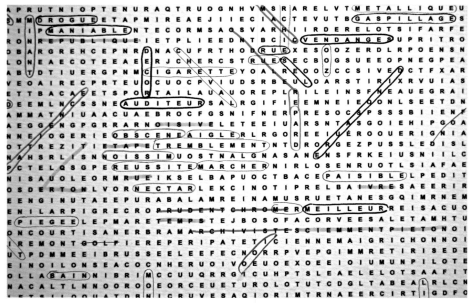

Here the user makes a physical and visual impact on the form of their product and environment, as they do on 'Snowbench' on p. 89.

Wallpaper Games
5.5 Designers
French

The surface of these wallpapers
is an area for play, because they
have familiar games, such as
word-searches and labyrinths,
printed on them. After time,
as the game progresses, the
surface becomes more elaborately
decorated with the marks of its
owner. The spontaneous graphics
demanded by each 'Wallpaper
Game' ensure each installation
is unique.

Wallpaper
Paper
www.cinqcinqdesigners.com
Location > France
In production
By > www.lutece-gpfb.com

Flutter
Catherine Hammerton
British

An antidote to commercial
wallpaper, 'Flutter' is made from
row upon row of ginkgo leaf-
shaped paper stitched onto
a wallpaper base. The result
is an ornate, textured surface
and a product that celebrates
preciousness and fragility in
opposition to disposable design.
'Flutter' is made to order in a
variety of papers and sizes for
commissioning clients.

Wallpaper
Base paper, soft-touch paper,
leatherette paper, thread
www.catherinehammerton.com
Location > UK
Available to order

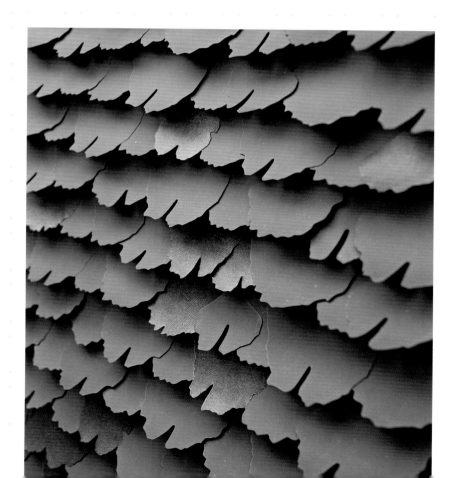

Cloud
Munchausen
French

Simon Pillard and Philippe Rossetti work together as Munchausen. For this wallpaper design, the duo were inspired by the famous Dürer engraving 'Melancholia'. The original engraving is heaped with symbolism and is said to represent heaven. Munchausen aimed to reflect the same theme in 'Cloud' while also updating the imagery through the addition of more graphic elements. Munchausen show a preference for using dream-like imagery in their work.

Wallpaper
Paper
Location > Denmark
In production
By >
www.sainthonorewallcoverings.com

Points de vue
Diane Steverlynck
Belgian

This curtain of woven polyester has a laser-cut panel in its centre. The addition of the panel plays with issues of transparency and opacity, and is meant to represent the open space between two curtains when one is pulled aside by an invisible hand. 'Points de vue' was originally created for a shop in Amsterdam and was intended to close off the space while also inviting the curiosity of passersby, setting intimacy against public space, privacy against curiosity.

Curtain
Polyester
www.dianesteverlynck.be
Location > Belgium
In production
By > www.verzameldwerk.be

Issues of privacy versus curiosity are also dealt with by Frank Flavell's 'Wingback Chair' on p. 78.

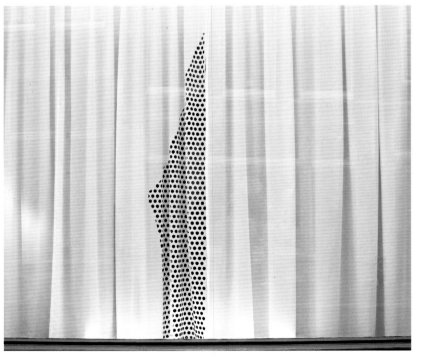

Jigsaw Wallpaper
Tracy Kendall
British

The common jigsaw puzzle has
'a low visual and economic value'
says Tracy Kendall. But by applying
jigsaw pieces to handmade
wallpaper, she illustrates that such
a perception can be quickly turned
around. The pieces have an
appealing colour range, induce
feelings of nostalgia, and provide
an unusual textured finish.

Wallpaper
Paper, secondhand jigsaw pieces,
nylon tags
www.tracykendall.com
Location > UK
Available to order

Interior Dialogue
Dorte Agergaard Jensen
Danish

The technique of digital printing
on textiles allows for the
production of unique designs.
For textile designer Dorte
Agergaard Jensen it has meant
freedom from the restraints of
working with repeated patterns.
The series 'Interior Dialogues'
includes unexpected motifs of
everyday items used in a new
context and to a decorative end.
Every piece (the collection includes
bedlinen, blinds and pillows)
displays a unique part of the
complete textile pattern.

Soft furnishings, bedlinen
Satin, polycotton
www.dorteagergaard.dk
Location > Denmark
Available to order

Meterware Carpet
Volksware
German

The 'Meterware Carpet' is made
from different kinds of clothes,
used and unused. They are stitched
together to form a running length
of carpet, which is then sold by the
metre (foot). A clever comment
on the current problem of excess
consumer goods, it is intended
to inspire consumers to live with,
and desire, surplus materials.

Rug
Mixed secondhand textiles
www.volksware.nl
Location > the Netherlands
In production
By > designer

For more Meterware products see 'Meterware Table' on p. 150.

Carpet
Carina Nilsson
Swedish

The pattern of this carpet is based
upon a doily or antimacassar,
but this oversized version of the
traditional object is made from
2 km (1.25 miles) of 4 mm (0.16 in.)
thick rope. The carpet, designed
for 70F in the Netherlands, can also
be used outside as in due to this
robust material.

Rug
Coreless polyester rope
Location > the Netherlands
In production
By > www.70F.com

PuzzlePerser
Katrin Sonnleitner
German

Persian rugs have been produced by the same method and using the same patterns for hundreds of years. Katrin Sonnleitner rapidly updates the familiar design by producing it in rubber and reinterpreting the graphic pattern as a giant jigsaw puzzle. The rug can be built, moved or adapted by its owner as desired.

Rug
Rubber
www.katrin-sonnleitner.com
Location > Germany
In development

This design updates a familiar pattern by breaking it down to its basic elements. See also 'Materialized Vase' on p. 233.

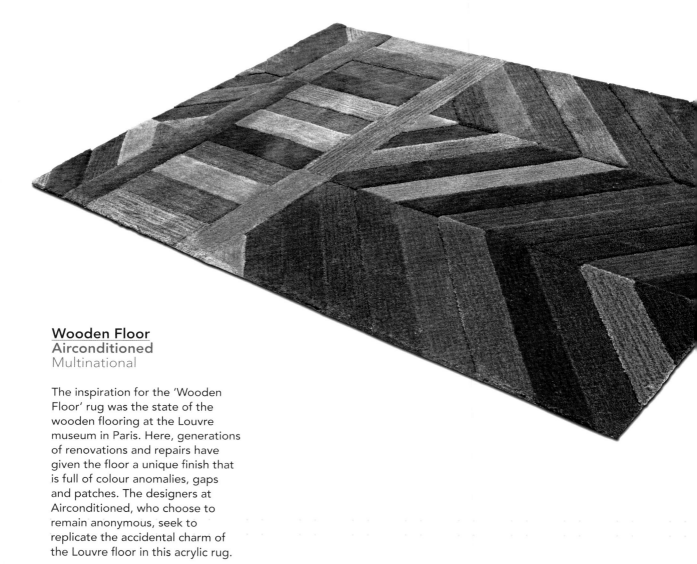

Wooden Floor
Airconditioned
Multinational

The inspiration for the 'Wooden Floor' rug was the state of the wooden flooring at the Louvre museum in Paris. Here, generations of renovations and repairs have given the floor a unique finish that is full of colour anomalies, gaps and patches. The designers at Airconditioned, who choose to remain anonymous, seek to replicate the accidental charm of the Louvre floor in this acrylic rug.

Rug
Acrylic
In production
By > www.bytrico.com

Some designers buck the trend of celebrity designers by remaining anonymous in order to emphasize the work. See more from the mysterious Airconditioned on p. 253.

JU87-G STUKA
Katharina Wahl
German

On the one hand a carpet, and on the other a model of the famous World War II Stuka dive-bomber: the 'JU87-G STUKA' carpet invites its user to play. This extraordinary textile design is directly influenced by 'the beauty that is found in the order of a model kit' says Wahl. The 2D object can later be transformed into a 3D living-room sculpture.

Rug
Felt
www.katharinawahl.de
Location > Germany
In development

Invitations to consumers to play are increasingly common. See the 'Miles' rug on p. 284.

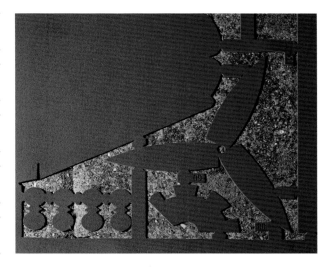

Landscape
Gaële Girault
French

When Swiss carpet manufacturer
Rucksthul asked Ecole cantonale
d'art de Lausanne (ECAL) students
to develop new ideas, Gaële Girault
produced a rug that represented
an island of comfort between
furniture. 'Landscape' is made
from wool felt layers, inspired
by topographic and relief maps.
The built up forms of the rug offer
a cosseting place for people to lie.

Rug
Wool
www.gaelegirault.com
Location > France
In production
By > www.ruckstuhl.com

More products with a distinct topographic
inspiration are 'Lounge Landscape' on p. 91
and 'Topography' on p. 238.

Miles rug
Big-Game
Grégoire Jeanmonod – Swiss
Elric Petit – Belgian
Augustin Scott de
Martinville – French

This rug takes the twists and turns
of a motorway interchange as the
starting point. The rug comes with
three small wooden cars; an apt
addition, because the design is
inspired by the gestures of children
at play. The rug is as much about
humour as it is a practical floor
covering – a considered intention
of the designers who make up Big
Game. Irreverence is an essential
ingredient in their work, as is taking
the basic element of either a
material, an archetype or a principle
and instigating a design that they
then strive to make functional.

Rug
Wool
www.big-game.ch
Location > Switzerland/Belgium
Limited edition

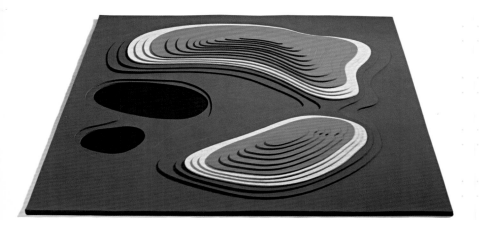

Irak
NEL
Mexican

International current affairs are a significant influence in this product from NEL, a Mexican design collective. The repetition of the image of Iraq, as a graphic element in newspapers and on television, together with the recurrent images of war, lent a 'game-like dimension' to what was serious and distressing visual information. As a deliberate extension of this peculiarity, the 'Irak' rug makes use of these now-familiar elements. 'With this piece we also wanted to address the fact that decoration is commonly perceived as apolitical.'

Rug
Wool felt, synthetic pile
www.nel.com.mx
Location > Mexico
Limited edition

Cable Carpet
Britta Böhne
German

The 'Cable Carpet' presents an ornamental solution to a typical domestic problem. The wires and cables from electrical items pass through the carpet, creating an abstract decoration and being kept tidy at the same time. Böhne says that utilizing the cables in this way gives them a 'higher value' than they might normally enjoy as they become decorative objects.

Rug
Polyamide rug, silicone
www.brittaboehne.de
Location > Germany
In development

Focusing on the unremarkable aspects of a household product can reveal ways of using them as decorative elements. See also Nick Fraser's 'Hall Stand' on p. 112 and 'Weave Your Lighting' on p. 183.

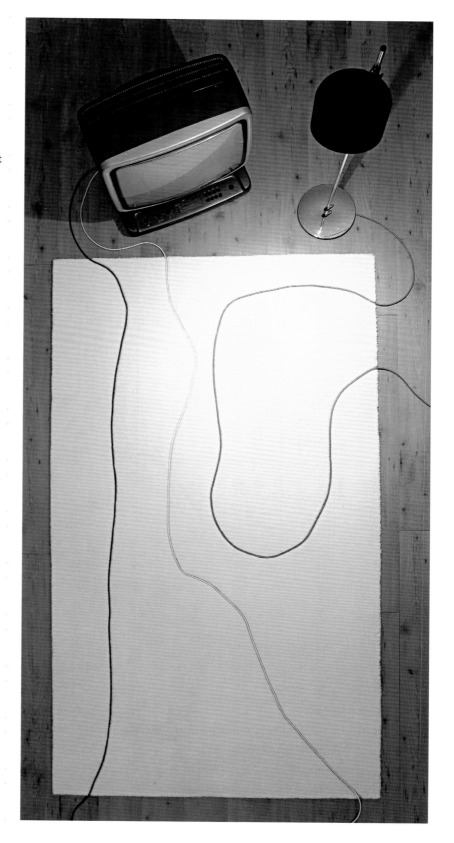

Utility

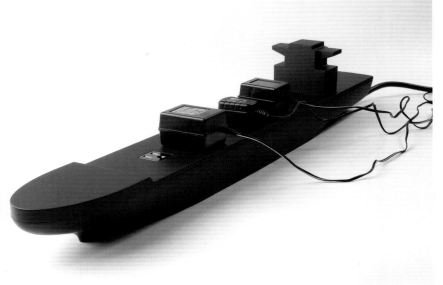

Containership Powersupply
giffin'termeer
American

The possibility of making a subject tangible through product design motivated artist Jess Giffin and industrial designer Jim TerMeer to produce the 'Containership Powersupply'. This product is intended to accommodate the many power adapters that clutter domestic spaces, while also offering a reminder of the infrastructure behind electrical consumption. The form represents the import of electronic devices delivered on giant ships and the energy that this requires.

Extension socket
Metal, rubber
www.giffintermeer.com
Location > USA
Available to order

Wattson
DIY Kyoto
British

The Wattson is a device that makes electricity consumption, usually invisible and intangible, a visible entity. A sensor attached to the household electricity supply reads energy flow and sends information to a wireless display unit, which shows the level of energy currently in use through a low-energy light emitting diode (LED) display. The Wattson 'enables you to learn about your own personal energy through interactive play' and together DIY Kyoto hope they 'can communicate something useful which will change the behaviour of the user for a greater good'.

Energy display
Polypropylene, polycarbonate
www.diykyoto.com
Location > UK
In production
By > designer

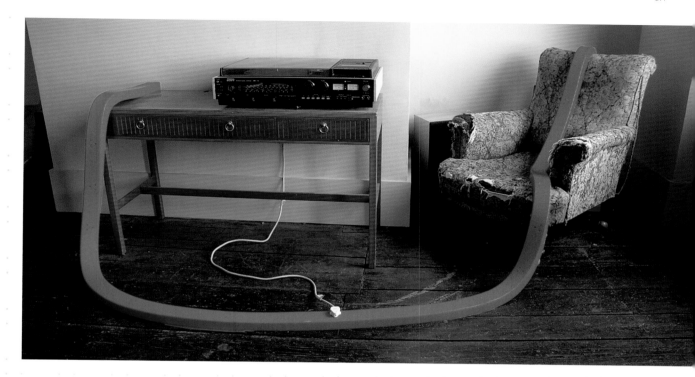

Standby Extension
&made
British

This exaggerated extension cable is designed to focus our attention on the energy consumption of our appliances. It prompts its owner to consider their responsibility to switch off appliances, and makes that task easier by bringing the switch into the centre of the room. 'Standby Extension' is one product from the Climatised Objects Series produced by David Cameron and Toby Hadden of &made with the aim of beginning an environmental dialogue with the consumer.

Extension socket
Silicone
www.and-made.com
Location > UK
In development

PowerBlock
Johann Aumaître,
Jérôme Lopé
French

The 'PowerBlock' is designed
to blend into the aesthetic of
a contemporary interior. Its job
is to conceal the wires and cables
that litter modern homes behind
a softly sculptural steel shell.
A flat piece of laser-cut steel is
bent into a form that is discreet
but nonetheless stylized, because
Aumaître and Lopé wanted the
'PowerBlock' to be more than
a simple box.

Extension socket
Steel, powder-coated finish
www.studiomanzano.fr
Location > France
In production
By > designer

A new genre of design object has been
invented to deal with the abundance
of electrical cables in the modern home.
Some designers choose to conceal these,
while others, such as 'Standby' on p. 291
and 'Plu' on p. 293, make them a feature
instead.

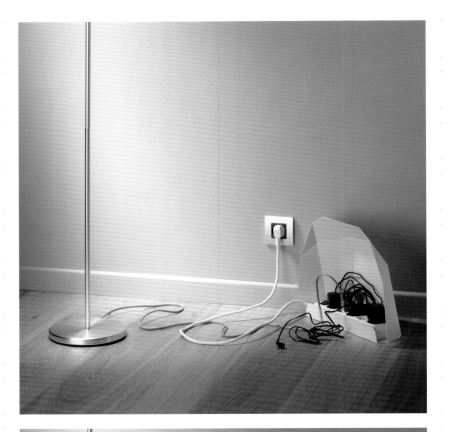

Plug Brother
Sdesignunit
Korean

Everyday we are using more and
more electrical appliances and,
by association, more plugs, yet the
humble plug has been offered very
little design attention up until now.
Sdesignunit in Korea have made
a plug that allows for a second
plug to be inserted into its back.
The result is a tidy meeting of
cables and plugs rather than the
unattractive scrum more usually
found at the socket.

Plug
Polycarbonate, acrylonitrile
butadiene styrene
www.sdesignunit.com
Location > Korea
In production
By > designer

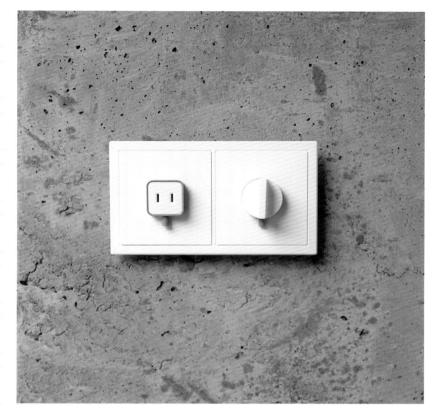

Plu
Line Depping
Danish

'Plu' is a contrary product: rather
than striving to tidy away electrical
cables, Line Depping has chosen
to accentuate their existence and
draw attention to them 'as a
positive part of our world today'.
With 'Plu', the socket becomes a
sculptural object in its own right,
'and maybe it will make us less
irritated about wires' says Depping.

Extension socket
Plastic
www.linedepping.dk
Location > Denmark
In development

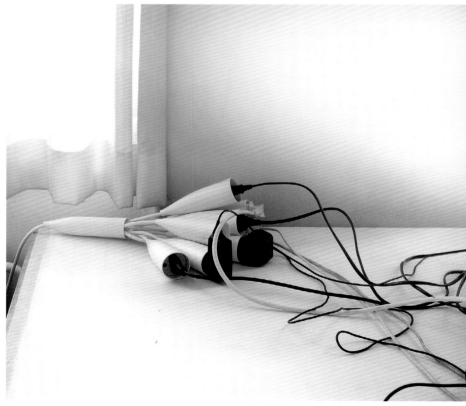

Radio dB
Ditte Kuijpers, Bas Geelen
Dutch

Ordo dB is a collaborative project between two Dutch designers, Ditte Kuijpers and Bas Geelen. This small series of handmade radios uses old radio parts and electrics and found plastic fuel cans. The influence of the exaggerated forms of ghetto blasters from the designer's youth is clearly seen.

Radios
Reused radio parts, plastic
www.ordodb.com
Location > the Netherlands
Limited edition

See another use for the recycled fuel containers in 'To Handle, To Pour, To Contain' on p. 207.

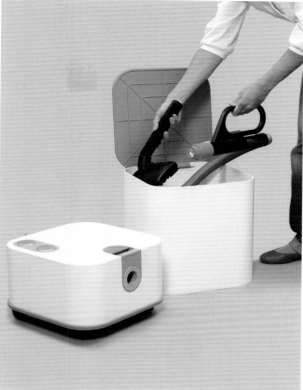

Stool Vacuum Cleaner
Jin Sang Hwang
Korean

There is little consideration
for storage in the design of
vacuum cleaners. Jin Sang Hwang
addresses this neglect with the
compact 'Stool' cleaner. The
machine fits neatly inside a stool,
which can then be integrated into
a living environment rather than
clumsily hidden away.

Vacuum cleaner
Acrylonitrile butadiene styrene,
aluminium, polypropylene,
glass fibre
www.jinsanghwang.com
Location > UK
In development

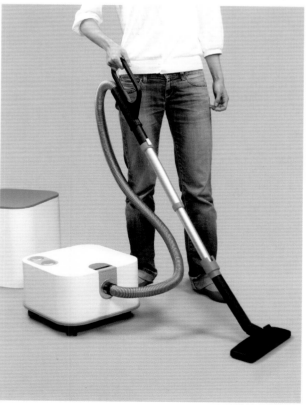

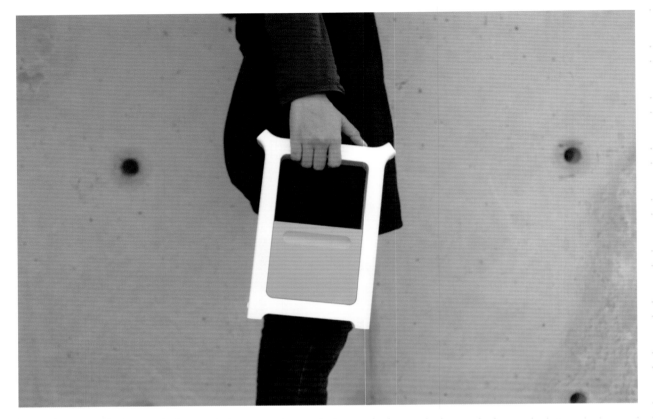

Portable Humidifier
Sdesignunit
Korean

A humidifier improves the immediate environment by freshening air. The innovation of this design is its portability. The mobility of the compact unit is made possible by its lightweight frame, which also functions as a built-in handle.

Humidifier
Polycarbonate, acrylonitrile butadiene styrene
www.sdesignunit.com
Location > Korea
In production
By > designer

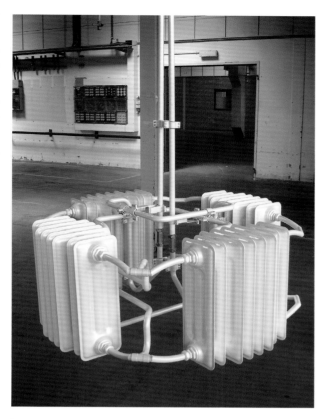

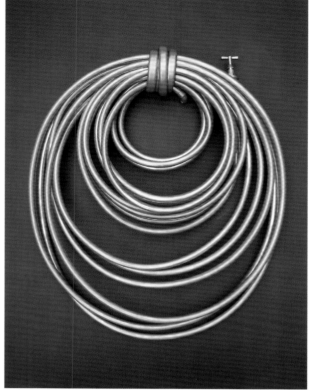

Heatingpoint
Bas van Raay
Dutch

This suspended radiator creates
a warm circle in a public space.
Concerned with the lack of meeting
points in social spaces, van Raay
used heat, rather traditionally,
as a focal point and and turned
the radiator into a contemporary
campfire. The radiator is made from
materials and parts available in the
heating industry, but van Raay has
pushed the limits and aesthetics
of these materials in this new form.

Radiator
Stainless steel, brass,
automotive paint
www.vraay.com
Location > the Netherlands
Available to order

Veins of the house
Liane Gaemers
Dutch

In any ordinary heating system,
piping will form an invisible network
through the house, the 'veins of
the house'. Gaemers decided that
these pipes were beautiful enough
to be the final product, and coiled
copper pipes to create a unique
but functional radiator.

Radiator
Copper
www.2design4.nl
Location > the Netherlands
In development

Public interaction is also the theme of 'Stuhlhockerbank' on p. 335.

Calimero
Manuel Kostrzynski
German

The process of percolating coffee is normally hidden behind the walls of a regular coffee machine but 'Calimero' was devised to make that process visible. By employing glass – an unusual material for appliance manufacturing – Manuel Kostrzynski adds a new dimension to a familiar kitchen object and combines utility with pleasure.

Coffee maker
Borosilicate glass, stainless steel
www.rinsky.de
Location > Germany
In development

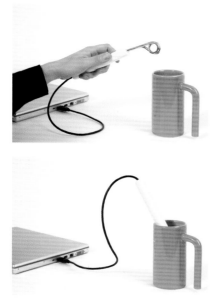

Heat Me
Key Portilla-Kawamura
Spanish/Japanese

Can our computers help us cook? Putting aside complex technologies, Key Portilla-Kawamura investigates the humble USB port, originally developed for data transfer. This function 'allows for a myriad of further applications that go beyond the strictly digital world' and here it is used as an everyday device to heat up drinks.

Cooking aid
Plastic, anodized aluminium, Teflon® coating
www.tik-tac.com
Location > Spain
Available to order

Computer technology is also employed for a surprising use in 'Spore 1.1' on p. 302.

Glas Gib Gas
Harry Thaler
Italian

To make a kitchen appliance from glass was a deliberately unusual application, says Thaler. 'The idea was to take the glass out of its usual context and to estrange it from its normal use.' The mobile gas cooker was a random choice, but the result is thoroughly functional. This product's compact design and ease of manufacture makes it democratic and accessible.

Hob
Borosilicate glass, stainless steel, steel braided hose
Location > Italy
Available to order

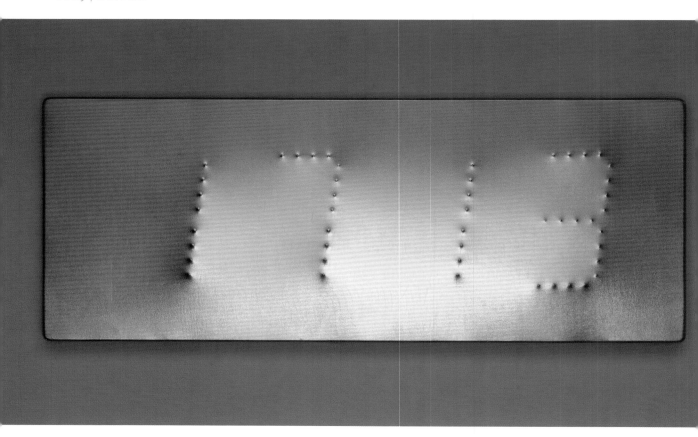

Digital Clock #2
Albin Karlsson
Swedish

'Time fascinates me, both as physical phenomena and as a philosophical and personal matter,' declares Swedish designer Albin Karlsson. Our perception of time has changed, as have our technical capabilities, and Karlsson makes full use of them both in this clock. Pins behind an elasticated textile are moved back and forth by a motor, and the time appears punched onto the surface.

Clock
Wood, elastic textile
www.albinkarlsson.com
Location > Sweden
Available to order

World Clock
André Klauser
German

This clock was designed for 'people with a longing for faraway places'. The clock face shows 12 cities of the world in their respective time zones: with your time zone at twelve o'clock, you simply count the hours between it and other time zones. For locations to the east, count clockwise, for locations to the west, count anticlockwise.

Clock
Steel, powder-coated finish, screen-printed face
www.andreklauser.com
Location > UK
In production
By > www.authentics.de

Use-It Dispose-It
Christian Kocx
Dutch

New, bigger and better televisions are launched every year with a view to enticing consumers to spend more and more often. Kocx was inspired to turn the packaging that surrounds televisions into the main feature of the product, thereby extending the lifespan of the less lavish television set.

Television casing
Cardboard, secondhand television
www.kocxontwerpen.nl
Location > the Netherlands
In development

Spore 1.1
SWAMP
American/New Zealander

Corporate health is most often reflected on charts and graphs, but this product was designed to reveal the relationship between corporate health and an individual. 'Spore' links the success of a large corporation to an ecosystem by forcing a direct interaction between stock-market data and a plant's life-support system. When the week-ending stock rises, the plant is automatically rewarded with water; if the stock remains the same or drops, the plant is not watered. SWAMP, which stands for Studies of Work Atmosphere and Mass Production, are Douglas Easterly and Matt Kenyon.

Interactive ornament
Plant, soil, acrylic, electronics
www.swamp.nu
Location > USA/New Zealand
In production
By > designer

Supper
Jin Kuramoto
Japanese

These are discreet speakers in the form of bottles or cups, produced with audio company Taguchi. The intention is that they integrate with other household objects and allow music to be moved to wherever you might be. Giving the speakers the form of tableware suggests their use at the dinner table to create ambience while you eat. Inverting the glass-shaped speaker switches off the music, and turning the bottle cap adjusts the volume.

Speakers
Resin, punched metal
www.jinkuramoto.com
Location > Japan
In production
By > www.taguchi-mk.com

Wooden Clock
Vinta
Japanese

Wanting to express the 'feeling
of time', Kohei Okamoto and
Toshitaka Nakamura of Vinta
created a moving, 3D clock.
The two leaning forms represent
the arms on a clock, and revolve
accordingly. The larger sphere
displays minutes and completes
its rotation in one hour, while the
smaller sphere displays the hours
and takes twelve hours to rotate.
The concealed mechanics move
the tactile wooden objects
smoothly and efficiently, and
produce an engaging and
unexpected manifestation
of timekeeping.

Clock
Kalopanax wood
www.vinta.jp
Location > Japan
In development

Time to Time
Tatsuhiro Sekisaka
Japanese

Designer Tatsuhiro Sekisaka's own
circumstances, living far away from
home, led him to invent this means
of maintaining awareness of dual
time zones. Either clock can be
obscured, or even both when you
might want to avoid seeing the
time, for example on a day off.
This is more than just a timepiece:
the process of opening the doors
or obscuring the time is
representative of a mental leap
for Sekisaka, who regularly moves
between two lives in Tokyo and
Eindhoven.

Clock
Medium density fibreboard (MDF)
www.hitsujiame.com
Location > Japan
In development

See André Klauser's approach to the issue
of multiple time zones in 'World Clock' on
p. 301.

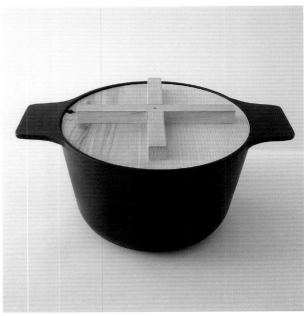

Alma, Orlando und Björn
Anita Meyer
Swiss

The use of existing furniture can be expanded and added to, especially if they support Alma (a repository), Orlando (a fan) or Bjorn (a light). These are parasitic helpers constructed from silicone and designed to be attached to many surfaces. They complement existing interior items, rather than replacing or overpowering them.

Fan, lamp, storage
Silicone
www.anitameyer.ch
Location > Switzerland
Available to order

Cast Iron Pot
Yuta Watanabe
Japanese

A simple observation led Yuta Watanabe to create a new version of an old cookery classic. He noted that after cooking, most of us place hot pots on chopping boards to protect work surfaces, but remove and leave aside their lids. His 'Cast Iron Pot' features an oak lid that doubles as a trivet.

Pans
Iron, oak
www.yutawatanabe.com
Location > Japan
In development

Waternetworks Collection
Fulguro
Swiss

Cédric Decroux and Yves Fidalgo of Fulguro have been developing products that deal with the relationship between man, water and vegetation. This collection consists of four products that offer solutions to water consumption or encourage plant growth. The 'reLEAF' gathers rain water, 'reFRESH' is a multifunctional vessel for water, 'reFLECT' both lights a room and becomes a light source for a plant, while 'reCOVER' redirects even the tiniest amount of water from coats and umbrellas.

Water-saving devices
reLEAF: aluminium, powder-coated finish
reFRESH: enamelled ceramic
reFLECT: steel, aluminium, powder-coated finish
reCOVER: beech, steel, powder-coated finish
www.fulguro.ch
Location > Switzerland
In development

Issues surrounding consumption demand awareness. See also 'Standby' on p. 291 and 'Divide It' on p. 310.

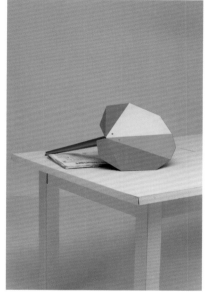

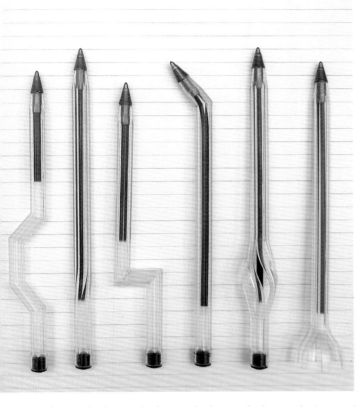

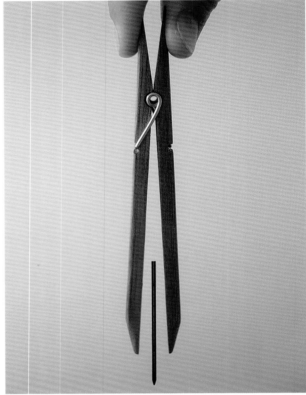

GH (Bic®) Pens
Gemma Holt
British

Holt was inspired by the ubiquitous and humble Bic® pen to create something that was at once beautiful, intriguing and instantly recognizable. The rapid manufacturing process used was ripe for adaptation, and Holt was seduced by the immediacy of the process and the possibilities it offered her, saying 'the variation between these six pens is an illustration of what this technique can achieve'.

Writing implements
Stereolithography resin, Bic® refill
www.gemmaholt.co.uk
Location > UK
Limited edition

Peg Pencil
Yuta Watanabe
Japanese

Yuta Watanabe designs gentle products that blend in seamlessly with the contemporary environment. 'No one has seen this "Peg Pencil", but everyone intuitively understands what it is and how it works' says Watanabe. It is the common understanding of both a pencil and a clothes peg that allows this new object to be recognized and accepted.

Writing implement
Oak, spring steel
www.yutawatanabe.com
Location > Japan
In development

Drain Eye-Catcher
Joana Meroz
Brazilian/Dutch

Joana Meroz describes the sink drain as 'on the edge' of our domestic world, and relishes the opportunity to add ornament to this area. She intends to bring into question the human relationship with beauty and provoke a debate around why we bring decoration into our homes at all; is it for personal pleasure or for others to see? The functional use is maintained but made beautiful by simply repositioning the necessary holes into a pattern.

Sink strainer
Plastic
www.theornamentedlife.com
Location > the Netherlands
In production
By > www.droogdesign.nl

The incidental elements of an interior can be used to decorative effect. See also 'Cable Carpet' on p. 287.

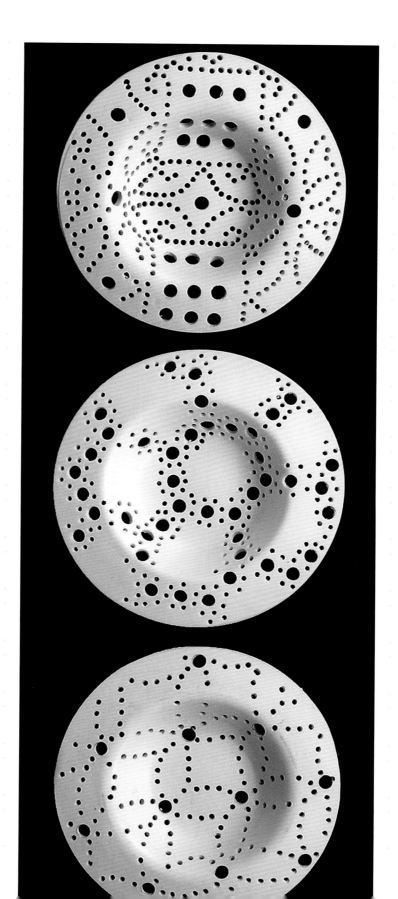

A-Zero
Martino d'Esposito
Italian/Swiss

Martino d'Esposito created this wastepaper bin from a single sheet of aluminium. The bin is constructed much as it would be were it made from paper, and the form, with an open vent, clearly demonstrates the bin's use for and relationship with paper.

Wastepaper bin
Aluminium, powder-coated finish
www.despositogaillard.com
Location > Switzerland
In development

Divide It
Ali Ganjavian
Iranian/Spanish

Though recycling policies are becoming stricter and more widely enforced, our immediate domestic environment has adapted little to cope with changing habits. Ali Ganjavian's simple design is intended to tackle this problem. The function of 'Divide It' is entertainingly unclear, until it is dropped into a wastepaper bin and becomes a tool for dividing different waste types.

Waste divider
Corian®
www.tik-tac.com
Location > Spain
Available to order

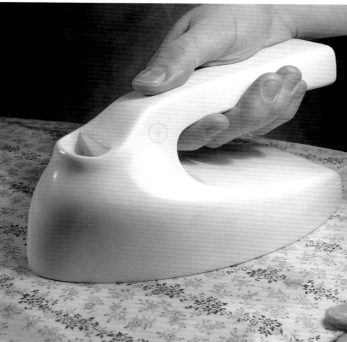

Tschoc
Fries & Zumbühl
Swiss

The 'Tschoc' watering can takes simple inspiration from its direct habitat. Kevin Fries & Jakob Zumbühl have designed a product that can be camouflaged between real plants when not in use. An extendable hose allows the can to be filled from any water source, and the two branch-like nozzles allow a direct flow or many fine jets of water to rain over houseplants.

Watering can
Biodegradable composites
www.frieszumbuehl.ch
Location > Switzerland
In development

Pressing Matters
George Pegasiou
British

Irons were once kitchen dwellers, says George Pegasiou. They were practical, attractive and tactile, most often made from ceramic and considered stylish products to be displayed rather than hidden away. Today's irons have little connection to the kitchen and, although ceramic is a material well suited to steam ironing, it is rarely used. Pegasiou's design is born from an examination of these past truths and an ambition to reintroduce the iron as a desirable object.

Iron
Ceramic
www.urban-shed.com
Location > UK
In development

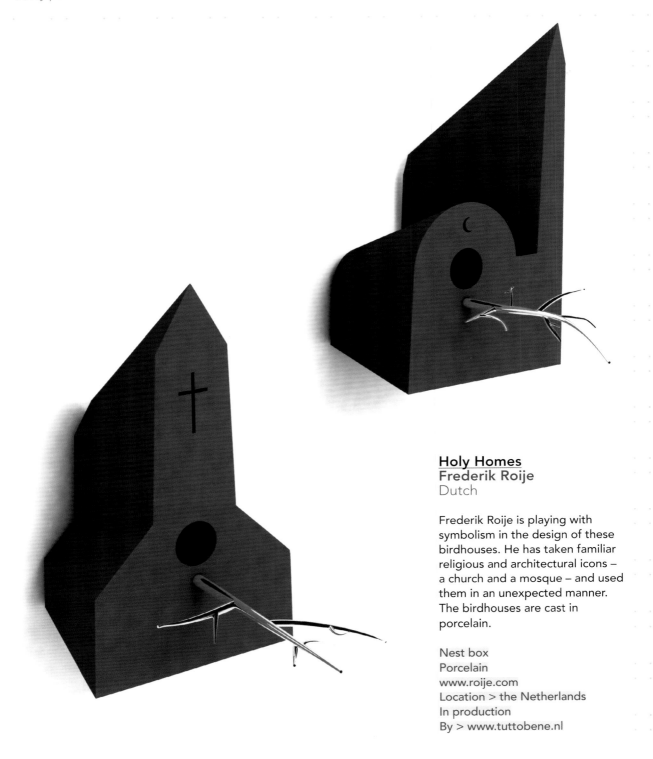

Holy Homes
Frederik Roije
Dutch

Frederik Roije is playing with symbolism in the design of these birdhouses. He has taken familiar religious and architectural icons – a church and a mosque – and used them in an unexpected manner. The birdhouses are cast in porcelain.

Nest box
Porcelain
www.roije.com
Location > the Netherlands
In production
By > www.tuttobene.nl

Birdy
Jaccard Vladimir
Swiss

A desire to make full use of the qualities of a hardwearing and resilient Eternit fibre cement led Jaccard Vladimir, a graduate of Ecole Cantonale d'Art de Lausanne (ECAL), to create this birdhouse. The design for the birdhouse uses just two moulded, U-shaped forms that sit together without the need for any fixatives, simplifying the production process.

Nest box
Fibre cement, polyester rope
Location > Switzerland
In production
By > www.eternit.ch

Lockvogel
Mareike Gast
German

Wild birds could do with a dumb friend like their caged cousins, thought designer Mareike Gast. She made a small model from porcelain to lure wild birds to a window and another 'sarcastic' version from seed.

Birdfeeder, bird decoy
Porcelain, stainless steel, seeds, fat
www.mareikegast.de
Location > Germany
In development

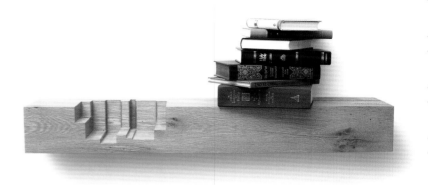

This design uses religious iconography to comment on cultural issues. Eric Morel also employs religious icons in his 'Coat hanger' on p. 244.

Juxtaposed: Religion
Curated bookshelf
Mike Simonian – Dutch
Maaike Evers – American

The objective of 'Juxtaposed Religion', say designers Mike Simonian and Maaike Evers, is to give books new meaning by juxtaposing them with other books. 'For the first time, the world's most influential religious texts are brought together and presented on the same level, their coexistence acknowledged and celebrated.' The arrangement of the books is symbolic in its attempt to place the titles on the same level and thereby suggest equality.

Shelving
Reclaimed hardwood, books
www.mikeandmaaike.com
Location > USA
In production
By > www.blankblank.net

Pinno hooks and shelves
Donald Holt
Australian

The different shapes and sizes of these sculptural wall pieces allows for personalized arrangements. The collection of shapes is intimate and tactile and devised to be ultimately functional. Mostly, this collection of helpful and humble household objects has been created to show off the possibilities of camphor laurel wood (Cinnamomum camphora). This is classified as a weed in Australia, the homeland of designer Donald Holt.

Hooks
Camphorwood, stainless steel
www.holtclifforddesigners.com
Location > Australia
In production
By > designer

From Above
Mathias Hahn
German

The hangers are held in position along the length of rope by friction. Because they are individually positioned, they allow for an increase or decrease in hanging capacity depending on what is needed. The ropes are suspended from the ceiling and take up no floorspace, making this an ideal installation for small living spaces.

Hanging system
Ash or pine, rope
www.mathiashahn.com
Location > UK
Available to order

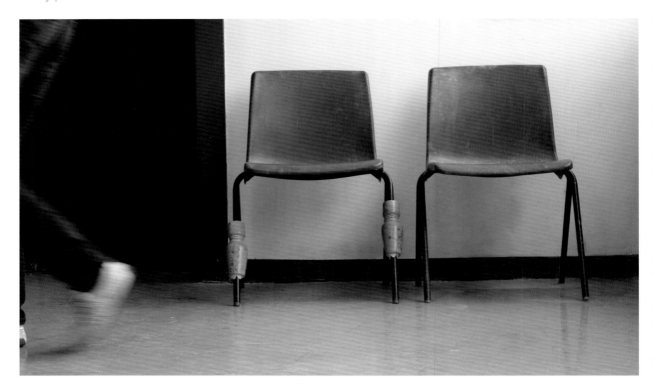

Adding decoration is a method of extending the lifespan of a furniture design. See also 'Plakbanterie' on p. 156.

Seeking To Embellish
Steffi Ong
Malaysian

What can be done if a piece of furniture becomes too 'cold' or 'tired' for your liking? Steffi Ong chose to address what happens when we no longer engage with a piece of our furniture. Her solution is to invite us to embellish redundant items and therefore reignite our affection for them. These bold ceramic beads can be slid onto furniture legs, turning a simple chair into a personalized, decorated beauty.

Decoration
Ceramic, rubber
Location > UK
Available to order

Leggs
Alfonso Merry
Spanish

Observing that 'our most common domestic companions have a scale that is not apt to our human height, nor do they grow organically as we do during our lifetime', Alfonso Merry invented 'Leggs'. These furniture accessories extend the height of everyday objects to make them more accessible. The legs themselves are a byproduct of the textile industry; they are recycled paper cones, which can be stacked to achieve any desired height.

Furniture legs
Paper
www.merry.es
Location > Spain
Available to order

Clampology
Jorre van Ast
Mexican/American

Jorre van Ast decided to develop a system that would allow existing pieces of furniture or structures to be 'added onto'. For him, a simple industrial clamp inspired a family of objects, each with a specific function. The collection of these informal utensils includes a book stop and book end, a hook and a rail that clamp onto the side of horizontal surfaces, a hook to clamp on to pipes and a candle holder. The spirit of 'Clampology' is functionality and economy of design. 'Clamp-a-leg' is the latest manifestation: a set of legs with built-in clamp technology offer an alternative to trestle legs, and can be combined with any surface to create a table.

Construction accessory
Clampology: polymer, spring metal
Clamp-a-leg: wood, sheet metal
www.jorrevanast.com
Location > UK
In development

Prop
Peter Marigold
British

Peter Marigold describes the function of 'Prop' as 'to elevate box-shaped objects above floor level. It is part product, part furniture and part architectural intervention.' Considerable observation of the domestic habits of people living in temporary accommodation was met by Marigold with this intelligent response. 'Prop' simply makes use of the architectural support of walls and allows objects to be stored away, freeing up floor space while avoiding the need to drill holes into walls or buy furniture. Marigold adds that 'Prop' can be supported by 'a stolen sand bag from local construction sites, or a locally bought bag of rice that can be eaten when it is time to move on'.

Storage aid
Hardwood, steel
www.petermarigold.com
Location > UK
Available to order

See more of Peter Marigold's storage work in 'Tilt' on p. 118.

Environment

Black Candy
Katharina Wahl
German

Pieces of black polyurethane foam cut to resemble slices of gateau are positioned together in a strange, graphic pattern. 'Black Candy' is intended as an installation for the floor or wall. Though it functions like a carpet and is resilient enough to walk over, the principal idea is that it evokes a decadent and surreal experience.

Floor covering
Polyurethane foam
www.katharinawahl.de
Location > Germany
In development

Floor Motion
Judith van den Boom
Dutch

'Floor Motion' is intended
to capture the sensation of
movement, the kind you might
experience when walking on
a ribbed, wet beach. The tiles can
be laid like a path across a floor
or as a ceramic rug. 'The inspiration
for this product was the fluidity
of material that is easily found in
textiles and soft material but not
in ceramic' says Judith van den
Boom. By freezing the natural flow
of ceramic, she achieved an illusion
of fluidity over the familiar and
classic grid pattern of ceramic tiles.

Floor tiles
Ceramic
www.judithvandenboom.nl
Location > UK
Available to order

For other work by Judith van den Boom
work see 'Qing Zuo!' on p. 26.

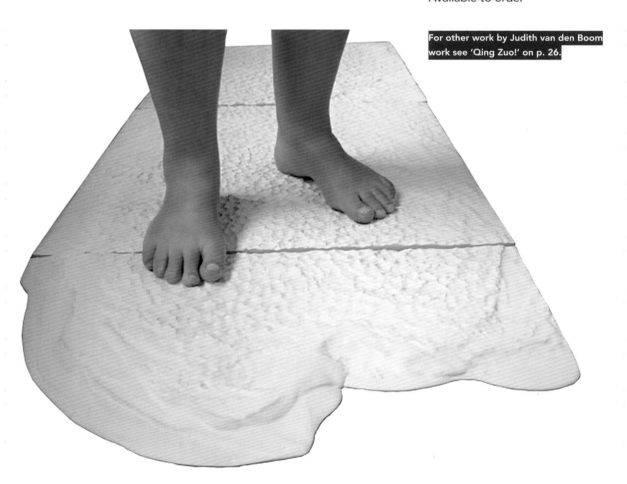

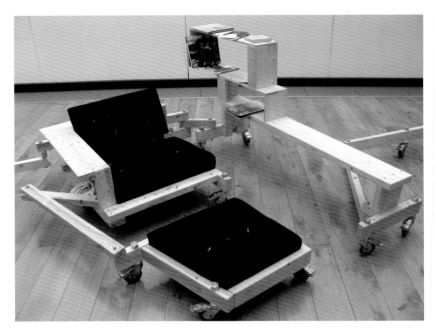

Endoskeletons
Alon Meron
Israeli

Alon Meron has a fresh perspective
on the dynamics of the home and
how furniture functions within it.
His design is a concept for a living
room that incorporates various
elements in a single, extendable,
structure. 'I have applied the
structural principle of a skeleton
to the domestic environment.
The space is now drawn around
the function rather than containing
it.' The skeletons allow different
elements – a seat, table, television,
library – to be rolled around an
interior space at the whim of their
owner. Meron says his concept is
about 'the subtle pleasure of having
the system move around you in
response to your movements,
all in a very analogue manner'.

Interior system
Wood, steel, upholstery
www.alonmeron.com
Location > UK
Available to order

Taste the edible
and the inedible
Carina Chi
Swedish

Taste and touch are as important
as vision to Swedish designer
Carina Chi. That's why this design,
incorporating wallpaper and
accessories together into an
interior installation, holds several
surprises. Digital print and flock
surfaces combine with scented ink
and concealed magnets within the
wallpaper. This is a playful product
intended to provoke interaction.

Installation
Wallpaper, magnetic wallpaper,
magnets, perspex, cotton, foam,
flock, polyester, blackboard paint,
gloss spray, scratch-and-sniff inks
www.carinachi.com
Location > Sweden
Available to order

Basic Baroque
Rachel Horrocks
British

Impermanence and play were two
themes occupying Rachel Horrocks
when she created 'Basic Baroque'.
This kit of felt parts is do-it-yourself
ornamentation for the home;
while suggested compositions
are provided, individual layouts are
encouraged. The forms are familiar
baroque motifs, but the material
and the application have more to
do with contemporary living styles
and disposable culture. This is 'poor
man's plasterwork', says Horrocks.

Decoration
Pure wool felt, hook-and-loop tape
www.rachelhorrocks.co.uk
Location > UK
In development

In its most modern manifestation, the word baroque is used,
fittingly, as a shorthand for decoration. See also 16&12's
'Bench for two' on p. 34.

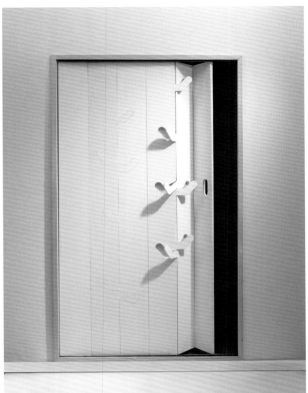

La désinvolture
Arnaud Lapierre
French

Observation of the habits we all adopt when staying in hotel rooms inspired Arnaud Lapierre to design this wardrobe, which legitimizes the ad hoc approach to clothes storage we so frequently adopt. The desire to leave an imprint on bland, unfamiliar surroundings, coupled with the break from regular domestic habits, often induces intense untidiness. Lapierre's wardrobe features a door with hidden hooks. When opened, the door presents a new, unrestrictive and, in some senses, decorative option for clothes storage.

Door
Beech
www.arnaud-lapierre.com
Location > France
In development

Waslijn
Charlotte Grün
Dutch

The drying process of laundry is cleverly articulated in this design. This clothes line responds to weight, stretching tighter as the washing becomes drier and lighter. The addition of rotating bone china wheels filled with steel balls, which chime as the clothes line shifts, transforms the drying process into an audio-visual experience.

Clothes line
China, aluminium
www.studio-ook.nl
Location > the Netherlands
Available to order

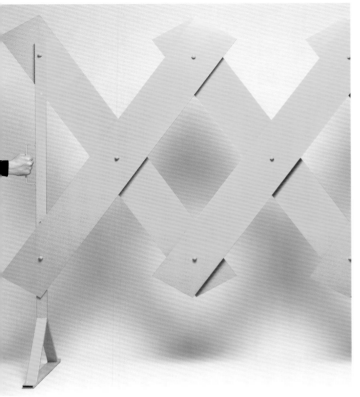

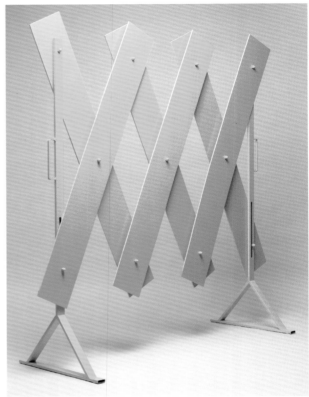

Divider (no.10)
TAF
Swedish

Gabriella Gustafson and Mattias Ståhlbom of TAF have produced a room divider with a recognizable industrial aesthetic; this metal frame is more than a little reminiscent of the safety gates found at road works. Extending the divider increases its size and therefore also its transparency. TAF have removed a piece of outdoor equipment from its usual context and adapted it for indoor use.

Room divider
Plywood, steel, lacquered finish
www.tafarkitektkontor.se
Location > Sweden
Available to order

Nomad Architectural System
MIO
Jaime Salm – Columbian
Roger Allen – American

Jaime Salm and Roger Allen of MIO are conscientious designers. This screening system is produced using renewable, recyclable and locally sourced materials. The kraft paper units are a modular architectural system designed to grow and adapt to any environment. This is intended as a democratic design, which can be easily implemented by anyone for any use and needs no equipment for its construction.

Room divider
Double-walled cardboard from recycled kraft paper
www.mioculture.com
Location > USA
In production
By > designer

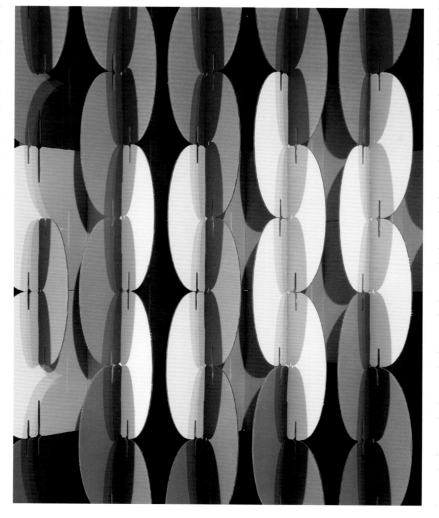

This work raises issues of privacy versus openness in the same way as the 'Points de vue' curtain on p. 276.

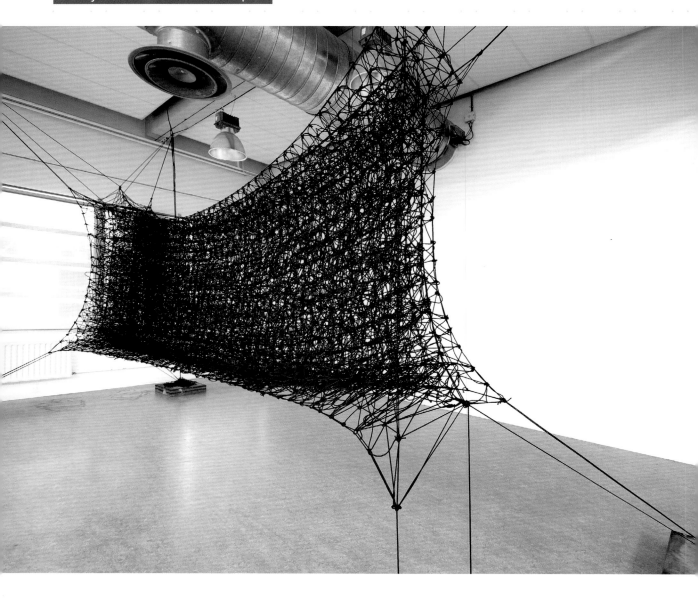

Dividing Veil
Lucas van Vugt
Dutch

The function of 'Dividing Veil' is to divide interior space. When looking through the divider, any detail is broken up by the pattern, in much the same way as it might be by a woman's veil. Events can be glimpsed on the other side of the veil, which stimulates curiosity, and the shape of the veil can be altered by adjusting the tension on the attached pull lines.

Room divider
Nylon elastic cord, nylon sailing cord
Location > the Netherlands
Available to order

Shades
Martin Born
German

'Shades' is a modular curtain system intended to manipulate daylight. Curved lengths of opaque textile are adjusted by a ceiling-mounted mechanism to control the daylight entering a room – from full to indirect exposure. 'The surfaces of a room become animated by being made responsive to natural light,' says Born. 'Shades' can also be used to divide interior space.

Room divider
Steel, fabric
mborn.com
Location > Finland/the Netherlands
In development

For another approach to the manipulation of light, see Daniel Rybakken's 'Daylight Comes Sideways' on p. 220.

Infinity
Samuel Accoceberry
French

This system is a new interpretation of the wall-mounted shelf. Just like a railway system, 'Infinity' is made up of tracks fixed upon a series of points, in this case brackets attached to the wall at intervals. This allows for a free-flowing installation of shelves that wind around interior walls. The shelving continues uninterrupted around angles or curves and can adapt to any interior architecture. The effect, says Accoceberry, is 'scenographic as much as functional'.

Shelving installation
Birch ply, metal, lacquered finish
www.samuelaccoceberry.com
Location > France
In development

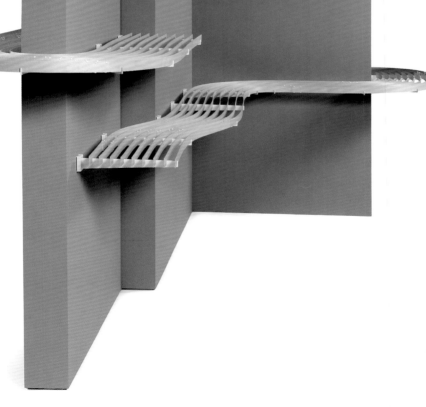

Entreciel
Sylvain Rieu-Piquet
French

It took Sylvain Rieu-Piquet two
years to realize this design for
a woven cane bed. The project
was to create a piece somewhere
between a nest, a mezzanine and
a shack, which would lift a bed
high above the ground leaving
floor space free for other uses.
Craftsmen more used to weaving
small cane baskets created this
giant 2.5 m (8 ft) structure, which
Rieu-Piquet describes as being
'near to nature.'

Mezzanine bed
Cane, steel
Location > France
In production
By > www.vannerie.com

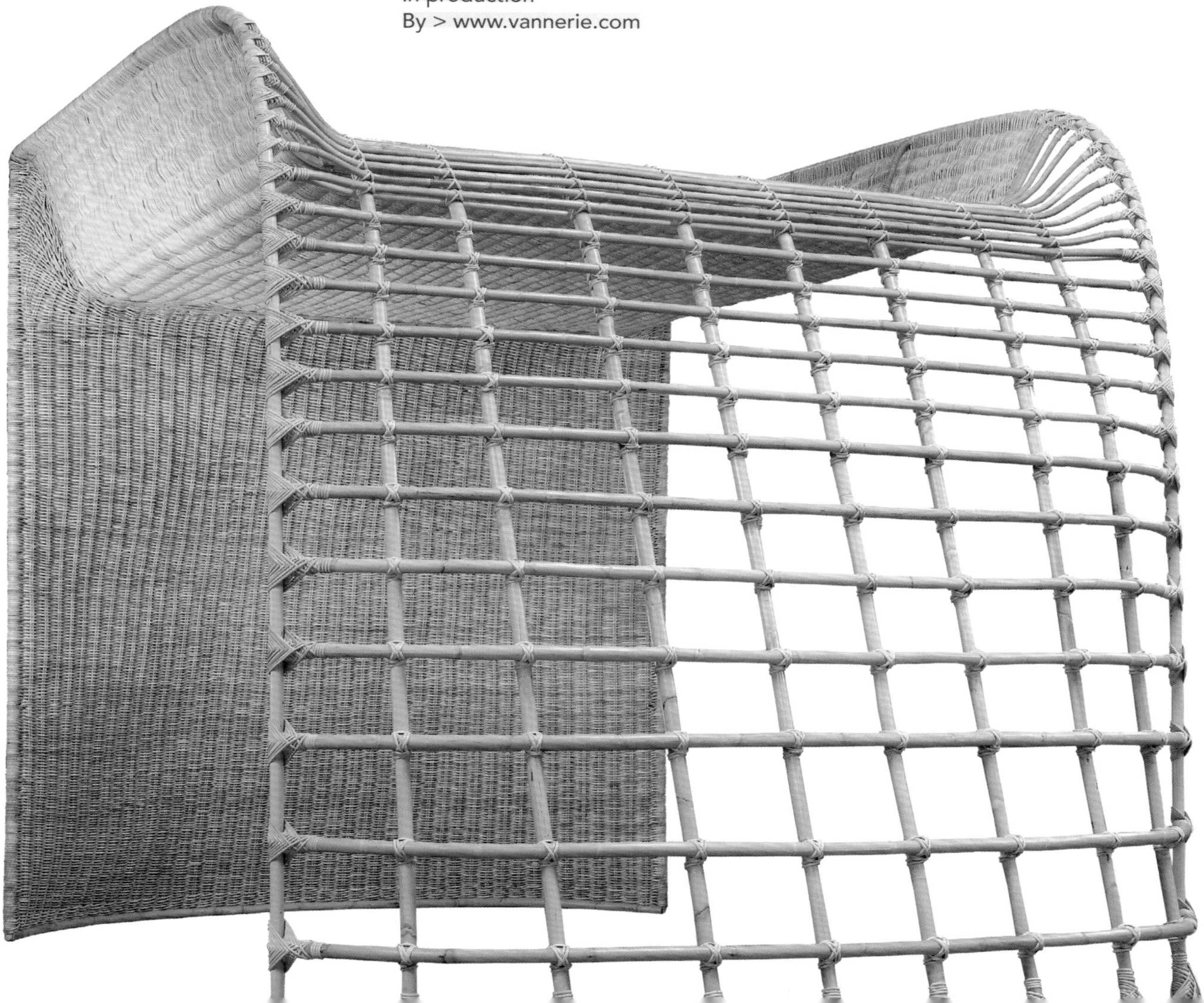

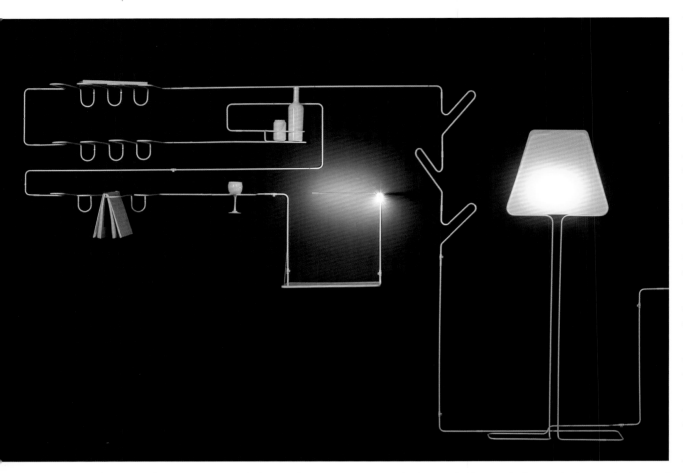

Another single structure that seeks to deal with all interior issues uniformly is 'Endoskeletons' on p. 324.

Line
Aykut Erol
Turkish

A single line extends indefinitely to create an entire interior system; a work table, coat rack, bookshelf and CD rack are all considered, as well as an integrated television stand and lighting. 'Line' is constructed from 1 cm (0.4 in.) thick aluminium bars fixed to interior walls and is able to meet basic furniture needs in one simple move.

Interior system
Aluminium
www.aykuterol.com
Location >Turkey
Available to order

Stuhlhockerbank
Yvonne Fehling,
Jennie Peiz
German

Fifteen different variants of the
'Stuhlhockerbank' benches are
available, but each shares the same
key characteristic: the division
between chair, stool and bench
has been eliminated. In its place is
one singular, mutated form. Fehling
and Peiz wanted to introduce a
narrative element to their design
– the 'Stuhlhockerbank' represents
a desire to interrupt and challenge
everyday public seating habits.
The benches are made for the
designers by a traditional German
chair manufacturer.

Seating installation
Oak, oil finish
www.kraud.de
Location > Germany
In production
By > designer

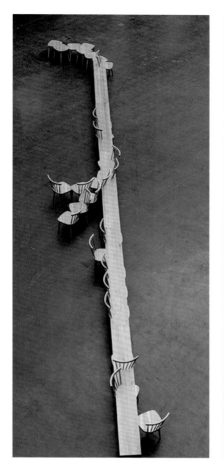

Instant Allotment
Louise Campbell
Danish/British

An idealistic design, the 'Instant Allotment' is designed to satisfy a variety of horticultural ambitions and is a reflection on the simple but often unfulfilled desire for a garden. The lightweight, mobile allotment is made from digitally printed textiles and offers its owners their own, albeit temporary, patch of green.

Boundary wall
Non-woven textile, quilting, bamboo
www.louisecampbell.com
Location > Denmark
Available to order

Willow Boughs
Christopher Pearson
British

Christopher Pearson has taken
'Willow Boughs', perhaps William
Morris' most renowned print, as
a subject for his series of projected
wallpapers. Pearson animates the
willow boughs of the design in a
short video, causing them to sway
and move and grow. Making a leap
from the handmade and traditional
to the technologically advanced,
Pearson accurately calls himself
a 'digital craftsman'.

Animated wallpaper projection
Projection
www.christopherpearson.com
Location > UK
Limited edition

Traditional iconography is used to promote
a cutting-edge technological application.
See also 'Speed Metal' on p. 250.

References

Glossary

Composites

Composites are engineered materials that constitute two or more existing materials with differing properties. This is a wide-ranging and expanding material palette that, thanks to new technology, offers an ever-increasing range of qualities, such as exceptional lightness, strength or pliability. Wood, carbon, glass, epoxy, ceramic and metals can all be used in composites, and plastic resins are commonly the binding component. The technology used in the manufacture of composite furniture and other products is frequently borrowed from innovations in other industries, such as aviation design.

Conceptual design

A form of design where the idea or concept behind the product (rather than its function) is its innovation and the principal motivation behind its creation, and is articulated as such. Conceptual design brings into question the role of function within contemporary design and stresses the idea of the designer as author.

Contemporary Arts and Crafts

The original Arts and Crafts movement was established during the late 19th and early 20th centuries. It was a reactionary cultural movement, championing the decorative arts and authentic craft manufacture against industrialization. Comparisons are increasingly drawn between this period in design history and a specific area of our current period: thanks to the resurgence and increased viability of the designer-maker, a return to craft production and rebellion against industrial processes is an important trend today.

Design art

This controversial term was coined to describe a specific type of design whose worth has begun to be measured in a similar way to that of contemporary art. The appearance of high-end design in art sales and galleries began the debate about whether this category existed. The discussion that has followed can be seen as the start of a wider discourse on what contemporary design is and where its parameters fall.

Designer-makers

This term has only recently entered the design vocabulary, but is now in widespread use. A designer-maker is a designer who produces their own work directly for market, rather than relying on a manufacturer to make it for them. Designer-makers apply craft manufacture to their work, but today this can include a wide range of new techniques beyond traditional skills.

The designer-maker is set apart from a traditional craftsperson by their self-valuation as a designer first and a maker second.

Digital craftsmen

In the work of the digital craftsmen, an interest in craft production and skills and the values with which they are associated collides with the possibilities for form and manufacture offered by digital design processes. This group of designers use a combination of computer software and craft techniques to produce contemporary forms with traditional qualities.

Frankenstein design

This term is sometimes applied to the popular trend for reappointing existing products and furniture – most often abandoned or trash products – to construct new designs. Using existing, found products as raw material offers designers an aesthetic choice that immediately suggests sustainability and recycling. It also brings nostalgia and sentimentality, which are inherent in existing objects, into a new design. The method of manufacture often includes the fusing together of furniture or products into a new, improved, rejuvenated form, hence the reference to Frankenstein.

Interactive product

Many designers seek to create an emotional attachment between object and person by creating products that respond to the presence or use of the consumer, so engaging them. This is most often a reaction to observations on the desensitized nature of contemporary culture. Designers may also seek to add value to their products or to educate the consumer in some way through such a relationship.

Limited edition

Products that are manufactured in a limited number, due to constraints imposed by the cost of or expertise in the manufacturing process, the materials or both. Limited edition designs have become a more widely recognized means of production; this is partly due to the fashion set by the established generation of designers, and leads to a recognized consumer-related desirability for individual, rare design pieces. Similarly, the trend for complex, hand-produced designs encourages limited-edition manufacturing techniques.

Modular designs

Modular works are a combination of individual units, rather than a fixed whole. Such designs are often developed as solution-driven products, offering either flexibility of use or ease of transportation and manufacture. Increasingly, modular products are championed because they encourage interaction between product and consumer as a by-product of their physical nature.

Monomaterial product

Limiting the number of materials used in a design – including any fixtures and fittings – to just one is a method employed to aid recycling and exaggerate the sustainable qualities of a product.

Rapid prototyping

This is the automatic construction of objects from computer-generated designs. The processes involved can create complex cross-sections without machining. Selective laser sintering, stereolithography and 3D printing are all popular variants of rapid prototyping. In all of these, the design is 'sliced' into thin cross-sections by the computer software, and these are then built in successive layers, each fused automatically to the last, to create the final shape. In 3D printing, each slice is printed and cured in turn on top of the last to form the final shape; in the other techniques, a laser traces the shape of each slice in turn in a liquid or powder, solidifying it. The process appeals to designers because of its ability to create almost any shape or geometric feature.

Reductionism

Reductionism is a particular school of design thinking and procedure that promotes function and engineering above all else. The design is reduced to its very core elements, at the expense of all decoration or unnecessary elements.

Sustainable design

In relation to contemporary design, sustainability is a goal that can be approached in any of several forms. Issues of sustainability can relate to the lifecycle or lifespan of a product, the materials that are chosen for its manufacture or the energy used in its production and transportation. Recently, efforts to achieve sustainability have started to be communicated in the outward form or function of a designed product. Similarly, a sustainable design might be a psychological or functional tool that facilitates the consumer's own sustainable activities in the face of energy consumption.

Contact information

5.5 Designers info@cinqcinqdesigners.com 275
16&12 contact@16et12.com 34

Aalto, Niina niina.aalto@taik.fi 262
Abe, Yuki yuki@howaboutviktor.com 71, 86
Accoceberry, Samuel akozign@hotmail.com 332
Adams, Annie otherannie@gmail.com 183
Aguiñiga, Tanya tanya@aguinigadesign.com 40
Airconditioned info@bytrico.com 253, 282
Akan, Erdem eakan@maybedesign.at 235
Alberdi info@outofstockdesign.com 31
Alkalay, Shay info@raw-edges.com 103, 106
Allen, Roger info@mioculture.com 329
Allmen, Raphaël von mail@raphaelvonallmen.com 72
Alonso, Tomás tomas@tomas-alonso.com 267
&made info@and-made.com 291
Anton, Siggi sgi@cu.is 143
Antonietti, Thomas thomas@thomasantonietti.com 238
Appelius, Julian mail@julianappelius.de 211
Ast, Jorre van info@jorrevanast.com 268, 318
Atelier Blink info@atelierblink.com 82
Aumaître, Johann presse@studiomanzano.fr 292

Bakırküre, Yesim y@ypstas.com 37
Bancroft, Helena miss-helena@hotmail.co.uk 251
Baptist, Maarten i@joine.nl 262
Bartels, Cris crisbartels@gmail.com 21
Bautier, Marina mail@lamaisondemarina.com 138
Beardshall, Jenny jenny.beardshall@alumni.rca.ac.uk 203
Becker, Daniel info@danielbecker.en 88
Berglund, Linus info@linusberglund.se 69
Bergmans, Pieke info@piekebergmans.com 229, 230
Bernabeifreeman info@bernabeifreeman.com.au 129, 165
Big-Game contact@big-game.ch 284
Bihain, Michael info@bihain.com 53
Böhne, Britta info@brittaboehne.de 287
Boo, Bram bramboo@skynet.be 75, 107
Boom, Judith van den info@judithvandenboom.nl 26, 323
Born, Martin info@mborn.com 124, 331
Bosch, Mareanne mareannebosch@gmail.com 138
Bovesse, Nicolas mail@nicolasbovesse.com 232
Bradley, Susan susan@susanbradley.co.uk 140
Braun, Mark info@markbraun.org 175, 261
Brogård, Hanna info@jba-design.se 218
Broom, Lee inof@leebroom.com 161
Brose, Joscha info@studiohausen.de 111
Brown, Jeremy jeremy@jeremybrowndesign.com 257
Brueckner, Christopher chris.brueckner@gmx.net 123
Bruninx, Johan Johan_bruninx@yahoo.com 156
Buchegger, Denoth, Feichtner office@bdf-ad.com 190
Bullus, Anna ab@annabullusdesign.com 23
Burggraf, Nicola loungelandscape@yahoo.de 91

Campbell, Louise studio@louisecampbell.com 337
Canet, César cesarcanet@hotmail.fr 62
Caperan, Fabien fabiencaperan@gmail.com 25

Cappello, Fabien contact@fabiencappello.com 188
Carbonell, Nacho info@nachocarbonell.com 85, 92
Carretero, Julien info@juliencarretero.com 98
Charlot, Michel michel.charlot@gmail.com 166
Chen, Min info@chenmindesign.com 156
Chi, Carina carina@carinachi.com 324
Chicherio, Gabriela gabriela@chicherio.com 246
Cihat, Sarah sarah@sarahcihat.com 235
Ciscar, Herme info@hermeymonica.com 100
Cullin, Mia mia@miacullin.com 141

Da Fonseca, Tiago mail@tiagodafonseca.com 147
Dayes, Céline contact@16et12.com 34
Degenhardt, Eric ask@eric-degenhardt.com 88
Delvigne, Guillaume guillaumedelvigne@hotmail.com 225
Deneufbourg, Benoît info@benoitdnb.com 129, 188
Depping, Line mail@linedepping.dk 139, 293
Derrider, Willem info@deridderdesignstudio.com 20
Design Drift info@designdrift.nl 65
Design Ship Tora info@designshiptora.com 212
d'Esposito, Martino desposito@despositogaillard.com 310
Dewez, Nathalie info@n-d.be 166
DFC Mexico City info@dfcasa.com 265
DIY Kyoto info@diykyoto.com 290
Duke, Ruby sather@hiveminddesign.com 30
Duke, Sather sather@hiveminddesign.com 30

Edmondson, Joel jedmon23@student.scad.edu 48
Eijk, Kiki van info@kikiworld.nl 38, 146
Eijk, Niels van info@ons-adres.nl 184, 232
El Oulhani, Mostapha mosweb7@hotmail.com 122
Emblin, David www.davidemblin.co.uk 33
Erdal, Eliz e.erdal@hotmail.co.uk 152
Ernstsen, Channa info@channa-ernstsen.nl 231
Erol, Aykut info@aykuterol.com 334
Estadieu, Alex alex_estadieu@yahoo.com 252
Eun, Oh Kyung kidi85@naver.com 247
Evans, Laura lauraeevans@hotmail.com 210

Fahmy, Shahira info@sfahmy.com 26
Farsen, Nina mail@ninafarsen.de 145
Faudet, Jochem info@jochemfaudet.com 198
Fehling, Yvonne mail@kraud.de 335
Feiz, Khodi info@feizdesign.com 214
Fernaeus, Jarl jarl@jarlfernaeus.se 132
Flavell, Frank frankflavell@hotmail.co.uk 78
Fleuren, Madieke info@madieke.com 230
Fokkink, Jesse info@jessefokkink.nl 154
Foussat, Eric eric.foussat@wanadoo.fr 143
Franco, Luciana Gonzalez loopaula@gmail.com 29
Fraser, Nick nick@nickfraser.co.uk 112
Freshwest Design info@freshwest.co.uk 253
Fries & Zumbühl mail@frieszumbuehl.ch 311
Frommeld, Max contact@ma-fro.com 127
Fujiwara, Keisuke hiramatsu@keisukefujiwara.com 68, 76
Fulguro info@fulguro.ch 307

Gaemers, Liane info@2design4.nl 297
Gagnaire, Valerian valerian_gagnaire@yahoo.fr 131
Gameren, Sarah van contact@sarahvangameren.com 251
Ganjavian, Ali info@tik-tac.com 310
García, Mónica info@hermeymonica.com 100
Garcia, Scott garcia_scott@hotmail.com 149
Gardener, David david@davidgardener.co.uk 189
Garzon, Jérôme djegarzon@gmail.com 122
Gast, Mareike info@mareikegast.de 79, 313
Geelen, Bas info@ordodb.com 294
Genton, Aude mail@audegenton.com 186, 240
Georgacopoulos, Alexis alexis@georgacopoulos.com 242
giffin'termeer info@p32.com 290
Ginder, Erich contact@erichginder.com 233
Girault, Gaële ggirault@designa4.ch 284
Giunta, Justin info@subversivejewelry.com 172
Gordijn, Lonneke info@designdrift.nl 65
Gövsa, Tugrul tugral@govsa.com 34, 142
Graas, David info@davidgraas.com 176
Greiling, Katrin info@katringreiling.com 174
Grew, Sofia sofia.grew@gmail.com 90
Grün, Charlotte charlotte@studio-ook.nl 327
Gschwendtner, Gitta gitta@gittagschwendtner.com 206
Gumpp, Hannes hg@hannesgumpp.com 130
Gunnlaughsdóttir, Gudrun Lilja gl@bility.is 126

Haar, Anna Ter annaterhaar@gmail.com 58
Hahn, Mathias info@mathiashahn.com 210, 315
Häll, Katarina info@katarinahall.se 102, 216
Hammerton, Catherine info@catherinehammerton.com 275
Hansandfranz info@hansandfranz.de 220
Harding, Matthew matthewharding@apex.net.au 84
Hardy, Christopher chris.hardy@canberra.edu.au 168
Harrison, James info@jamesdesignuk.co.uk 80
Harrison, Jon jon@jon-harrison.com 43
Hasan, Simon info@simonhasan.com 226
Hashimoto, Jun hashimoto_ju@ybb.ne.jp 71
Heikkilä, Mikael info@mikaelheikkila.com 141
Henriksson, Elisabeth info@elisabethhenriksson.se 167
Herkner, Sebastian info@sebastianherkner.com 80, 217
Herrenknecht, Joa joa@yoma.de 50
Heusser, Gabriel info@pervisioni.it 118
Heykoop, Pepe pepe@pepeheykoop.nl 43
Hildebrandt, Leslie leslieh@gmx.de 188
Hill, Demelza mail@demelzahill.com 61, 254
hivemindesign sather@hivemindesign.com 30
Hoegner, Christiane mail@christianehoegner.com 86
Hoff, Dick van dick@vanhoffontwerpen.nl 270
Hoffmann, Susanne loungelandscape@yahoo.de 91
Holt, Donald mail@holtclifforddesigners.com 315
Holt, Gemma gemma.holt@network.rca.ac.uk 308
Holzapfel, Martin info@holzapfel-moebel.de 142
Horrocks, Rachel rachel@rachelhorrocks.co.uk 325
Horsfall, Gaël info@gaelhorsfall.com 154
Hovers, Floris vorm@florishovers.nl 95
Hu, Yan huyan1978@hotmail.com 95

Hüttner, Mirjam mirjam.huettner@huettners.com 181
Hwang, Jin Sang jinsangh@gmail.com 295

IAFR (Interior Adventures for Real) info@iafr.nl 100
INOUT info@inoutdesigners.ch 28, 149
Interactive Institute info@tii.se 205
Irinarchos, Anna info@wisdesign.se 70
Irwin, David info@davidjirwin.co.uk 65

Järvinen, Elina elinatjarvinen@gmail.com 195
Jeglinska, Maria mail@mariajeglinska.com 125, 228
Jensen, Dorte Agergaard mail@dorteagergaard.dk 278
Jeppsson, Frida mail@fridajeppsson.se 51
Jirou-Najou, Joachim mail@joachimjirounajou.com 106
Jo, Daniel slowhanz@hotmail.com 249
Jukanovic, Admir info@jukanovic.de 115

Kaisin, Charles info@charleskaisin.com 67
Karlsson, Albin albin@albinkarlsson.com 300
Karvonen, Kaisa kaisa.karvonen@nuoska.org 248
Kawase, Kazuyuki kazu@link-design.org 137
Kayser, Aylin aylinkayser@yahoo.de 171
Kehrer, Cordula mail@cordulakehrer.de 97
Kellermann, Elina office@productlove.org 108
Kendall, Tracy info@tracykendall.com 277
Kim, Wanju contact@wanjukim.com 27
Kinmond, James info@jamesdesignuk.co.uk 80
Kirby, Chris info@chriskirbydesign.com 123, 170
Klauser & Carpenter info@klauserandcarpenter.com 187
Klauser, André info@andreklauser.com 301
Knecht, Tété ttknecht@bluewin.ch 63, 82
Knüppel, Silvia silviaknueppel@web.de 105
Kocx, Christian info@kocxontwerpen.nl 79, 302
Kogelnig, Paul info@pervisioni.it 118
Koivula, Jani jani@mutu.tv 56
Kools, Bas bas@baskools.com 256
Kostrzynski, Manuel info@rinsky.de 298
Koz, Defne defne@defnekoz.com 266
Kral, Tomas mail@tomaskral.ch 191
Kro, Ronen Ronenkro@hotmail.com 258
Küçükgürel, Kerem info@keremkucukgurel.com 68
Kuijpers, Ditte info@ordodb.com 294
Kumagaya, Akihiro info@alekole.jp 236
Kuramoto, Jin info@jinkuramoto.com 303
Kurrein, Lucy lucy@lucykurrein.com 158
Kwon, Hyock hmkhmk@gmail.com 120

Lai, Sylvia info@studioroom906.com 35
Lamb, Max max@maxlamb.org 46, 60
Lapierre, Arnaud contact@arnaud-lapierre.com 327
Larmaraud, Edouard info@larmaraud.com 201, 204
LauberDeAllegri info@lauberdeallegri.com 149
Laymond, Antoine lesdieuxvivants@free.fr 130
Lee, Kwangho spainbar@gmail.com 183, 273
Lee, Seongyong designlsy@gmail.com 260
Legge, Jonathan mail@jonathanlegge.com 27

Contact information

Leif.designpark italwoth@w4.dion.ne.jp 87
Le Moigne, Nicolas nicolas_lm@hotmail.com 28, 36
Lepistö, Tiia tiia.lepisto@nuoska.org 248
Li, Han huyan1978@hotmail.com 95
Libertiny, Tomás Gabzdil info@studiolibertiny.com 227, 229
Lie, Stefan contact@stefan-lie.com 240
Lifegoods info@lifegoods.ch 137
Lixfield, Alexa info@alexalixfeld.com 260
Ljungsten, Maria marialjungsten@gmail.com 50
Loebach, Paul paul@paulloebach.com 120, 250
Lopé, Jérôme presse@studiomanzano.fr 292
Lubbe, Miriam van der info@ons-adres.nl 184, 232
Lundmark, Malin malin@malinlundmark.com 102

McCarthy, Ben ben@benmccarthy.com 22
McConnell, Anna anna_mcconnell@hotmail.com 202
McElhinney, Ryan ryan@ryanmcelhinney.com 193
Made By Midas info@madebymidas.com 144
Maezm zeezeec@hotmail.com 59
Magee, Finn finn@finnmagee.com 221
Maggio info@outofstockdesign.com 31
Malouin, Philippe info@philippemalouin.com 135
Mantila, Mikael mikael@coolcorporation.fi 54
Marguerre, Eva info@eva-marguerre.de 24
Marie, Romuald contact@16et12.com 34
Marigold, Peter info@petermarigold.com 118, 319
Mathies, Arno mathiesarno@hotmail.com 54
Meesters, Jo post@jomeesters.nl 239
Megson, Richard richardmegsondesign@hotmail.co.uk 72
Meier, Martin isabelleolsson@gmail.com 215
Mer, Yael info@raw-edges.com 93
Meron, Alon alon@alonmeron.com 324
Meroz, Joana info@theornamentedlife.com 309
Merry, Alfonso amerry@mac.com 317
Metzner, Christian chrische.metzner@web.de 171
Meyer, Anita info@anitameyer.ch 306
Mike and Maaike info@mikeandmaaike.com 314
Milewicz, Luiza luiza@luminadesign.net 178
Millar, Andrew andrew.r.millar@gmail.com 63
Minale-Maeda office@minale-maeda.com 159
MIO info@mioculture.com 329
Misiak, Christine misiak2005@gmail.com 258
Mitrani, Vanessa contact@vanessamitrani.com 230
Mittra, Bikram bmittra@gmail.com 20
Mohaded, Cristian mohadedc@gmail.com 29
Moïse, Bernard moiseb@wanadoo.fr 57
Monchy, Laura de ldemonchy4@hotmail.com 207
Moorer, Eelko eelkomoorer@yahoo.com 226
Morel, Eric info@ericmorel.com 244
Mori, Takesui takesui@hotmail.co.jp 60
Moxham, Tony info@dfcasa.com 265
Muilwijk, Huib info@madebymidas.com 73
Mul, Marlie office@productlove.org 108
Muller, Claude mail@huettners.com 181
Munchausen philipperossetti@hotmail.com 276

Murakoshi, Jun mail@junmurakoshi.com 121
Murphy, Mike timestable@formular.com.au 150

Nakamura, Ryuji info@ryujinakamura.com 243
Narud, Oscar Magnus oscar@oscarnarud.com 113
Nash, Heath elevator3000@mweb.co.za 248
Nauta, Ralph info@designdrift.nl 65
NEL info@nel.com.mx 286
Nemme, Anton timestable@formular.com.au 150
Nenonen, Marko marko@howaboutviktor.com 180
Nieuwendijk, Wouter info@wouternieuwendijk.nl 105
Nigro, Philippe phil@philippenigro.com 90
Nilsson, Carina design@70F.com 280
Nistelrooy, Henny van info@hennyvannistelrooy.com 77
Normal Studio contact@normalstudio.fr 146, 271
Nosigner info@nosigner.com 164
Nunn, Joe www.tobeofuse.org 76

Office Origin Air info@officeoriginair.com 30
Oirschot, Suzanne van suzannevanoirschot@gmail.com 105
Oki, Emiko emikooki@aol.com 239, 264
Olsson, Isabelle Isabelleolsson@gmail.com 215
Ona, Hideyuki walkstation1983@gmail.com 25
Ong, Steffi steffiong@gmail.com 316
Oooms info@oooms.nl 174
Oshiro, Kensaku info@kensakuoshiro.com 32
Outofstock info@outofstockdesign.com 31
Ovalle, Liliana info@lilianaovalle.com 92, 224

Paniagua, Mauricio info@dfcasa.com 265
Pawlofsky, Tom tom.pawlofsky@gmx.de 173
Pearson, Christopher studio@christopherpearson.com 337
Pegasiou, George gpegasiou@urban-shed.com 201, 311
Peiz, Jennie mail@kraud.de 335
PeLi Design info@pelidesign.com 157
Pelikan, Alexander peli@pelidesign.com 157
Perryman, Laura lauraperryman@hotmail.com 73
Philippson, Susanne info@philippson.org 148
Pliessnig, Matthias pliessnig@wisc.edu 44
Polka office@polkaproducts.com 269
Portilla-Kawamura, Key info@tik-tac.com 299
Praet, Jens info@jenspraet.com 101
Price, Ashley Design@ashleypricedesign.co.uk 96
Price, Tom info@tom-price.com 83

Quiroga, Isabel info@isabelquiroga.com 128

Raay, Bas van bas@vraay.com 297
Rahm, Marie office@polkaproducts.com 269
Rampelotto, Patrick design@patrickrampelotto.com 192
Reichert, Steffen loungelandscape@yahoo.de 91
Reinhardt, Nico loungelandscape@yahoo.de 91
Rice Design info@rice-design.com 195
Riehling, Philippe riehling@hotmail.com 52
Rieu-Piquet, Sylvain srieupiquet@hotmail.com 333
Rijswijck, Lonny van info@ateliernl.com 255

Robling, Karin info@karinrobling.se 216
Roeder, Tina info@tinaroeder.com 254
Roije, Frederik info@roije.com 312
Rönkönharju, Saana sannamaria@hotmail.com 50
Rooijackers, Björn post@bjornr.com 127
Rovero, Adrien mail@adrienrovero.com 22, 243
Rowe, Adam adam@adamrowedesign.com 78
Rusydin, Haris roosydinharis@gmail.com 46
Rybakken, Daniel me@danielrybakken.com 132, 220

Salm, Jaime info@mioculture.com 329
Salvatore, Daniel Marcelo salvatoredaniel@ciudad.com.ar 259
Sato, Tomohiko info@tomohikosato.com 117
Scheublin, Wouter wouterscheublin@yahoo.com 151
Schlierkamp, Tanja tanja.schlierkamp@gmail.com 42
Schneck, Shane ss@shaneschneck.com 55
Schöllhammer, Isabel mail@farsen-schoellhammer.de 145
Scholz, Philipp pscholz@hfg-karlsruhe.de 237
Schwarzbauer, Bernhard contact@bernhardschwarzbauer.com 41
Sdesignunit sdesignunit@hotmail.com 293
Sealac office@sealac.com 110, 209, 296
Seitz, Mats info@matsseitz.com 69
Sekisaka, Tatsuhiro info@hitsujiame.com 117, 305
Sellars, Moko moko@mokosellars.com 28
Seng, Judith mail@judithseng.de 134
Seyppel, Milia info@frenchknicker.de 213
Sies, Sjoerd Info@sjoerdsies.com 109
Sigel, Marcel marcel@zuii.com 194
Singer, Monica office@polkaproducts.com 269
Sionis, Fred fred.sionis@gmail.com 122
Slater, John info@john-slater.com 133
Smånsk Design Studio inga@smansk.com 155
Smith, Nick nick@nicksmithfurniture.co.uk 261
Smith, Oliver info@oliversmith.com.au 266
Sonnleitner, Katrin info@katrin-sonnleitner.com 98, 281
Southcott, Robert rob@robsouthcott.com 47
Spitshuis, Lidewij hallo@lidewij.net 234
Staps, Marieke mariekestaps@hotmail.com 198
Sterk, Nadine info@ateliernl.com 179
Steverlynck, Diane info@dianesteverlynck.be 276
StokkeAustad info@stokkeaustad.com 81, 224
Strasser, Laura info@frenchknicker.de 213
Studio Gorm mail@studiogorm.com 99, 176
Studio Libertiny info@studiolibertiny.com 229
Studioroom906 info@studioroom906.com 35
Subic, Rainer info@pinkpinguin.com 115
SWAMP douglas.easterly@vuw.ac.nz, mck16@psu.edu 302

TAF info@tafarkitektkontor.se 158, 328
Takeuchi, Shigeichiro shige@shigeichiro.com 212
Takkinen, Jussi jussi@jussitakkinen.com 42
Tan+Chua info@outofstockdesign.com 31
Terada, Naoki info@teradadesign.com 168
Thaler, Harry thalerharry@hotmail.com 299
Thomas, Anna mail@loyalloot.com 245
Tiem, Greetje van info@greetjevantiem.nl 272

Tilbury, Oliver ot@olivertilbury.com 114
Todo Design mail@tododesign.com 110
Toida, Yu walkstation1983@gmail.com 25
Tolstrup, Nina info@studiomama.com 160
Tolvanen, Mika info@mikatolvanen.com 216
Tromp, Jan jan@valvomo.com 173
Tsagkas, Kostas kostastsagkas@yahoo.com 44
Tseng, Wen-Ting frank791376@hotmail.com 75
Tsuboi, Hironao info@100per.com 177
Tsujimura, Tetsuya t-t@t-products.jp 219

Ünal & Böler Studio info@ub-studio.com 153

Vaahtera, Merit Milla meritmilla@hotmail.com 49
Vaskivuori, Rane rane@valvomo.com 209
Vaugh, Shannon studio@vaughshannon.com 204
Vautrin, Ionna ionnavautrin@hotmail.com 225
Vince, Edward ed@kith-kin.co.uk 170
Vinta info@vinta.jp 304
Vladimir, Jaccard vladimir.jaccard@gmail.com 313
Volksware silkewawro@gmx.de 150, 279
Vugt, Lucas van lucasvanvugt@gmail.com 331

Wahl, Katharina info@katharinawahl.de 283, 322
Wai, Hunn info@hunnwai.com 66
Warren, William william@williamwarren.co.uk 104
Watanabe, Yuta info@yutawatanabe.com 306, 308
Wech, Jason jason@jasonwech.com 74
West, Katy katy@katywest.co.uk 126
Whatels els@whatels.net 55, 187
Widén, Lisa info@wisdesign.se 70
Wieringen, Laurens van info@laurensvanwieringen.nl 197
Willems, Frank frank@frankwillems.net 81
Willenz, Sylvain info@sylvainwillenz.com 185
Wilson, Duncan duncan@duncan-wilson.com 89
Winkel, Dirk mail@dirkwinkel.com 39, 144
Woldhek, Els els@whatels.net 55, 187
Wood, Bethan Laura heinzmeanzbeanz@yahoo.co.uk 257
Wu, Wei-Cheng charles.woo@mas.hinet.net 75

Xavier, Rui mail@ruixavier.ch 196
Xu, Yanbo loungelandscape@yahoo.de 91

Yamaguchi, Makoto mail@ymgci.net 96
Yar, Pinar pinaryar@gmail.com 34, 142

Materials

3D oak veneer **96**
3D polyester mesh **91**

aluminium **22, 28, 43, 54, 72, 75, 101, 117, 120, 129, 130, 132, 138, 143, 149, 153, 165, 180, 181, 188, 190, 194, 196, 210, 214, 216, 219, 228, 251, 267, 271, 295, 307, 310, 327, 334**
acrylic **167, 226, 282, 302**
acrylic half mirror **219**
acrylobutadiene styrene **168**
acrylonitrile butadiene styrene **295, 296**
aluminium, anodized **299**
ash **43, 65, 89, 139, 151, 210, 315**

bamboo **337**
basswood **120**
bean-starch vermicelli **164**
beech **30, 32, 55, 66, 70, 78, 100, 118, 121, 135, 147, 307, 327**
beech ply **52, 78**
beeswax **227**
Bic® refill **308**
biodegradable composites **311**
birch **42, 49, 69, 71, 95, 99, 132**
birch ply **44, 69, 121, 145, 146, 332**
bonding agent **72**
books **314**
borosilicate glass **166, 264, 265, 298, 299**
brass **47, 76, 112, 149, 195, 235, 240, 297**
brick **118**
bronze **46**
bronze alloy **250**
brown paper tape **156**
bungee cord **113**

camphorwood **315**
cane **27, 333**
canvas **130**
car paint **228**
cardboard **29, 137, 176, 302, 329**
cement, fibre-reinforced **36**
ceramic **26, 28, 34, 126, 146, 230, 232, 236, 243, 251, 252, 257, 258, 270, 271, 307, 316, 323**
china **251, 253, 327**
china, bone **253, 257**
clay **249, 255**
coal **206**
coating **73**
composite **34**
concrete **113, 149**
copolyester sheet **220**
copper **112, 198, 224, 230, 235, 297**
copper finish **187**
Corian® **43, 132, 146, 168, 310**
cork **243**
cotton **89, 141, 201, 204**
cotton webbing **27**

Creacrete™ concrete **260**
crystal **172, 183**

deal **95**
double-sided tape **54**

ebony **34**
elastic **88**
elastic textile **300**
electric cable **182**
electronics **302**
enamel **175, 210, 269**
epoxy **239**
epoxy lacquer **201**
epoxy resin **24**
eternit fibre cement **166**
extruded terracotta **122**

fabric **139, 331**
fat **313**
felt **63, 114, 121, 239, 273, 283, 286, 325**
fibre cement **313**
fibreboard **95, 102**
fire hose **25**
flock **79**
flock velvet **240**
foam **25, 31, 55, 81, 85, 88, 90, 105, 188**
foam coating **81**
Formica® laminate **105**

galvanized metal wire **154, 248**
gel coat **143**
glass **131, 141, 174, 177, 196, 198, 203, 207, 214, 225, 229, 230, 252, 257, 262**
glass fibre **24, 48, 295**
glass-reinforced acrylonitrile butadeine styrene **260**
glass-reinforced plastic **50, 84, 90, 91, 212**
glaze **34, 249**
glazed earthenware **232**
glue **239**
goat leather **110**
gold foil **184**

hardwood **106, 134, 314, 319**
hook-and-loop tape **325**

ink **170**
iron **145, 248, 306**

kalopanax wood **304**

lacquer **30, 31, 40, 42, 69, 71, 100, 102, 106, 107, 108, 158, 161, 188, 204, 234, 239, 328, 332**
lacquered steel **158**
laminate **48, 74, 129**
laminated birch **47**
laminated scrap material **30**
laminated teak **20**

latex **81, 82, 92, 185**
latex foam **88**
lead **145**
leather **20, 38, 55, 60, 78, 80, 127, 148, 174, 209, 217, 226**
linen thread **226**

magnets **108, 148, 247**
mahogany **161**
maple **117, 120, 156, 245**
medium density fibreboard (MDF) **23, 26, 95, 100, 102, 104, 105, 109, 121, 127, 128, 133, 142, 143, 144, 201, 305**
melamine veneer **95**
meranti **95**
metal **37, 108, 127, 139, 141, 154, 167, 176, 177, 188, 192, 195, 205, 252, 258, 290, 303, 332**

neon **161**
newspaper **272**
nylon **40, 145, 277, 331**

oak **23, 30, 44, 79, 80, 96, 114, 138, 146, 154, 158, 270, 306, 308, 335**
oil finish **30, 335**
opal glass **218**
optical fibres **178**
OSB **78, 100**

paint **32, 53, 54, 55, 70, 71, 109, 110, 125, 130, 143, 155, 166, 170, 195, 209, 297**
paper **61, 67, 93, 101, 108, 121, 170, 189, 206, 229, 239, 275, 276, 277, 317**
paraffin wax **171**
pigment **98, 230**
pigmented epoxy clay **66**
pine **27, 30, 102, 157, 160, 315**
plant **302**
plastic **21, 83, 108, 110, 117, 146, 157, 176, 185, 192, 193, 206, 207, 244, 247, 268, 293, 294, 299, 309**
plexiglass **64**
plywood **34, 42, 48, 49, 53, 55, 56, 57, 65, 68, 73, 79, 95, 100, 103, 107, 110, 114, 118, 123, 128, 137, 150, 156, 159, 184, 328**
polyamide **77, 224, 235**
polycarbonate **168, 173, 185, 209, 290, 293, 296**
polycotton **278**
polyester **115, 276, 280, 313**
polyethylene **22, 51, 248**
polyethylene terphthalate **73**
polymer **318**
polypropylene **39, 72, 83, 86, 106, 135, 178, 186, 187, 290, 295**
polyrey laminate **23**
polystyrene **73, 82, 86, 108, 117, 124, 254**

polyurethane 43, 58, 60, 70, 87, 90, 93, 98, 124, 130, 135, 168, 193, 226, 322
polyvinylchloride (PVC) 115
poplar 30
porcelain 62, 218, 225, 233, 235, 237, 238, 246, 254, 256, 259, 261, 266, 312
powder-coated finish 38, 54, 71, 75, 97, 111, 120, 129, 140, 142, 143, 149, 165, 180, 181, 187, 204, 205, 210, 215, 216, 242, 261, 292, 301, 307, 310
press board 123
projection 337

quilting 337

rattan 46
resin 77, 101, 243, 262, 303
rice paper 240
rope 113, 315
rotating colour wheel 178
rubber 72, 85, 135, 281, 290, 316

sand 86, 92
sandstone 60
satin 278
screen-print ink 128, 301
secondhand jigsaw pieces 277
secondhand materials 202
secondhand textiles 279
seeds 313
semi-transparent acrylic 220
sheet metal 318
silicon carbide 271
silicone 174, 183, 212, 226, 287, 291, 306
silk 210
silver 170
soft-touch polyurethane 41, 216
soil 198, 302
spring metal 308, 318
stain 69, 71
stainless steel 20, 25, 42, 115, 126, 129, 142, 148, 149, 165, 171, 191, 198, 266, 297, 298, 313, 315, 331
steel 27, 31, 33, 38, 40, 41, 43, 50, 54, 66, 71, 72, 74, 75, 80, 81, 88, 92, 97, 106, 107, 111, 112, 114, 124, 125, 129, 131, 133, 138, 140, 141, 143, 144, 145, 151, 166, 170, 171, 175, 179, 180, 187, 188, 201, 202, 204, 210, 212, 215, 217, 242, 261, 269, 292, 297, 299, 301, 307, 319, 324, 328, 333
stereolithography resin 308
stone 192
straw 63, 82, 239
suede 31
sycamore 57, 76, 98
synthetic pile 286

teak veneer 143
Teflon® coating 299

terracotta 234
textile 21, 30, 50, 59, 60, 73, 80, 81, 82, 86, 87, 88, 159, 204, 248, 337
thermoplastic remnants 79
thread 68, 275
titanium 76
transfers 232
tubular steel 133

upholstery 60, 324
urethane rubber 226

varnish 57, 128
vinyl 197
visco-elastic polyurethane foam 89
viscose 149
vulcanized paper 25

wallpaper 93
walnut 30, 92, 117, 157, 210
water 198
wax 206, 251
whitened oak veneer 53
wick 251
wood 26, 33, 34, 46, 49, 56, 58, 63, 67, 68, 75, 80, 81, 87, 88, 90, 98, 106, 113, 118, 125, 127, 130, 131, 132, 144, 150, 152, 155, 156, 158, 192, 193, 201, 203, 206, 216, 236, 240, 248, 300, 318, 324
wool 63, 90, 106, 179, 284, 286, 325

Xorel® textile 173, 209

zinc 198
zip-ties 46, 248

Designer locations

Argentina
29, 31, 259

Australia
129, 150, 165, 168, 178, 240, 266, 315

Austria
190, 192, 269

Belgium
53, 67, 75, 79, 82, 86, 107, 129, 138, 156, 166, 185, 188, 232, 276, 284

Canada
47, 245

China
35, 95

Denmark
50, 60, 84, 139, 276, 278, 293, 337

Egypt
26

Finland
42, 49, 54, 56, 71, 86, 90, 124, 141, 173, 180, 195, 209, 216, 248, 252, 262, 331

France
34, 52, 57, 62, 90, 106, 110, 122, 125, 130, 143, 146, 188, 201, 204, 209, 225, 228, 230, 271, 275, 284, 292, 327, 332, 333

Germany
24, 33, 39, 41, 50, 79, 80, 88, 91, 97, 98, 105, 111, 123, 130, 134, 142, 144, 145, 148, 171, 173, 175, 181, 188, 211, 213, 217, 220, 237, 244, 254, 260, 261, 281, 283, 287, 298, 313, 322, 335

Hong Kong
22

Iceland
126, 143

Indonesia
46

Ireland
204

Israel
258

Italy
32, 90, 101, 118, 156, 266, 299

Japan
25, 68, 71, 76, 87, 96, 117, 121, 123, 137, 164, 168, 170, 177, 195, 212, 219, 236, 238, 243, 303, 304, 305, 306, 308

Korea
183, 247, 249, 260, 273, 293, 296

Luxembourg
181

Mexico
92, 224, 265, 286

Netherlands
20, 21, 30, 35, 38, 43, 44, 55, 58, 65, 73, 81, 85, 92, 95, 98, 100, 101, 105, 108, 109, 115, 124, 127, 128, 138, 144, 146, 150, 151, 154, 157, 159, 174, 176, 179, 184, 187, 197, 198, 207, 213, 214, 227, 229, 230, 231, 232, 234, 239, 255, 262, 270, 272, 279, 280, 294, 297, 302, 309, 312, 327, 330, 331

New Zealand
302

Norway
224

Singapore
31, 66

South Africa
248

South Korea
59

Spain
31, 100, 299, 310, 317

Sweden
51, 55, 69, 70, 81, 102, 132, 141, 155, 158, 167, 174, 205, 215, 216, 218, 220, 300, 324, 328

Switzerland
22, 25, 28, 36, 54, 63, 72, 82, 131, 137, 166, 186, 191, 196, 215, 240, 242, 243, 246, 284, 306, 307, 310, 311, 313

Taiwan
75

Turkey
34, 37, 68, 142, 153, 235, 266, 334

UK
20, 23, 26, 27, 28, 31, 33, 42, 43, 46, 60, 61, 63, 65, 72, 73, 76, 77, 78, 80, 83, 89, 93, 96, 103, 104, 106, 112, 113, 114, 117, 118, 120, 126, 127, 133, 135, 140, 147, 149, 152, 154, 158, 160, 161, 170, 187, 188, 189, 193, 194, 198, 201, 202, 203, 206, 210, 221, 226, 239, 251, 253, 254, 256, 257, 258, 261, 264, 267, 268, 275, 277, 290, 291, 295, 301, 308, 311, 315, 316, 318, 319, 323, 324, 325, 337

USA
30, 40, 44, 48, 74, 99, 110, 120, 172, 176, 183, 233, 235, 250, 266, 290, 302, 314, 329

Index

118 **25**
1, 4 **219**
(nothing to) HIDE **20**
£250 Million Topless Table **147**
1 X 1 **160**
2D-Furniture **105**
3 Poäng **215**
5pm in the Spring **76**
800mm Chair Series **73**

A Restless Chairacter **43**
A Stacking Homage **39**
A4 **90**
A4 lamp shade **170**
accessories, cooking **268, 298, 299, 309**
accessories, decorative **242, 244, 245, 246, 247, 248, 249, 265, 302, 309, 314, 316, 317, 318, 325**
accessories, tabletop **264, 268, 269, 270, 306**
Accidentels **187**
Adam Wardrobe **111**
Adapt **127**
All About Hanging **117**
Alma **306**
Amorphous Lamps **183**
Apartment **260**
Around **106**
Ash and Corian Chair **43**
Avestruz **259**
AWARE Laundry Lamp **205**
A-Zero **310**

B45 **213**
Backstage **107**
Bag stuck in a tree light **170**
Barbaric Cut **266**
Basic Baroque **325**
Bastard **55**
bed **333**
Being Floorlamp **209**
bench **34, 35, 36, 37, 159, 335**
Bench for two **34**
Benches [Sylvia Lai] **35**
Bespoke **210**
Big Dipper chandelier **251**
birdhouse, birdfeeder **312, 313**
Birdy **313**
Björn **306**
Black Candy **322**
Blockhead **42**
Boa-constrictor **216**
Boox **95**
Borrod **139**
bowl **232, 234, 235, 236, 239, 261**
Bowl [Alexa Lixfield] **260**
Boxed Body **127**
Brace Angle Furniture **131**
Branch Stools **27**
Brick-a-bowl **234**

Brickshelf **118**
Brodie Table **129**
Bronze Poly Chair **46**
Budak **153**
Buitenbeentje **58**
Bulging Box **96**
Bullet **54**
Bureau [Martin Holzapfel] **142**
Butterfly **68**

Caba **273**
cabinet **95, 100, 101, 102, 105, 106, 107, 109, 156**
Cable Carpet **287**
Cage Lamps **201**
Calamare Light **173**
Calimero **298**
Campanula **180**
candle holder **250, 251, 264, 318**
Carpet [Carina Nilsson] **280**
Cast Iron Pot **306**
Ceramic Paper **236**
Ceramiko **28**
Chainwork Porcelain Bowl **235**
chair **31, 39, 40, 42, 43, 44, 46, 47, 48, 49, 50, 51, 52, 53, 54, 55, 56, 57, 58, 60, 61, 62, 63, 65, 66, 67, 68, 69, 70, 71, 72, 73, 74, 75, 76, 77, 78, 81, 120, 121, 123, 144, 154, 157, 158, 161, 335**
Chair [Frida Jeppsson] **51**
chaise **82, 90, 91**
chandelier **159, 251**
Character Lamps **203**
Cheap Cheap **220**
Chip Chair **74**
Chorus **249**
Clampology **318**
Clipping Rod **191**
clock **300, 301, 304, 305**
clothes line **327**
Cloud **276**
Clutter Shelf **123**
CMYK **242**
coat hanger **113, 244, 327**
Coat hanger [Eric Morel] **244**
Coma **190**
Construction Chandelier **172**
Containership Powersupply **290**
ContemPlates **253**
Coulure **130**
Creep **140**
Cup **88**
Cushion [Matthew Harding] **84**
Cushion [Office Origin Air] **30**
Cut 'n' Paste **73**
cutlery **266, 267**

Daylight Comes Sideways **220**
Dazzle 003 **100**
desk **133, 138, 142, 143, 151**

Desk and Chair **138**
Digital Clock #2 **300**
Digital Dishes **237**
dining table **128, 131, 151**
Discu **144**
Divide It **310**
Divider (no.10) **328**
Dividing Veil **331**
Do Re Mi **76**
Dog Bowl **65**
Double Backed **65**
Drain Eye-Catcher **309**
Drawer **96**
drawers **96, 102, 103, 106**
Dream of sand **92**
dressing table **146**
Drückeberger **105**

Easel Chair **70**
easy chair **41, 78, 79, 80, 81, 82, 83, 84, 85, 86**
Ebb Table **132**
Elbow Room **65**
Embedded Meanings Side Table **149**
Endoskeletons **324**
energy display **290**
Entreciel **333**
Eternit **36**
Everyday Sunday **262**
extension socket **290, 291, 292, 293**

Fabbrica del vapore **225**
Fairy, tale **126**
fan **306**
Five **23**
Flame Lamps **206**
Flexible Ceramics **256**
Flexible Light **212**
Flock & Brass **240**
floor covering **322, 323**
Floor Flower **212**
floor lamp **195, 202, 203, 204, 205, 206, 207, 209, 210, 211, 212, 213, 214, 216, 217**
Floor Motion **323**
Flor **246**
Flower Vases **224**
Flowers **181**
Flutter **275**
Foldable **128**
Fono Light **187**
Forest Vase **224**
Fortuna **192**
Fossile **122**
Frank Desk **133**
From Above **315**
Fuga **37**
Fukidashi Box **240**
Fullcolourball **248**
Fusion **261**

Index

Garav Teapot **258**
GH (Bic) Pens **308**
Ghost Chair **65**
Giraffe **195**
Glas Gib Gas **299**
Glassbulb Light **174**
Gold Toy Lamp **193**
Gori Stool **27**
Grace Duo **110**
Grace Table **135**
Grandma's Revenge **141**
Grid Vases **228**

Hadji Bowl **235**
Hairy Chair **67**
hall stand **112, 114**
Hall Stand [Nick Fraser] **112**
Hallstand [Oliver Tilbury] **114**
Hanabi **86**
hanging lamp **164, 165, 166, 167, 168, 170, 171, 172, 173, 174, 175, 176, 178, 179, 180, 181, 183, 184, 185, 306**
Hanging Out **154**
hanging system **115, 245, 315, 327**
Happy Lamp **204**
Happy Porcelain **254**
Hardwood Wingback **80**
Hat Plate **239**
Heat Me **299**
Heatingpoint **297**
Heavy Metal Table **143**
High Amphora, Jug, Pot **232**
Hoist **113**
Holy Homes **312**
hooks **315, 327**
Hotspot **184**
humidifier **296**
Hunting Lines **88**

Ikarus **171**
Image Collection **230**
Infinity **332**
Informal Dining Range **158**
InnerTube **185**
Insect Cage **243**
Instant Allotment **337**
Interior Dialogue **278**
Interior Furniture **126**
interior installation **307, 324, 334**
Intersection **90**
InterVases **231**
Irak **286**
iron **311**
itti & ette **79**

Jar Tops **268**
Je m'appelle Moustache **174**
Jewellery Drawer **102**
Jigsaw Wallpaper **277**
JU87-G STUKA **283**

Jungle Vase **226**
Juxtaposed: Religion Curated bookshelf **314**

Kate Chair **80**
Keyboard **148**
KuKunochi **87**

La désinvolture **327**
La Liseuse **188**
Ladycross Sandstone Chair **60**
Lamp and Table Adapted **202**
Lamp, Lamp **177**
Landscape **284**
Launch Stool **22**
Le bureau cube **143**
Le Cercle Lumineux **209**
Le Coffre **110**
Leather Vases **226**
Left or Right BIG **211**
Leggs **317**
Letters **25**
Lia **149**
Light Box **201**
lighting **160, 177, 198, 201, 307**
Lighting Bug **176**
LIINA chair **50**
Line **334**
Lingor **175**
Lockvogel **313**
Loop Chair Series **75**
Lost Model **188**
Lotus **261**
Louise **262**
Lounge Landscape **91**
Lux_it **252**

Magazine Mixte **95**
Magnet Light **198**
Maneki Chair **71**
Mary Joe 2 **188**
Materialized Vase **233**
Max **115**
Meltdown Series **83**
Meterware Carpet **279**
Meterware Table **150**
Miles rug **284**
mirror **159, 161**
mme **60**
Möbelette **98**
Mold Lamp **166**
Molto Beene **33**
Monsieur DressUp **245**
Mosquito **53**
Mu **156**
Mugroso **92**
My Truss **54**

Nabeshima Variations **253**
Néo Noé **52**

Neo Rococo **155**
NeoNeon **161**
Nido **24**
Ninho **100**
Nix **123**
Nomad Architectural System **329**
Non-woven **79**
Not A Box **176**
Nuoska **248**
Nymphéas **129**

occasional table **129, 140, 141, 149, 152**
Octopus **82**
Office **108**
One Day Paper Waste **101**
Oona **97**
Orlando **306**
P'tite Lulu **57**
Packaging Lamp **189**
Pantheon Light **168**
Paper Vases **229**
Patches **134**
Patchwork Pieces **152**
Pearl **218**
Peg Pencil **308**
Petal Spoons **266**
Pétrifié en porcelaine **62**
Pimp **22**
Pinno hooks and shelves **315**
Pint Glass Series **264**
Pivot **106**
Plakbanterie **156**
plant pot **246, 247**
Plastic Back Chair **72**
Plu **293**
plug **293**
Plug **217**
Plug Brother **293**
Plus Collection **142**
Plus de Madam Rubens **81**
Ply-Ply **56**
PointOfView Cabinet **109**
Points de vue **276**
Polka Pots **269**
Portable Humidifier **296**
pots and pans **269, 306**
Pouf de Paille **82**
PowerBlock **292**
Pressing Matters **311**
Profile Shelves **125**
Pro-injection-table **130**
Prop **319**
Public Garden **232**
Pulp **239**
Pulp Everyday **61**
Pump it up **85**
PuzzlePerser **281**

Qing Zuo! **26**
Quilt Chair **38**

Quilt Stool 38
R.A.W. Chair 46
radiator 297
radio 294
Radio dB 294
Recycling Daily News 272
Re-love project 1 59
rocking chair 38
Rolling 243
RU Chair 55
Rubber Up 72
rug 279, 280, 281, 282, 283, 284, 286, 287

Sandbank 86
Save 102
Science Series Glassware 265
Seam Lights 165
Seeking To Embellish 316
Serie 137
Shades 331
Shadow Lamp 204
Shed 99
Shelf Space 120
shelving 95, 118, 120, 121, 122, 123, 124, 125, 126, 127, 142, 314, 315, 318, 319, 332
Shelving Chair 121
Shuffle Chair, The 42
sideboard 104
Silent Chair 69
Sissi 63
Skinny 194
Skinterior 21
Sled 49
Sleeping Beauty 179
Snap and Dine 254
Snowbench 89
sofa 59, 86, 87, 88, 89, 90, 92, 93
Soft dressing table 146
Softy 197
Soil Lamp 198
Solid Honey-comb System 137
space divider 328, 329, 331, 336
speakers 249, 303
Speed Metal 250
Splinter 141
Spool Chair THONET #14 68
Spore 1.1 302
SpringRain 164
Stack 103
Stack Stool 30
Stackbox 124
Stain 257
Stamp Cutlery 267
Standby Extension 291
Stella 166
Stile Stool 33
Stitched Chair 77
stool 20, 21, 22, 23, 24, 25, 26, 27, 28, 29, 30, 31, 32, 33, 38, 157

Stool [Kensaku Oshiro] 32
Stool Vacuum Cleaner 295
storage 96, 97, 98, 99, 108, 110, 117, 127, 137, 154, 155, 156, 161, 240, 243, 306, 319
Streamer 41
Stuhlhockerbank 335
Subconscious 132
Sunda 173
Suppenkaspar 145
Supper 303
Survival Furniture 159
Swirl Light 178

table 22, 23, 24, 33, 36, 37, 129, 130, 132, 134, 135, 137, 138, 139, 142, 143, 144, 145, 146, 147, 148, 149, 153, 154, 155, 156, 157, 158, 159, 160, 271
table lamp 185, 186, 187, 188, 189, 190, 191, 192, 193, 194, 195, 196, 197, 198, 201, 206, 207, 210, 214, 216
Table-Chair 144
Tablescape 271
tableware 230, 232, 237, 238, 239, 252, 253, 254, 255, 256, 257, 258, 259, 260, 261, 262, 265, 268, 271
Tafel Tafel 138
Tak Light 214
Taste the edible and the inedible 324
Tea by candlelight 251
Tea Set Noir 258
teaset 258, 259
Teddy Bag 63
Teo Stool 29
Teotitlan 1 40
Terrace Sideboard 104
textiles 272, 273, 276, 278
The Flat Light 221
The Honeycomb Vase 'Made by Bees' 227
The king in I died 44
The PlasticNature 157
The Unexpected Visitor 210
Thin Chair Version 2 71
This Is (Not) 257
Thonet No.18 (homage) 44
TIK & TAK Stools 26
Tilt 118
Time to Time 305
Times Table 150
To be continued 98
To Contain 207
To Handle 207
To Pour 207
Topography 238
Torch 185
tray 238, 242, 260
Tre di Una 66
Tre1 195
Tree House My House 120
trestle 158, 318

Trestle 158
Triangular Stool 28
Tschoc 311
Twinlampshade 186
Two Lamps 196
Ty-bihan 154

U Form 167
Uit de klei getrokken 255
Unintended Ladder 117
United We Stand 47
Unlimited Edition 230
Upholstered Chair 81
Urchin 168
Use-It Dispose-It 302

vacuum cleaner 295
vase 224, 225, 226, 227, 228, 229, 230, 231, 232, 233, 265
Veins of the house 297
Victorian Grandfather Chair 78
Vitra Virus 229
Volume 93
Vuoka 216

W Lounge 48
Walking Table 151
wall lamp 218, 219, 220, 221
wallpaper 275, 276, 277, 337
Wallpaper Games 275
wardrobe 111
Waslijn 327
waste container 310
watering can 307, 311
Waternetworks Collection 307
water-saving devices 307
Wattson 290
Weave Stool, The 20
Weave Your Lighting 183
Willow Boughs 337
Window Story 247
Wing Chair 50
Wingback Chair 78
Wings Bench 34
Winter Arrives 31
Witte Non 75
Wooden Clock 304
Wooden Floor 282
Work Collection 270
Worktop 146
World Clock 301
writing implement 308

Credits

20 (nothing to) HIDE, fotografie-johanneke
20 The Weave Stool, Bahbak Hashemi-Nezhad 21 Skinterior, Mark van Gennip
22 Launch Stool, Holly McCarthy 22 Pimp, Fabrice Gousset 24 Nido, Ulrike Myrzik
26 TIK & TAK Stools, Amr Hamza 27 Gori Stool, Hyock Kwon 28 Triangular Stool, Thomas Adank 31 Winter Arrives, Wendy Chua 34 Wings Bench, Huseyin Harmandali 35 Benches, Claus Lehman 36 Eternit, Thomas Adank 37 Fuga, Fethi Izan 38 Quilt Chair and Stool, Frank Tielemans 41 Streamer, Silvester Busazi 42 Blockhead, Kristiina Kurronen 42 The Shuffle Chair, Martyn Lello 43 Ash and Corian Chair, Jon Sneddon 44 The king in I died, Paul Scala 47 United We Stand, Josh Cornell 48 W Lounge, Savannah College of Art and Design Photography Dept. 51 Chair, Frida Jeppsson and Karl-Oskar Karlsson 52 Néo-Noé, Patrice Thomas 53 Mosquito, Pierre-François Gérard 54 Bullet, Timo Ripatti 55 RU Chair, Johan Fowelin 56 Ply-Ply, Olli-Pekka Härmä 57 P'tite Lulu, Filloux & Filloux 63 Sissi, Andrés Otero 65 Elbow Room, Dog Bowl, Double Backed, Leon Maurice 68 Spool Chair Thonet #14, Satoshi Asakawa 68 Butterfly, ILGIN AKARSU 69 Silent Chair, Daniel Frisk 70 Easel Chair, Niklas Palmklint 71 Thin Chair Version 2, Satoshi Asakawa 71 Maneki Chair, Ville Palonen 72 Plastic Back Chair, Florian Joye 75 Witte Non, Lode Saidane 76 Do Re Mi, Aya Imura 76 5pm in the Spring, Satoshi Asakawa 77 Stitched Chair, Sylvain Deleu 82 Pouf de Paille, Andrés Otero 83 Meltdown Series, Christoph Bolten 85 Pump it up, Lilian van Rooij 86 Hanabi, Ville Palonen 88 Cup, Tillmann Franzen 90 A4, Jani Mahkonen 90 Intersection, Marie Flores 92 Mugroso, Liliana Ovalle 92 Dream of sand, Lilian van Rooij 94 Boox, Han Li 97 Oona, Evi Kuenstle 103 Stack, Peter Mallet 105 2D Furniture, Anne Luciari 105 Drückeberger, Michael Anhalt 106 Around, Baptiste Heller 107 Backstage, INK 108 Office, Simon Irgens 111 Adam Wardrobe, Andreas Velten 112 Hall Stand, Philip Vile 114 Hallstand, Roddy Paine 115 Max, Luis Menke Finsterbusch 120 Shelf Space, Jeremy Frechette 123 Clutter Shelf, Alin Huma 123 Nix, Jessica Schäfer 124 Stackbox, Rene van der Hulst 126 Interior Furniture, Alan Dimmick 126 Fairy/tale, Gunnlaugsdóttir,

Flash Gordon 127 Boxed Body, Lisa Klappe 129 Brodie Table, Dieu Tan 129 Nymphéas, Lode Saidane 131 Brace Angle Furniture, Missika Adrien 136 Serie, Milo Keller 138 Tafel Tafel, René van de Hulst 139 Borrod, Kristine Funch 140 Creep, J. J. Hunt Photography 141 Grandma's Revenge, Designer 141 Splinter, Mathias Nero 144 Discu, koelnmesse GmbH 145 Suppenkaspar, Andreas Velten 146 Soft dressing table, Frank Tielemans 146 Worktop, Fillioux & Fillioux 148 Keyboard, Katja Hiendlmayr 149 Lia, Michel Bonvin 150 Times Table, Penny Shek 154 Hanging Out, René van der Hulst 157 The PlasticNature, Michael Anhalt 164 SpringRain, Masaharu Hatta 165 Seam Lights, Dieu Tan 166 Mold Lamp, Milo Keller 166 Stella, Jacky Lecouturier 167 U Form, Emma Nilsson 168 Pantheon Light, Yuki OMORI 172 Construction Chandelier, Mortimer Lebigre 175 Lingor, Guido Mieth 178 Swirl Light, Chris Sorrell, Brendan Cook 179 Sleeping Beauty, René van der Hulst 180 Campanula, Ville Palonen 183 Amorphous Lamps, Erik Gould 185 InnerTube, Julien De Wilde 185 Torch, Julien De Wilde 186 Twinlampshade, Tonatiúh Ambrosetti 188 La Liseuse, Philippe Lermusiaux 188 Mary Joe 2, Reinhard Dines 188 Lost Model, Philippe Jarrigeon 189 Packaging Lamp, Claire Pepper 191 Clipping Rod, Milo Keller 192 Fortuna, Szilveszter Busazi 193 Gold Toy Lamp, Morten Schjolin 194 Skinny, Legis Lecram 195 Giraffe, HIROYUKI OHNO 195 Tre1, Kristiina Kurronen 196 Two Lamps, Milo Keller 198 Magnet Light, Angela Moore 199 Soil Lamp, Rene van de Hulst 204 Happy Lamp, Colm Howley 207 To Handle, To Pour, To Contain, Robert Alexander 208 Being Floorlamp, Tuomas Marttila 211 Left or Right BIG, Thomas Koy 216 Vuoka, Timo Ryttäri 219 1/4, George Tsuru 220 Daylight Comes Sideways, Designer 220 Cheap Cheap, Max Geuter 224 Forest Vase, Cecilia Ovalle 228 Grid Vases, Tonatiuh Ambrosetti 229 Paper Vases, René van der Hulst 231 InterVases, Vincent van Gurp 232 Public Garden, Peer van de Kruijs 233 Materialized Vase, Neil Lukas 235 Hadji Bowl, Serdar Samli 237 Digital Dishes, Simon Roth 238 Topography, Baudoin Charles 239 Pulp, Ingmar Timmer 240 Fukidashi Box, Paul Pavlou 241 Flock & Brass, Catherine

Leutenegger 242 CMYK, Milo Keller 246 Flor, Gabriela Chicherio 248 Fullcolourball, Dave Southwood 248 Nuoska, Samuli Pulkkinen 249 Chorus, Myungwook Heo 250 Speed Metal, Jeremy Frechette 252 Lux_it, Aino Huhtaniemi 253 ContemPlates, Abigail Sidebotham 254 Happy Porcelain, Rudi Funk 255 Uit de klei getrokken, Nadine Sterk 257 This Is (Not), Jean Michel Massey 258 Garav Teapot, David Risenberg 260 Apartment, Yongjin Choi 261 Fusion, Guido Mieth 262 Louise, Alain Baars 263 Everyday Sunday, Chikako Harada 265 Science Series Glassware, David Franco 268 Jar Tops, Royal VKB 269 Polka Pots, Michael Stelzhammer 271 Tablescape, Morgane Le Gall 272 Recycling Daily News, Vincent van Gurp 276 Points de vue, Olivier Lamy 278 Interior Dialogue, ANDERS WICKSTROM 279 Meterware Carpet, Petra Warrass 280 Carpet, Alexander van Berge 285 Miles rug, Milo Keller 287 Cable Carpet, Andreas Velten 292 PowerBlock, Sophie Carles 298 Calimero, Curzio Castellan 299 Heat Me, Alfonso Herranz 299 Glas Gib Gas, Curzio Castellan 302 Spore 1.1, Luke Hoverman 303 Supper, Takumi Ota 306 Alma, Orlando und Björn, Bernard-René Gardel 307 Waternetworks Collection, Geoffrey Cottenceau 310 A-Zero, Geoffrey Cottenceau & Régis Tosetti 310 Divide It, Alfonso Herranz 313 Birdy, Eternit AG 315 Pinno hooks and shelves, Pia Richardson 316 Seeking To Embellish, Pacharapong Suntanaphan 318 Clampology, Lucas Hardonk 329 Nomad Architectural System, Robert Hakalski 331 Shades, Mark van Gennip 332 Infinity, Marie Flores 333 Entreciel, Christophe Fillioux 334 Line, AHMET GÜL